P9-BZT-740

DATE DUE

MAY 1 1 '89			
APR 1 4 '93			

STRANGER IN THE FOREST

On Foot Across Borneo

ERIC HANSEN

A Yolla Bolly Press book published by

HOUGHTON MIFFLIN
COMPANY
Boston
1988

A YOLLA BOLLY PRESS BOOK

Stranger in the Forest was produced in association with the publisher by James and Carolyn Robertson at The Yolla Bolly Press, Covelo, California. Assisting the producers: Barbara Youngblood; Diana Fairbanks. Composition was provided by Wilsted & Taylor, Oakland, California. Maps were drawn by David Fuller, EarthSurface Graphics, Los Angeles.

All photographs in this book were taken by the author unless otherwise credited. Chapter One: Mr. Das. Chapter Two: *Tambang* operator, Kuching River. Chapter Three: Abat, Penan Pa Tik. Chapter Four: Pedera Ulun. Chapter Five: Penan boy hunting. Chapter Six: Building a temporary rainforest shelter. Chapter Seven: Penan with traditional rattan backpack. Chapter Eight: Dugout canoe and equipment, Bahau River. Chapter Nine: Nomadic Penan. Chapter Ten: Kenyah woman at Long Sungai Barang. Chapter Eleven: Spear-tipped blowpipe, poison darts and parang. Chapter Twelve: Ascending a cataract, Temaha River, Kalimantan (William Conley). Chapter Thirteen: Longboats near Data Dian. Epilogue: Logging road, Tutoh River.

LIBRARY OF CONGRESS CATALOGING-IN-PUBLICATION DATA

Hansen, Eric.
Stranger in the forest.

Bibliography: p.
Includes index.
1. Sarawak—Description and travel.   2. Hansen,
Eric—Journeys—Malaysia—Sarawak.   I. Title.
DS597.364.H36   1988   915.95'40453   87-17011
ISBN 0-395-44093-9

PRINTED IN THE UNITED STATES OF AMERICA

Q   10   9   8   7   6   5   4   3   2   1

For Stephanie and Mr. Das

CONTENTS

BORNEO

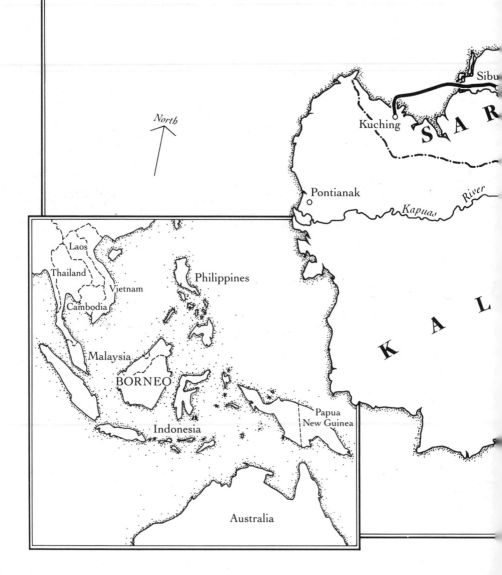

North

Sibu
Kuching
S A R
Pontianak
Kapuas River
K A L

Laos
Thailand
Vietnam
Cambodia
Philippines
Malaysia
BORNEO
Indonesia
Papua New Guinea
Australia

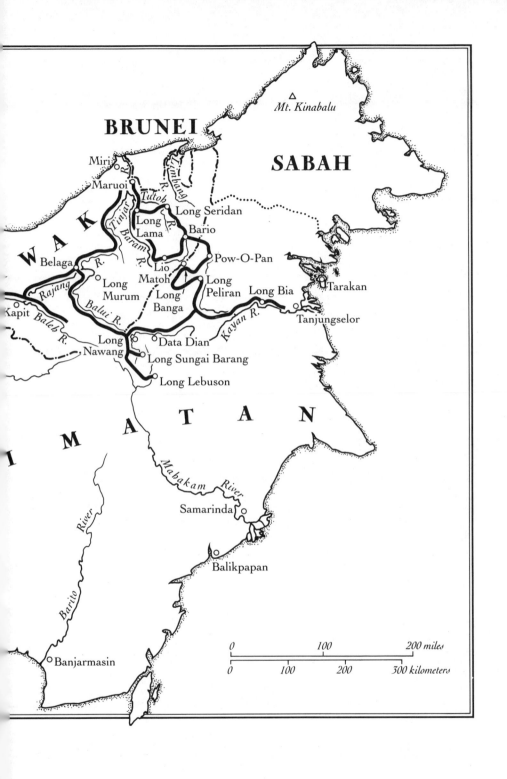

PROLOGUE · CHILD'S PLAY

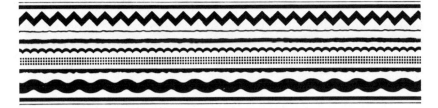

WHEN I WAS EIGHT years old, I found a piece of bamboo in my parents' garage. It was yellow with age and five feet long. It may have been an old rake handle, but from jungle movies on television I knew what to do. With my pocketknife I sharpened one end of the bamboo and made a spear.

The house where my three sisters and I grew up stood on a corner lot separated from the street on two sides by a footpath and a hedge five feet high. The hedge was well trimmed and very dense, and sometimes I would wait behind it with my spear. When a neighborhood child was foolish enough to pedal by on a bicycle, I would stick the spear through the hedge and into the spokes of the front wheel. There was a cherry plum tree in the front yard, and when the fruit came into season, I crouched behind the hedge and fought one-sided battles with passing traffic and old people walking their dogs. Bicyclists and pedestrians learned to give our hedge a wide berth.

My parents had planted lawn and a beautiful flower garden behind the hedge. I remember the pink, yellow, and white poppies perched precariously on their slender, furry, green stalks. There were tiger lilies — and the orchids. People would bring my father orchids that wouldn't bloom, mostly cattleyas and cymbidiums. He doctored the plants back to health and kept them in an old bathtub in a shaded corner of the yard. The owners of the orchids sometimes came to see the blooms, but never asked for the plants back. Each year the number of orchids and the variety of colors increased, until the bathtub overflowed and a forest of potted orchids threatened to take over the backyard.

Near the bathtub was a Gravenstein apple tree. It wasn't much for climbing, but the apples were good for pies and apple butter. The half-rotten apples on the lawn were used for spear practice. One afternoon I grew tired of stabbing apples and directed my attention to a nearby camellia bush. Before my eyes it transformed itself into a rhinoceros. I stood brave, then buried my spear in its leathery hide. Retrieving my weapon, I crouched like a hunter—motionless, listening—then crept silently into the front yard. My mother, preoccupied with an afternoon tea party, was oblivious to the wild animals lurking in her yard. I wrestled with a king cobra garden hose and left it with a broken back. A bear and a lion were soon dispatched, and for each new victory I cut a notch in the spear shaft. I became excited and began running around the house faster and faster, spearing everything in sight. There was a terrible loss of life. Suddenly a huge bull elephant reared up in my path and trumpeted a frightful challenge. I knew from the *National Geographic* magazines stacked next to the toilet that I was a goner if I missed the one vulnerable spot near the elephant's temple. I took aim and with all my strength threw the bamboo spear—clean through the bush that obscured the big living-room window. The sounds of breaking glass and overturned teacups were followed by startled screams. That brought me out of the jungle fast—but only momentarily. The next thing I knew I was being chased by natives. Hundreds of them—all with spears—and so I ran for my life. Down the empty street I went, dodging between parked cars until I finally gave them the slip, and hid in a neighbor's basement until eventually I had to go home for dinner. That night my mother listened as I explained about the jungle and the animals and the spear. My mother understood my hunting fantasies and excused the spear incident because it was she who would sit on the edge of my bed most nights and read to me from Kipling's *Jungle Book*.

It wasn't until twenty-five years later in the Sarawak rain forest that I learned about real spears and what it feels like to look at the receiving end of one when it is held in the hands of an expert.

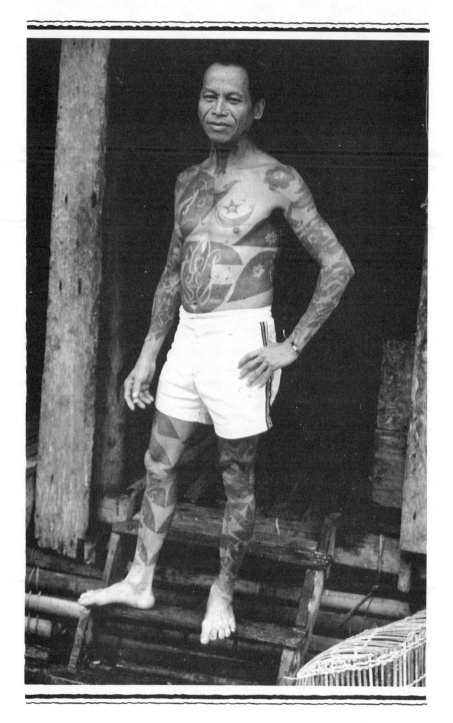

CHAPTER ONE · PRELUDE TO A JOURNEY—CHRISTMAS WITH MR. DAS

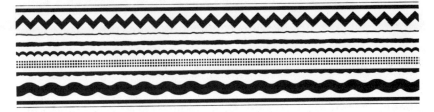

I N AUGUST 1976 I was faced with a simple choice: to fly directly from Djakarta to Singapore or to go to Singapore by way of Kuching, Sarawak, on the island of Borneo. I had never heard of Kuching, but was told that from there I might catch the *M. V. Perak*, a 30-year-old, 211-foot-long Borneo trader that cruised the South China Sea between Kuching and Singapore.

"Four first-class staterooms," some traveler had told me long before. "White enameled walls, polished mahogany furniture, crisp bed linen, and caged ceiling fans. Somerset Maugham stuff." I had listened to his descriptions of meals with the uniformed Malay officers, of tattooed Dayak stevedores swarming the decks, and of a white-haired Chinese steward who announced morning tea at sunrise by running his knuckles gently down the hardwood louvers of the cabin door. It had sounded too good. For the extra ten dollars I decided to go by way of Kuching. An easy decision, but one that would six years later totally transform my life.

I was traveling at that time with my friend Robyn, an Australian from Brisbane, Queensland. She had never been out of Australia before, and this trip was her introduction to Asia. We arrived in Kuching on the weekly flight from Djakarta, having changed planes in Pontianak, West Kalimantan. From the tiny airport shed it was a short bus ride into town. A warm tropical rain sprinkled the muddy Kuching River as *tambangs*, the distinctive double-oared river taxis, crisscrossed the main current, picking their way through huge nipa palms and other debris that had swept downstream.

Morning shoppers in search of fish and meat and vegetables

wandered through the covered markets that were conveniently perched along the riverbank. At day's end much of the refuse from the markets was thrown into the brown current. Across the street from the markets was a row of shop fronts typical of Anglo/ Malay Colonial architecture. These two- to three-story stuccoed brick buildings enclosed a walkway a block long that opened onto the street through a series of wide archways. Within these shaded archways hung plastic buckets, carry bags, and children's toys. The cool passageway was packed as quiet milling crowds bargained with vendors over cooking pots and bicycles, sacks of rice and dried *bêche-de-mer*. The street itself had that distinctive Southeast Asian smell of dried, fermented prawns and sump oil. The acrid fumes stung my nose at first, but I found them pleasant. Chattering swiftlets darted through the shopping arcade as lumbering blue-and-white buses nudged through the pedestrians and traffic. Rising above this morning scene was the golden dome of the Great Mosque.

On a hill commanding a strategic bend on the river was Fort Margherita with its whitewashed battlements; just upriver was the Istana, the former residence of the White Rajahs. Three generations of benevolent rule by James Brooke and his successors, Charles and Vyner Brooke, had come to an abrupt end with the Japanese invasion of Kuching in 1941.

The rain began to come down in sheets, and Robyn and I ducked into a coffee shop across from the main wharf area. A man bicycled past with what appeared to be a machete placed in the wicker basket attached to the handlebars. The man, cheerfully oblivious to the downpour, was drenched, and his arms and legs were covered with glistening blue-black floral tattoos. He also had distended earlobes. A transistor radio, hidden from sight in the bicycle basket, was playing the Beach Boys' "Surfin' USA." I was beginning to like Kuching. The machete, I later learned, is called a *parang* and is the universal tool of the people of the upriver communities. It is modeled after the traditional headhunting swords.

The rain cleared and we started walking. A few blood-warm droplets continued to fall as we made our way down India Street past curry houses and fabric shops. There were fruit and ice cream vendors on bicycles ringing their bells, but they would attract few customers until midday. On one corner a man with waist-length, matted, black hair was selling amulets. His neck was strung with bits of multicolored paper packets and brass and silver containers. Men of the motorcycle-helmet, necktie-and-polyester-trouser cult were handing over one dollar each for a thumbnail-sized piece of bark, which the amulet man tied to their biceps with a length of colored cloth. Thus armed, the men climbed onto their motorcycles and disappeared into the light morning traffic.

After leaving our bags in the hotel, we found the local agent for The Straits Steamship Company Ltd. From behind a desk stacked with yellow files the man informed us that the *M.V. Perak* was indeed still operating and yes there was a stateroom available. The ship was scheduled to leave Kuching in eleven days. We bought the tickets and that afternoon visited the fabulous Sarawak Museum. Out of general interest we had been collecting giant beetles and other bugs on peninsular Malaysia a few months earlier, so when we saw the insects on display, our interest in the interior of Sarawak was immediately aroused. Then, on the second floor of the museum, we found a full-size, walk-in mock-up of a longhouse room on display. All the domestic items were in place — the rice pots, the spears, the rice-wine jars, and the human skulls. After a short discussion with a member of the museum staff and a glance through the airport tourist literature, we decided to go upriver to visit a real longhouse. No more thought went into our plans, and like most extraordinary journeys, this one was completely innocent and spontaneous. No one could have foreseen what followed.

Two days later the river trader *Ovaltine Super Express* deposited us a couple of hundred miles up the Rajang River at the Kapit wharf. The first thing we encountered was a 16-foot-long crocodile stretched out on its back on the raised walkway that surrounds the central square of this upriver trading post. There was a very large bullet hole through the crocodile's head, and its yellow belly scales were as large as bathroom tiles.

Mr. Das was watching us. He was seated at a table twenty feet from where we stood gaping at the former river monster. He waved us over to join him for tea. Mr. Das was dressed in a pair of freshly pressed blue slacks and pink rubber bathroom thongs. His white shirt was open at the neck, revealing a tattooed garden of stars and flowers. He wore a gold wristwatch, and a black fountain pen with gold clip stood by in his shirt pocket.

Tea arrived and I asked Mr. Das if he was afraid of crocodiles.

"No," he replied. "I am safe from crocodile." He pulled up his trouser leg to display a large tattoo of a hook on his ankle. "We Iban catch the crocodile with hook tied to bamboo raft. When crocodile see this hook—no bite."

"What a good idea," I replied, wondering if I could have a facsimile drawn on my ankle with a laundry marker.

And did Mr. Das know an interesting longhouse for us to visit?

"Yes, you come with me," he replied immediately. Mr. Das was returning to his Iban village in the interior after two years of work on an oil-drilling platform off the coast of Brunei. We left the crocodile to the men with the sharp knives and strong stomachs, and with Mr. Das leading, we went shopping for the journey.

"Tobacco," said Mr. Das. We bought tobacco. "Sugar," he continued, and the Chinese shopkeeper smiled. We bought enough tinned food to last our anticipated two-day visit.

When the essential shopping was finished, I asked what special gifts might be appreciated. Mr. Das led me to a nondescript door on a passageway behind the main bazaar. I knocked. The door opened to reveal an old Chinese man dressed in striped pajamas.

"*Arak*," I said, following Mr. Das's instructions.

The man half-shut the door and disappeared. A minute later he returned with an old, brown beer bottle filled with an unidentifiable liquid. Without handing me the bottle so I could inspect the contents, the man delivered his sales pitch: "One bottle — enough four man. Maybe one bottle enough six man. No walk." He glanced up and down the laneway. "One bottle five dollar."

I bought five bottles at four dollars a bottle, and with our new friend Robyn and I climbed aboard the late-afternoon river trader. This elongated diesel version of *The African Queen* took us upstream to the jungle trading post where the Balch River flows into the Rajang. There the big trees began to dominate the river, and I had the sensation that this was the gateway to the great forests of the Iban homelands that I had read about in *Vanishing World* by Hedda Morrison, Leigh Wright, and K. F. Wong.

We hopped ashore and hitched a ride in a dugout canoe powered by a twenty-horsepower Johnson outboard motor. The journey took about two hours, and we arrived at the gravel beach below Mr. Das's longhouse just before nightfall.

The longhouse was 200 feet long, with a continuous thatched roof running the length of the building. Sections of the roof could be propped open from the inside to let out smoke from the cooking fires and to admit light. A row of evenly spaced identical doors opened onto a 40-foot-wide, springy, bamboo-slat verandah that overlooked the river. Behind the doors were the private family quarters for cooking, eating, storage, and sleeping. The entire structure was built off the ground, on 8-to-10-foot-tall hardwood posts, to facilitate cooling and ventilation. There were other functions of this raised design. Traditionally everything that Westerners would put in the garbage can or down the sink or toilet would be disposed of by sliding a floorboard aside . . . then "bombs away." Pigs, chickens, and dogs roamed and scavenged the underworld of the longhouse, keeping it relatively clean.

The longhouses were originally built on stilts for defense, and the slippery, notched, pole ladders at either end of the common verandah could be pulled up quickly in times of danger. Building off the ground also provided protection from snakes and leeches, as well as from the voracious bacterial fungi that inhabit the jungle floor. Any structure built on the ground would be consumed by microorganisms in a very short time.

We sat down on the verandah; the longhouse seemed deserted. Only a few children and dogs were in sight. Mr. Das disappeared into one of the doors and returned a few minutes later to announce that everyone had gone to another longhouse. The last longboat would be leaving soon, and there was room for us. But this had been an exhausting day, and I wasn't sure I wanted to go anywhere. I asked Mr. Das what was happening at the other longhouse.

"We go to celebrate Christmas," he replied.

Christmas in August? How could we refuse?

The jungle was very dark as we felt our way down the muddy riverbank and into a smaller dugout canoe. Four men had joined us. No one had a flashlight, and as the men paddled downstream, rocks and giant snags began to appear. They loomed up beside the dugout without warning and then disappeared back into the darkness. I couldn't see anything beyond five feet, and when we arrived at the second longhouse twenty minutes later, the dugout was half-full of water.

There were at least two hundred people gathered on the big common porch. Most of them appeared to be drunk. We were introduced to the headman and his wife. Our hostess was fat and formidable. She was also bare breasted and covered with sweat from the dinner preparations over an open fire. Her breasts looked like giant, greased, brown papayas. She smiled at us and broke out in a hearty laugh. Everyone seemed friendly enough, but we didn't speak a word of Malay or Iban and had to depend on Mr. Das for translations.

When we sat down, an Iban *Pua* blanket was laid out in front of us. A dozen or so small dishes of food were placed on the blanket, and Mr. Das showed me how to arrange the offering. The eggs, glutinous rice, popcorn, salt, feathers, and fried bananas were auspiciously rearranged to everyone's satisfaction; then I was handed a live rooster.

"What do I do, Mr. Das?"

"Hit everyone on the head," came his emphatic reply.

"I'm just a visitor," I tried to explain, "I can't . . ." But the headman's wife was coming for me. She pulled me to my feet and nudged me towards the seated throng. I was uncertain what to do, but people bowed down as I approached, so I tentatively tapped a few heads with the struggling rooster. The idea was to bestow a blessing.

"Hummmmmmph!" scoffed Big Mama. She grabbed the rooster by the legs and began beating people over the head as if she were swatting tennis balls. She waded into the seated crowd thrashing left and right with sizzling backhands, overhead smashes, and brilliant volleys. The frantic squawks soon subsided, and after this brief demonstration, she shoved the half-dead rooster back into my hands.

"That's how we do it in Texas!" (or the Iban equivalent), she seemed to say with a look of disdain.

I beat heads with the limp rooster for a few minutes, and everyone seemed to enjoy that. When I finished with the blessings, I handed the bird to a man nearby as if he were a golf caddy; then I sat down on the floor mat next to Mr. Das. Soon Big Mama and the caddy were rolling about the porch wrestling for possession of the rooster. The man ended up with the body, and Big Mama came up with the head, which she proceeded to rub in the man's face. She was strong, and the man couldn't escape her grip.

"Party joke," explained Mr. Das.

"What's going on?" asked Robyn.

I was beginning to feel uneasy, but also slightly amused.

"*Minum-lah! Minum-lah!*" (Drink! Drink!), ordered our hosts, and so we drank — too much. Our glasses were continually filled, and soon I began to feel quite relaxed. A young Iban girl knelt directly in front of me and fixed me with a sweet gaze. She also set two large glasses at my feet. One full of *tuak* (rice wine), the other of *arak* (rough distilled spirits). She then began to sing a haunting Iban song. Mr. Das explained that it was a song of welcome and that when the song was finished I would honor the girl by drinking both glasses at a single go. That was impossible. I was already very drunk, and as the song progressed, I began to perspire with nervousness. I didn't want to offend anyone, but what were the alternatives? Before the song was finished a man crept up behind the singer and pulled her over backwards,

21

smothering her face with two handfuls of pot black mixed with sump oil. When she sat up, her pretty face was completely covered with black muck. The song hadn't been finished, so I didn't have to drink.

I asked Mr. Das if the girl was upset over the incident. "Oh, no!" he replied. "It is only for fun. She was lucky — sometimes we use pig shit and pot black."

The evening was clearly getting out of control, and by midnight Robyn was gripping my arm tightly. We watched as a man called out for food. In response a charred leg of wild pig was thrown across the porch and hit him square in the chest. To my left I saw a young man of no more than sixteen leap onto a woman in her seventies and force her onto her back. Fully clothed, he humped her two or three times before rolling off. Everyone roared with laughter, including the woman.

"Party joke?" I asked Mr. Das hopefully.

I glanced at my pretty, strawberry-blonde, fair-skinned friend and felt a slight shudder of apprehension.

"Great Christmas party," I whispered to her, laughing.

"Christmas," as it turned out, was Mr. Das's English translation for *Gawai Antu*, the Iban tribute to the departed spirits. In simple terms this party was to mark the end of mourning for anyone whose relative had died in the previous six months. Dietary and other restrictions had been observed by the mourners. One man had not cut his hair from the day his wife had died, and that evening he sat in the middle of the crowd and wept publicly for his wife. His hair was then cut off. The headman collected donations for a poor old widow, and another woman was allowed to use soap for the first time in four months.

The subtleties of the rituals were beyond my understanding, but as the evening wore on, I became enchanted by the Iban sense of fun. The night blossomed into a series of ludicrous and bizarre scenes.

The drinking continued, and a man went berserk. He punched two men before being restrained by five others. Ten feet from where we sat he was tied to a post with jungle vines. They left him to kick and scream, and he exhausted himself in about fifteen minutes. No one took any notice, and half an hour later he was sitting peacefully at the base of the post. A man then approached him to see if he had calmed down, and after a short, whispered conversation he was untied. The man who had gone berserk joined the party as if nothing unusual had happened; he was fine for the rest of the evening.

By this time my confused and *arak*-sodden companion had been escorted to the headman's room by a sympathetic older woman. Mr. Das assured me she would be safe, and anyway, I was beginning to enjoy myself. What a delightful bunch of maniacs I had discovered! Three A.M. arrived, and no end to the party was in sight. One man passed out, and his friends propped him up and poured more rice wine down his throat to revive him.

The festivities continued to heat up. Men were now indiscriminately firing guns into the jungle night and screaming. Men, women, and children were getting sick over the railings. Then the longhouse caught fire. Something was burning beneath the bamboo-slat floor. There was a lot of smoke, and everyone laughed. *Tuak* was poured onto the flames, but to no effect. A vomiting man was directed to the spot, but that didn't help either. Buckets of water were sent for, and I watched a man who imagined his penis was a fire hose set to work on the spreading flames. The fire was soon put out, and the party continued.

In stages I let down my defenses, and, finally, when the people realized I was willing to join the insanity, the party really took off for me. I thought I had been to wild parties, but nothing before or since has come close to what I experienced that evening. I remember Big Mama pinning me to the floor with one knee on my chest as she rubbed the clammy rooster head in my face.

"Party joke!" I told myself. A group of us grabbed the big cooking pots (empty) from the kitchen area and set upon people too drunk to defend themselves. They were held down by many hands as the pot black was ground into their clothing. Sometime later, in my *arak*-inspired state, I heard, or at least I thought I heard, a scream of terror coming from the headman's room. I suddenly remembered my mate. "Where's Robyn?" I mumbled. "Must find Robyn." I staggered to my feet and in the darkness bounded down the longhouse bamboo porch as far as the first clothesline.

"Narrrrrrrrgh!" The wire caught me at neck level and laid me out cold. I came to hours later, nauseated and shivering in the thick jungle mist. The predawn light revealed a silent, body-strewn verandah. Guns, broken dishes, animal bones, charred floorboards, and an overturned rice-wine jar littered the scene as chickens and dogs picked over the remains. Now that's what I call a party! I got to my feet.

"Mr. Das, Mr. Das, where are you?" I called out weakly, but there was no response. I found Robyn dozing safely in bed, and I climbed in next to her, reeking of *arak* and pig fat.

"What happened last night?" she muttered in a half-sleep. "Are you all right? The shooting and yelling . . . I was afraid."

"Not now," I moaned, then fell asleep.

We had been in Sarawak four days.

We returned to Kapit, and there I met upriver agent Jimmy Sing. He informed me that he had been a border-patrol scout during the 1960s confrontation with Indonesia and had been up every major river in the Seventh Division. He knew the country, and he had maps. One rainy night, after a dinner of fried noodles in the Kapit Hotel, he told me the story of a lush highland valley where there was an open border area between Sarawak and Kalimantan. "The Apo Kayan — Kenyah country," he said, indicating the approximate location on the map.

According to Jimmy Sing the highland climate was cool, the people were hospitable, and, most important, they still observed *adat* (traditional law). The people also grew giant pineapples and owned the best hunting dogs and antique porcelain rice-wine jars on the island. Jimmy Sing mentioned that the area was beyond government control and that a passport wouldn't be necessary. My ears pricked up at that. I had worked and traveled in the Middle East and Asia for five years, and the thought of visiting a place untouched by Western visitors filled me with excitement. It is every traveler's dream to find an undiscovered area, and as I listened to Jimmy Sing's stories, I convinced myself that this was the place. There was no mention of the hill logging industry that was just beginning, the cult of the Holy Ghost, or the hydroelectric schemes that were to create the major social and political issues of the 1980s.

A week later Robyn and I boarded the *M.V. Perak* and steamed down the Kuching River, bound for Singapore. Steward Boon Kok Peng stowed our bottles of tonic water and Bombay gin in the galley refrigerator in preparation for the languid three-day crossing of the South China Sea. The welt on my neck gradually faded, and during the voyage I realized I had fallen in love with Sarawak. One hundred years of benevolent rule by the White Rajahs showed in the character of the people. The harmonious mix of Malay, Chinese, Indian, and indigenous tribal people from the interior gave the country an easy-going, relaxed feel. Walking down a street in Kuching was like walking back to a forgotten era or into a dream. The waterfront and Chinese and Indian sections of Kuching had retained their 1920s Colonial appearance, and as soon as I traveled up my first jungle river, winding its way into the rain forest, I felt as if I had returned to one of my childhood jungle fantasies.

On day two of the voyage, I glanced overboard in an attempt to gauge our progress in relation to the banded sea snakes that seemed to be keeping pace with the boat. The shallow-draft *M.V. Perak* rolled heavily in the inky blue swell as flying fish hurried on their way. The aroma of smoked raw rubber and coconut oil permeated the first-class cabins, where we sat sipping afternoon tea beneath a raucous oscillating fan.

We were both silent. Robyn read a book, and I thought about our visit to Sarawak. During our stay I had a familiar sensation in my stomach, the one we all get when we return to a familiar and loved place. I felt as though I had "come home." If a two-week visit was so full of wonderfully strange events, what would it be like to live in Sarawak? I wanted to find out and made the decision to return. I didn't know when, but I knew I would come back to search for that highland valley.

CHAPTER TWO · A LITTLE PREPARATION, SARAWAK 1982

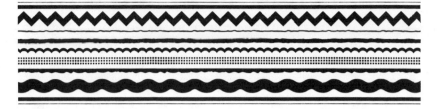

THE DEAFENING roar and vibration of the twin 500-horsepower Detroit Diesel engines suddenly ceased, and at idle the 60-foot, aluminum-hulled express launch began to drift to a standstill. It nudged the floating log dock below the main market square of Marudi and nestled in with half a dozen similar boats. From the air they might have looked like a string of giant, silver fish, bows facing upriver in the slow-moving, muddy current.

By midmorning the Baram River was already dotted with a wide assortment of river craft. Tugboats were hauling massive log rafts from the interior to the downstream timber mills, and at the main wharf black-and-white battered coastal tramp freighters with lines of rust running from the scuppers to the waterline were being unloaded. I watched as a cloud of blue-gray smoke erupted from an ancient deck crane on one of the boats. Gears gnashed and steel cables groaned under the weight of wooden pallets loaded with tinned goods and compact Japanese cars. Stevedores struggled across the splintered wood jetty wheeling gigantic sacks of rice and cement. Four-foot-long cylindrical pig baskets woven of rattan were being lifted from the hold of one ship. The baskets swung through the air, and the pigs squealed in terror before being stacked five deep in the back of a decrepit motor lorry. Handsomely constructed longboats and simple dugout canoes jostled for space between the big boats to unload their cargoes of rattan and freshly killed wild game.

I walked up the wooden ramp from the dock and crossed the

street to a cafe facing the river. I selected a chair at an empty table and ordered *kopi susu*, the Malay version of café au lait, strong black coffee mixed with sweetened condensed milk. From where I sat at the circular, marble-topped, hardwood table, I had a view of the river traffic and the main bazaar area, which was enclosed on three sides by two-story, arcaded shop fronts. Projecting from the peeling facades of these buildings were faded canvas awnings bearing advertisements for an assortment of products. My imagination was set to work by Great Wall Canned Chicken Claws, Skyscraper Filter Cigarettes, Masculine Pills for Men, and Medicated Brylcream.

The variety of river craft reflected the racial diversity of the people moving through Marudi's central market square. Four major tribal groups — Iban, Kelabit, Kayan, and Penan — come to Marudi to do business with the Chinese, Malay, and Indian merchants. Marudi is the farthest upriver major trading post and services all the longhouses in the Tutoh, Tinjar, and Baram river basins. These modest shops also attract people from the central highlands, hundreds of miles away across trackless rain forest.

Borneo is the third largest island in the world. It is approximately eight hundred miles by six hundred miles and straddles the equator. Nearly 80 percent of the island is covered in steaming tropical rain forest filled with valuable species of hardwood and inaccessible mineral deposits, including gold, diamonds, uranium, and coal. Until the late 1970s the exploitation of the interior was limited because oil and timber, the major natural resources, were readily obtainable near the coast. The jungle appears lush at first glance, but the ground is infertile because of the heat and constant leaching of the soil by the daily rain. The plants and trees receive nutrients by recycling their own leaves and rotting vegetation.

Six great rivers drain the island, and at the headwaters of these rivers, the central highlands of Kalimantan are isolated from the coast by huge sets of rapids. The confusion of mountain ridges that rise to thirteen thousand feet is divided by smaller rivers that flow in all directions. To the north, facing the South China Sea, the tiny, oil-rich sultanate of Brunei is wedged between the East

Malaysian states of Sarawak and Sabah. Kalimantan, which occupies the southern two-thirds of the island, is claimed by Indonesia.

The people of the interior are classified as Proto-Malays and Deutero-Malays and are divided into at least twelve distinct tribal groupings, including Iban, Murut, Melinau, Bidayu, Kenyah, Kayan, Kelabit, and Penan. The men are about five and a half feet tall, and the women are an inch or two shorter. They have light brown skin and straight black hair. Traditionally both men and women distend their earlobes with brass weights for beauty, and practice extensive body tattooing. For the longhouse people the staple diet is hill rice, which is cultivated with slash-and-burn, long-fallow farming techniques. There are still bands of nomadic hunters and gatherers who wander through the rain forest in groups of twenty-five to thirty-five to hunt wild pigs and search for sago palms (*Eugeissonia utilis*) from which they extract their staple food, sago flour. These forest nomads, commonly referred to as Penan, are considered to be the jungle experts by all the inland tribes. Because they live in the shade of the forest, their skin is very fair. They have a great affection for the coolness of the forest and until the 1960s would not come into the open even for five minutes. For them sunlight is extremely unpleasant. They are broad and much more stocky than the river people. The Penan are extremely shy and have had little contact with the outside world. Most of their trade is conducted with remote Kayan, Kenyah, and Kelabit longhouse communities on the edge of the rain forest.

An observer, seeing me at that riverside cafe, might have concluded that I was absorbed in the waterfront activities before me, but I was actually trying to unravel the sequence of events that had brought me to this place. Six years had passed since the Christmas party with Mr. Das, yet the events of that evening were still unusually clear to me. Upon my return to the United States from what became a three-year journey through Southeast Asia, I attempted to settle in San Francisco, but I continued to fantasize about Jimmy Sing's vague account of an isolated highland community. The allure of Borneo grew in stages. One

of the principal attractions of the central highlands of Kalimantan was its inaccessibility. I found the blank spots on the maps
irresistible. Of the many places I had visited in the Middle East
and Asia between 1971 and 1978, Sarawak was one area that I
felt might have escaped the standard Western influences: tourists, missionaries, the Peace Corps, Marine Corps, and U.S.
AID. A quiet, little backwater that existed in a British Colonial
twilight was what I had in mind.

My assumptions reveal only how hopelessly ignorant I was of
the actual situation in Sarawak and Kalimantan in the 1980s. In
1973 a fanatical Christian revival had ripped through the longhouse communities in Sarawak. The profound effects of that revival were still in evidence in 1982. In some villages people went
to church three times daily, and drinking and dancing were forbidden. Priceless family heirlooms, such as dream beads,
charms, and old headhunting swords, were thrown in the rivers
or burned because of their magical power to cure sickness and
control weather or to bring good luck on the hunt. Special beads
are used to interpret dreams and divine the future. These objects
are an indispensable part of animist beliefs and wholly incom-
patible with modern Christian teachings.

In 1979 hardwood-log prices doubled on the world market,
and timber extraction from Sarawak increased dramatically,
with Japan, Korea, and the United States providing the market.
The local people provided cheap labor. By 1982, when I was
contemplating that "Colonial twilight," the timber industry in
Sarawak was exporting 583 million U.S. dollars' worth of logs
and milled lumber annually. A similar scenario had developed in
East Kalimantan. Over the previous decade timber extraction in
that area increased by fifty times in volume and nearly nine thousand times in value. These timber operations in East Kalimantan
have grown to represent approximately 50 percent of the total of
Indonesian timber exports. Not bad, considering only 1 percent
of the population of Indonesia lives in the area.

I was blissfully unaware that these things were happening as
I organized my trip. I had the good fortune of being able to make
my plans in near-perfect ignorance of my destination. From 1978

through 1982 I fed my Borneo fantasy with regular visits to the libraries of the University of California at Berkeley, where I had once been a student of industrial art and environmental design. One day while I browsed through the stacks, I happened upon a complete collection of *Sarawak Museum Journals* from 1912 onwards. Everything one would like to know about Sarawak is contained in those thirty-five wonderful volumes.

In one of the papers submitted by Herbert and Patricia Whittier, "The Apo Kayan Area of East Kalimantan," two themes stood out: migration and trade. The Whittiers included with their article a small map detailing the traditional trade routes from the highlands to the coast, and a brief mention was made of desirable trade items. This obscure reference, combined with a map of British paratrooper Tom Harrisson's 1945 route through the highlands — and Jimmy Sing's stories — gave birth to my unlikely journey. Using these three sources of information, I linked together a pathway over the spinal range of mountains that divides Borneo northeast to southwest. In the library the pencil line that I effortlessly drew across the map connecting villages and traversing mighty mountains looked promising. It was not until I stood at the very edge of the Sarawak rain forest that I discovered most of the trails no longer existed and many of the longhouses were abandoned. It was then I also realized I had no idea what I was doing.

The aim of the trip was to cross the island, following old trade routes, collecting jungle products and medicinal plants of value, and exchanging these and Western goods for what I needed. The concept was a masterful piece of scholarly lunacy based on anachronistic information and my own half-baked notions of Sarawak that had been gleaned from a twelve-day drunken visit six years earlier. I was to learn later that Jimmy Sing had never been to the highlands and that there was an open border between Sarawak and Kalimantan for a very simple reason: it was almost impossible to move through that uninhabited, wild, jungle-clad mountain country. A passport wasn't necessary because there was no one to look at it. I anticipated the "Lost World" of Arthur Conan Doyle, and in doing so I made a thorough job of setting myself up for some breathtaking surprises in the jungle when it had long become too late to turn back.

⚑ ⚑ ⚑

I must have been sitting at the Marudi waterfront cafe staring into space for some time, because I was suddenly startled by a voice nearby. It was the Chinese proprietor asking me in English if I would like something more to drink.

"Yes, I'll have an iced lemon tea, please," I told him. The man nodded and shuffled away. A light rain was falling on the river, but it gave no relief from the hot, damp air that was being nudged around the room by the wooden blades of an overhead fan. My drink arrived in a tall, frosty glass packed with ice, and I took a long sip. I wasn't ready to search for a hotel room, so I occupied my thoughts by reviewing the setbacks and mistakes that had led up to my present effort to enter the rain forest from Marudi. I winced at the thought of my incredible naiveté when I stepped off the plane at Kuching airport two months earlier.

The first mistake I had made upon my return to Sarawak was to take a nostalgic trip up the Rajang and Baleh Rivers in search of Mr. Das's longhouse. I didn't expect to see Mr. Das, but I anticipated that a few days spent at the scene of the "Christmas Party" would put me in the right frame of mind for my journey to the highlands. I caught an express boat to Sibu and then continued up the Rajang River to the riverside town of Kapit.

Kapit had not changed appreciably in the six years since I had last seen it. The shops seemed to have a wider range of goods, and the local Iban youths had discovered jogging shorts and Adidas warm-up suits. I spent the night in a small hotel and left early next morning for the Baleh River. A cool mist hung over the river and diffused the sunlight as we motored upstream. The sleek new river-boat was built of metal — very different from the original wooden-hulled launch that I remembered from my first visit. Piled on the roof of the riverboat were rolls of linoleum and cheap living-room furniture upholstered in bright orange vinyl. Wedged between sacks of rice was a television set bolted to the top of a small gasoline-powered Honda generator. I noticed the

32

longhouse roofs were now covered with corrugated metal, rather than traditional *attap* thatch. At least the Iban passengers on the riverboat lived up to my exotic memories. The men carried the jungle knives and woven rattan backpacks, and between the men and women there were more than enough tattoos and brass ear weights to occupy a bevy of *National Geographic* photographers. Without introducing myself, I took a few photos and then smiled to mask my discomfort. I didn't speak any Iban, and my Malay was then so poor that I was unable to understand their comments. I was still blinded by my *Sarawak Museum Journal* fantasies, but the setting I found myself in was pretty impressive: white man travels slowly upriver in Chinese river trader; all the appropriate props were in place — the brown-skinned natives, the spears, the woven-leaf sun hats, and an acrid-smelling cheroot in every mouth. And outside the "Heart of Darkness" slipped by. What a starry-eyed fool I must have seemed to those people. They were simply returning from a shopping trip to Kapit bazaar, the only market within fifty miles.

I couldn't remember the name of Mr. Das's longhouse, but the memory of the two days recovering from *Gawai Antu* had become branded in my mind, and I felt sure I would recognize it. Periodically the Chinese helmsman would run the bow of the boat into the slick, muddy riverbank. He held the boat steady in the current while individuals or small groups gathered their belongings. The angle of the bow was specially designed to match the slope of the riverbank. From the wide, flat foredeck it was an easy step ashore. The people would struggle up the mud slope and disappear into the forest. The engines would be thrown into reverse, and with a loud sucking sound the boat would pull free from the mud. We continued upstream, and I found myself dreaming about my first visit to this beautiful river — the *arak*, the rooster head, even the clothesline. Within a couple of hours of leaving Kapit, I realized we must be getting close to Mr. Das's longhouse.

Log rafts were lining the banks, but eventually I recognized a distinctive turn in the river, where a tall rock cliff stood at the water's edge. The realization that I had been to this same spot

33

before sent a shudder of excitement through my body. The long-house would be around the next bend on the right-hand side of the river. I pulled my bag onto the foredeck and waited excitedly in the fresh air. I visualized the scene — children swimming in the shallows and the longboats pulled up on the banks, the long-house itself obscured by the wild tangle of lush jungle, but iden-tified by dozens of roosters crowing. The riverboat churned around the last bend, and my eyes came to rest on a gigantic log-loading station. I was stunned, disbelieving the evidence of change my eyes were registering. Tugboats stood by as barges of Singapore registry were being piled high with hardwood logs. Bulldozers and huge lumber trucks moved back and forth over the large clearing, arranging the giant logs. The barren ground was soaked with sump oil to keep down the dust, and raw, red-earth logging roads radiated into the denuded hillsides. The longhouse was nowhere in sight. I felt as though I had returned to my childhood home only to find it replaced by an auto-wrecking yard.

What a stupid idea it was to come back. I should never have returned to this river, I told myself. Memories of my wonderfully innocent first visit to Sarawak were shattered in an instant by this scene of devastation. For the first time I began to realize that the obscene greed and short-sightedness of the logging industry in Sarawak was ruining the forest. The boat eased next to the log landing stage and unloaded boxes of engine parts and soft drinks. I didn't bother getting off the riverboat to find out what had hap-pened to all my mad friends. I assumed they were employed as chain-saw operators or truck drivers. I stood on the bow with my bag, and above the roar of the engine, the helmsman yelled for me to jump ashore. I told him I would take the roundtrip and return to Kapit. Six years had been too long to wait. With in-creasing feelings of uncertainty, I was wondering if the country had been turned into one big timber concession.

Back in Kapit I looked up Jimmy Sing. He greeted me cor-dially, though I doubted that he could remember me. We sat in a coffee shop drinking lukewarm Carlsberg beer while I explained

34

my plans. Jimmy proudly announced that he had gone into the tourist business and would love to help me get upriver. For an old friend, a special price. Boat, guides, food, gasoline, gifts, and tobacco for one week: 2,400 Malay dollars, the equivalent of about 1,000 U.S. dollars. I laughed at his joke. Jimmy smiled. He wasn't kidding, and he wouldn't lower the price. Since my first visit large numbers of tourists had discovered Kapit as "The Gateway to the Iban Longhouse Experience." I was being treated like your standard 30- to 45-day mail-order-catalog adventure traveler.

After more talk and beer Jimmy eventually confessed that he had . . . well . . . um . . . never actually been to the highland communities that he had so colorfully described to me years earlier. But, he tried to reassure me, the area did exist. He had heard the stories himself. I ended up paying for the drinks and decided that I would have to find my own way. I would move farther inland, and perhaps there I would find the jungle of my library fantasies.

For the next eight weeks I struggled up one river after another trying to reach the big mountains that separate Sarawak and Kalimantan. I got close on three occasions, but something different stopped me each time. On my first attempt I traveled up the Baleh River as far as Rumah Entawau, a distance of about seventy miles, which took me two days. From there I couldn't find guides, and I hadn't brought enough longboat gasoline to reach Long Singgut, the Kenyah village located another seventy-five to eighty miles upriver, near the headwaters and within a three- to five-day walk to the first village in Kalimantan. The extra gasoline was necessary to get to Long Singgut and back to Rumah Entawau. I was disappointed by this first setback, but I had expected some initial problems. The upper Baleh River had been beautiful, and I had the opportunity to practice Malay for four days. Still full of optimism, I told myself I must be on the wrong river. It was a simple matter of finding the correct river. Then everything would be fine, or so my fantasies assured me.

I returned to Kapit for the second time and then tried the Balui river above Belaga. In their article the Whittiers had indicated that this river was the major trade route from the Apo Kayan to the commercial centers of Sarawak. In the Belaga bazaar I bought a ridiculous amount of salt and also flashlight batteries because I had read they were very valuable in the interior. I caught a ride on a shallow-draft cargo boat, similar to a landing craft, and we left Belaga before noon.

We made good time that first day and successfully powered through the treacherous Bakun Rapids before nightfall. The cargo boat was returning to Belaga the next day, and my plans were to find another boat headed upriver. I was asked where I wanted to get off, and at random I said Rumah Bawang, the Kayan village at Long Murum. I chose this village, from my limited knowledge, because it appeared to be the largest village in the area. This, I reasoned, meant more people, more boats, and more upriver travel opportunities.

I couldn't have selected a worse village. I was stranded there for a week, and during that time no one took any interest in me or my laughable plans. In all of Sarawak I never stayed in a more unpleasant village. My possessions generated a great deal of interest, and I was soon fleeced of most of them. I was charged for accommodations and meals, which is unheard of in longhouse communities, but the worst thing about my situation was that there was no independent way for me to leave. The village wasn't connected by footpath to the only nearby longhouse, Long Linau (or so I was told), and no one would take me upstream or downstream by boat. Make the best of the situation, I told myself, practice speaking Malay. Unfortunately everyone insisted on my teaching them English and how to do The Twist to their Rolling Stones tapes.

On day eight I had literally to take the shirt off my back and give it to one of the sons of headman Lihan Hawang so that he would take me ten minutes downriver to a government work camp. The shirt, by the way, was a gratuity, a special thank you, in addition to the quadruple-rate fee for gasoline, rental of long-boat, and hire charge for the driver. The roundtrip couldn't have taken half an hour, and I was charged for the entire day. I left that village feeling like a walking dollar sign. I wasn't angry, just confused. Seldom have I felt so totally inadequate. I was doing everything wrong.

I later learned why the people in Rumah Bawang might not have been feeling particularly hospitable and friendly. At the time of my visit, those people were in conflict with the government over a bitterly contested land-compensation claim. Just downriver, at Bakun Gorge, a 2,400-megawatt dam was to be built. The lake formed by the dam would flood six hundred square kilometers of virgin jungle, agricultural land, sacred burial sites, and prime hunting grounds. Four thousand people in fifty-two longhouses would be displaced, and the people of Rumah Bawang were to be among them.

With construction due to commence, the people up and down the Balui River valley didn't know what cash compensation would be paid or where they would be resettled.

The concept of the project is staggering. Sarawak's current annual electrical consumption is less than 200 megawatts. One may well ask where all the excess power is going to go. The answer: to industrial, energy-starved Singapore and Peninsular Malaysia via a 650-kilometer submarine cable. Plans for construction are going ahead despite claims by German engineers on the site that the local rock may not be strong enough to hold the water pressure from the 190-foot-high cement dam. The possible benefit of a dam with an anticipated operational life estimated to be thirty-five to fifty years — when weighed against the complete environmental and social devastation of such a large area — is difficult to understand. Government officials claim the large reservoir will improve fishing and encourage tourism in the area. Water skiing also has been suggested by the government. The World Health Organization, commenting on water-borne and communicable diseases associated with huge dams in tropical areas, suggests that typhoid, cholera, dysentery, viral infections, schistosomiasis, opisthorchiasis, malaria, and filariasis are much more likely than a tourist industry based on water sports.

A Kayan woman expressed the local concern succinctly when she said, "We want a doctor more urgently from the government than a big dam."

And I thought I had problems. I was merely trying to travel back in time, to reconcile my fantasies of Borneo with the realities of the place. I was learning about Sarawak very quickly.

I returned to Belaga bazaar with the ten kilos of salt. No one in Rumah Bawang had wanted it. The shopkeeper in Belaga who had sold it to me smirked and looked away when I suggested a refund, so I gave the five-year supply to my hotel manager, who laughed when I told him about the people at Rumah Bawang. The man had already seen a few white people try to get up the river, and he sympathized with me.

Out of obstinancy I decided to try the next major river to the north, the Baram. Looking back, I'm astounded at how easily I gave up on the first two rivers. But I was still operating under the illusion that there *was* an easy way to get into the interior. All I had to do was find it.

Once again I bought a selection of inappropriate gifts and trinkets, this time based on advice from the dreaded, smiling shopkeepers. The third journey started off well. After seven days in a longboat, I succeeded in reaching Lio Matoh, at the headwaters of the Baram River. From there I started overland on a wide trail accompanied by four Kenyah men returning to their village, Long Banga. We walked for one and a half days, and then it happened. I suspect I was preoccupied with patting myself on the back for my good progress and forgot to watch where I was stepping. Less than a kilometer from the village I fell off the trail and sprained my ankle badly. One of the men took my load, and I managed to limp to the village. Fortunately the people of Long Banga were hospitable and kind. I was deliciously pampered for a week, but my ankle didn't improve. I became alarmed when the swelling turned black and blue around the ankle bone and I could put little weight on it. I thought I might have chipped the bone.

My confidence was badly shaken by the experience, and for the first time I realized how vulnerable I was to injury. Even a simple thing like a toothache could turn into a nightmare. And what if I cut myself badly or got appendicitis or scrub typhus or broke a bone? Even if I were fortunate enough for someone to find me, would they take care of me, a total stranger? I must be very careful, I told myself, never to let my thoughts wander while walking. If I were to hurt myself in the deep jungle, there would be no way to get out or call for help. I imagined I would just lie where I fell and wait for the insects and animals of the jungle to come for me. The mosquitoes, the leeches — I couldn't imagine a slower death.

These thoughts made me recall a rather grim obituary I had read in the *Borneo Research Bulletin*. In 1975 Bruce Sandilands, an Englishman and government surveyor with twenty-three years experience in Borneo, was abandoned by his guides when they became disoriented in uninhabited rain forest. They left him with one can of sardines and badly infected feet. He could no longer walk, and his guides evidently didn't feel like carrying him. His remains were found two months later by a patrol of border scouts. According to his diary and self-winding watch, he died eighteen days later. He was eaten by animals. If a man of his experience was incapable of finding his way out of the jungle alone, what hope would there be for me in a similar situation?

I wasn't willing to continue into the trackless jungle of Kalimantan until my foot was better. I was only two days' walk from the Sarawak/Kalimantan border, but I made the bitter decision to return to the coast. I could have stayed in the village, but I wanted a doctor to look at my ankle. I should have hired some people to carry me, but my pride wouldn't allow it. There is a small airstrip at Long Banga, but the flights are unreliable even when scheduled, and no planes were expected for a month. I'm still not sure how I managed, but I taped my ankle as high as my calf and spent two days walking through the jungle to Lio Matoh in excruciating pain. I had a guide to carry my bag. He cut a walking stick for me, but the pain became so bad that it caused me to tense up my entire leg. As a result, my knee began to spasm from the strain, and by the time we reached Lio Matoh I was a mess.

I hitched a ride downriver to the coast with eighteen people in a magnificent 70-foot longboat. The anticipated three- to four-day journey went askew on day two when the big, green boat, without warning, ran up on a submerged rock in the Mawit Rapids and capsized. Everyone managed to leap overboard before the longboat rolled over, but most of the baggage was lost. The cooking pots, food, bedding, and gasoline drums for the outboard motor sank to the bottom of the swift-moving, brown river. I managed to grab my small bag with my notebooks, camera, clothes, and mosquito net, but my large pack, which contained several hundred dollars' worth of fabric, tobacco, and batteries, had gone into the river. That was the last thing I needed. I could barely walk; for the third time I had failed to reach the mountains, and now my trade goods were gone. With them went my last trace of optimism. I felt utterly defeated.

A few hundred yards downstream we found the battered longboat still intact, but minus its roof. Our sorry group paddled to the first longhouse to buy more rice, and two days later we arrived in Long Akah, where we could get gasoline for the outboard motor. It was a depressing journey, and I lay in the longboat and slept as much as possible.

I began to think that I would never make my dream journey through the highlands. The rivers were proving to be my nemesis. If there was too much rain, the logs and branch debris made river travel unsafe. Too little rain, and the water would be low, exposing long stretches of dangerous rapids. Even when the river conditions were ideal, accidents could happen as a result of a moment's inattention. The gasoline prices upriver were astronomical, and guide fees were draining my resources. Standard fees (in Malay dollars) in Sarawak for longboat and crew were: driver, $18, plus food and tobacco; crew member, $15, plus food and tobacco; bow lookout, $10, plus food and tobacco; outboard motor, $1 per horsepower (20 horsepower, $20); longboat (25 to 35 feet) rental, $10 per day; and dugout canoe, $5 per day. These fees were in addition to gifts for people in the longhouses along the way and gasoline.

I was also beginning to be suspicious of people's motives. During the first two months I had tried to reach the highlands on some of the smaller rivers, and I'm certain that on a few of those occasions my guides agreed to take me upriver with the knowledge that we would never be able to reach our destination. They would earn their wage for a week or so and have an all-expenses-paid hunting and fishing trip. I was doing something wrong, but I didn't know what it was. I became irritated because I had so little to show for my efforts. I struggled to contain my frustration because, as I quickly learned, any outward expression of anger or displeasure is considered in Sarawak to be the ultimate in bad manners. Even a slight outburst reduces these people to stony silence, and if this becomes a habit, you can forget about getting any further cooperation or sympathy. The temptation to raise my voice or use anger was very great at times, yet I concluded, after much internal debate, that it was totally inappropriate. I had spent too much time and energy to abandon the trip, but the stockbroker's golden rule kept coming to mind: Get out and cut your losses. I wasn't enjoying myself. Most of the time I was on edge and felt that I was trying to live out a sham that I had lost confidence in, but my pride wouldn't allow me to quit. I hadn't come all this way to turn back; yet there was a growing sense of my own inadequacy, a lack of control over situations that was ruining the trip. Maybe I was trying too hard? But however hard I tried it seemed as if I was getting nowhere. One of the most demoralizing aspects of the journey so far was that no one shared my dream or took my goal seriously. It was becoming increasingly difficult to sustain my fantasy without a trace of positive reinforcement. One of the few things that sustained me during this time was the knowledge, gained from eight years in Asia, that complications go on for only so long. With patience, and more patience, a way is eventually found.

For eight weeks I had been on the move, and as the longboat approached the mouth of the Baram River, I decided to return to Kuching for a rest. I needed to rethink what I was doing. If my ankle didn't improve, I would have no choice but to abandon my plans. I flew back to Kuching from Miri feeling miserable, if not yet defeated. I was to stay in Kuching for a fortnight.

I took a room in an old, 1930s-style guest house that had originally been the home of a wealthy Chinese family. The building was situated on a hill amidst spacious gardens and tall shade trees. When I opened the floor-to-ceiling louvered shutters I looked out over a roofscape of private porches and terra-cotta tiles that extended to the waterfront. The word *kuching* means cat in Malay, and over the expanse of rooftops that spread below me prowled cats of every description. Some of them seemed to spend entire days napping on the roof tiles, but at twilight they began to prowl. Throughout the night sounds of feline courtship and savage battles drifted across the darkened city.

The visit to Kuching went well. My favorite fruit, the mangosteen, was in season, and I discovered the reference library in the Sarawak Museum. This small library has arguably every book ever written about Sarawak, and many of them appeared to be first editions. My stay in Kuching allowed me to distance myself from the jungle and what had happened over the previous two months. My ankle got better, and I decided to give up on river travel for the time being. Instead I planned to walk overland on one of the old footpaths between Marudi and the Kelabit highlands. From readings in the museum library I knew that these trails were in use at the end of World War II, but I had no idea whether they still existed in 1982.

In the relative comfort of Kuching, I was eventually forced to ask myself why I was still trying to reach the highlands. Now that my preconceived notion that Sarawak was a quiet backwater full of happy natives who knew how to party had been obliterated, what was the purpose of the journey? So much had changed in six years. Resource-development projects based on agriculture, timber, oil, and natural gas had changed traditional village economy. The longhouse communities used to live in what anthropologists call "primitive affluence." With few exceptions everything the people needed came from the jungle. There was an abundance of fish and wild game and building materials; medicine and plant foods and fruits were easily obtainable. Jungle products such as rattan, tree resins, and edible bird nests were traded on the coast for steel tools, salt, brass gongs, cooking pots, and rice-wine jars from China. Until the 1930s these jungle products were the primary commercial products of Sarawak and Southeast Asia. By 1982 the villages were tied to a coastal cash economy and Western subculture that I had no interest in whatsoever.

I played with the idea that in the far interior things would be better. Perhaps because of the extreme inaccessibility of the mountain communities I would find another longhouse similar to the one that I had visited with Mr. Das. Insurmountable travel problems had so far kept me from my goal, but even if I did manage to cross the mountains, there was no guarantee that I would find a remote community cut off from the big development projects.

My journey had a pretty vague purpose, considering the extreme discomfort and uncertainty I was putting myself through. What was to be gained? Tricky one, that.

In her book *The Oblivion Seekers*, Isabelle Eberhardt, that eccentric North African traveler, wrote about the freedom to wander: *To have a home, a family, a property or a public function, to have a definite means of livelihood and to be a useful cog in the social machine, all these things seem necessary, even indispensable, to the vast majority of men, including intellectuals, and including even those who think of themselves as wholly liberated. And yet such things are only a different form of slavery that comes of contact with others, especially regulated and continued contact.*

I have always listened with admiration, if not envy, to the declarations of citizens who tell how they have lived for twenty or thirty years in the same section of town, or even the same house, and who have never been out of their native city.

Not to feel the torturing need to know and see for oneself what is there, beyond the mysterious blue wall of the horizon, not to find the arrangements of life monotonous and depressing, to look at the white road leading off into the unknown distance without feeling the imperious necessity of

43

*giving in to it and following it obediently across mountains and valleys!
The cowardly belief that a man must stay in one place is too reminiscent
of the unquestioning resignation of animals, beasts of burden stupefied
by servitude and yet always willing to accept the slipping on of the harness.*

*There are limits to every domain, and laws to govern every organized
power. But the vagrant owns the whole vast earth that ends only at the
nonexistent horizon, and his empire is an intangible one, for his domi-
nation and enjoyment of it are things of the spirit.*

Boredom — perhaps that is what made me return to Borneo?
I have an extraordinarily low tolerance for boredom and routine.

Isabelle was right about there being no destinations. Travel is
the act of leaving familiarity behind. Destination is merely a by-
product of the journey. I guess what I wanted from my journey
was a unique experience, something so far beyond my compre-
hension that I would have to step completely out of my skin to
understand and become a part of my surroundings. That idea,
more than anything else, had motivated me to pack my bag and
leave San Francisco. The comfort and security of a successful
business and a long-term relationship with a wonderfully tal-
ented, kind, and creative woman were not enough to hold me.

⚓   ⚓   ⚓

In Kuching I had plenty of time to think, and I eventually realized that, despite myself, I had made some progress during those
first three attempts to penetrate the highlands. I had acquired a
working knowledge of *bahasa pasar*, a basic form of modern Malay that is the trade language of the interior of Sarawak and Kalimantan. From previous travel I knew that I needed approximately three hundred words plus a few dozen basic sentence
constructions. With these I could build up my fluency through
everyday conversations with non-English speakers. There are
many tribal languages, but with *bahasa pasar* I could communi-
cate with nearly everyone.

I had also learned the basics of village etiquette: how to enter
a longhouse, what gifts to offer to whom, how to change clothes
in public with a sarong, to bathe upriver and defecate downriver.
Dancing, I discovered during the June rice-harvest celebra-

44

tions, is the most common expression of village socializing, as well as fun, so I learned to imitate a graceless version of *ngajat*, the traditional solo male dance. But the two most important things I learned, and these I had to learn from observation, were persistence and patience. By patience, I'm not referring to the grin and bear it, the Western sort, or the patience of resignation, but rather the fatalistic Asian variety that has a meditative, soothing quality. Patience, the use of silence, the art of masterful inaction — these are very important skills in a society where so much is communicated on an intuitive, nonverbal level. I was beginning to understand how the inland people thought.

It had also dawned on me that what I was attempting was extremely difficult. Maybe I wasn't such a bumbler after all. Dr. A. W. Nieuwenhuis, two associates, and 110 porters and body-guards had preceded me to succeed in crossing the island, but that had been in 1897, and it had taken them a year. Certainly some local people and perhaps even some Westerners have crossed the island. There are many stories, but the point of my trip was not to be the first, or the fastest, or the straightest. The challenge was to do it alone, to make myself completely vulnerable, and to be changed by the environment.

In addition to the uncertainties of travel, I was faced with some practical problems. It was illegal to cross the Sarawak/Kaliman-tan border, and legally I had to renew my visa every thirty days at an immigration office. This precluded any authorized ex-tended journeys into the interior of Sarawak because the few immigration offices were on the coast. I had no visa or permission to enter the highlands of Kalimantan, and that meant I would have to avoid the police and army outposts.

Food provided another difficulty. If I was going to walk, I couldn't carry more than fifty pounds comfortably. Fifty pounds of food would get me only three or four weeks into the rain forest, and I anticipated a journey of three months. And what of my clothes, camera, and trade goods? Who was going to carry them? There were still some major problems to unravel.

I hadn't anticipated so many delays, and by the time I felt ready to start my journey, my passport was due to expire in two months. The nearest place to renew an American passport was Kuala Lumpur in Peninsular Malaysia, and I wasn't about to fly all that way for a document that was absolutely useless where I was going. I solved the first two problems by putting my passport away and forgetting it.

♠   ♠   ♠

What a sense of freedom and relief to be able to disregard that document. In nine years of work and travel in Asia, the Middle East, and Australia, I had constantly been irritated and burdened by visa applications, visa deadlines, renewals, rubber stamps, and the nuisance of having to protect this highly overrated piece of identification. My main fear of flying comes from my fear of being singled out by a terrorist because of my American citizenship. I resent being held responsible for U.S. government policy.

The popular misconception, of course, is that if a traveler gets into trouble, he or she can always turn to the embassy or consulate for assistance. In 1978 I had the misfortune of testing this theory in North Yemen. I had been shipwrecked for two long weeks on a real desert island in the Red Sea between Eritrea and North Yemen. I was eventually rescued by a 40-foot Arabian dhow filled with sixty goats and four Eritreans. Once safely ashore, I was arrested by the North Yemen marines for ten days as a suspected Soviet spy. Upon my release I went to the American embassy in San'a to report the incident. After I waited for more than an hour beneath the arrogant gaze of a pimple-faced American marine guard behind bullet-proof glass, the consular official made his appearance. Sweeping into the reception area, he first pointed out that the embassy was normally closed on Friday (the local weekend holiday); then he informed me that I had interrupted his meal at an "official diplomatic luncheon." With a condescending indifference that I still remember with astonishment, he asked me what I wanted. Looking at this man's ample midsection, striped silk tie, starched collar, immaculate fingernails, and perfectly shined shoes, I recalled how many turtle eggs I had eaten on the island. After a brief discussion I was ushered to the street and directed to the nearest hotel. My passport, that cherished lifeline to the motherland, has yet to regain its former mystique.

♣   ♣   ♣

In Long Banga, where I sprained my ankle, I had met a group of Saban from Kalimantan who told me money was of little value in the highlands. The people there would accept cash, but were largely self-sufficient and were much more interested in goods. They practiced an intricate system of barter trade. It was obvious that in many areas I would have to take trade goods to pay for guide fees and gifts. Certain items from the coast could be sold in the highlands for five to ten times their purchase price, but I hadn't been able to find anyone who knew or was willing to tell me what those items were. The advantages to the traveler with the appropriate goods were obvious. For a long trip the goods should have a high profit-to-unit-weight ratio. What I needed was a sympathetic local expert to explain these things to me.

All of these thoughts and more about the intricacies of inland travel, as well as my motivations for coming back to Sarawak, had occupied my mind as I sat in the Marudi cafe. In Kuching I had made the decision that Marudi was to be my jumping-off point for the highlands. The afternoon rain had finally stopped, and I strolled through the steaming wet streets in search of a room. That afternoon I found not only a room, but also a man by the name of Syed Muhammad Aidid: the man with the plan.

I had asked a fruit vendor in the market if there was anyone in Marudi who knew about upriver travel. Leaving his stall, he walked me a short distance to a narrow doorway, pointed up the darkened steps, then left me. The stairway was unlit, but I had no difficulty climbing the steep stairs. Muhammad Aidid was seated behind a large hardwood desk when I walked into his first-floor office. He was a big man with laughing eyes and a luxurious black mustache twisted at the ends. I liked him at once. Glass-fronted hardwood gun cabinets lined the walls and were filled with long rows of shotguns and rifles. Every bit of available wall space displayed Japanese swords, animal skins, and a collection of curiously misshapen deer antlers. Muhammad Aidid ran a successful business selling guns and ammunition and Western-style fishing equipment. He was a collector of paramilitary magazines from the United States, and on his desk was a very old life-size, carved-stone penis that he used as a paperweight.

I later examined this artifact. Hindu statuary has been found in Sarawak, but this was not a Shiva lingam, and it had not fallen off a statue. For lack of a more sophisticated or delicate analysis, it appeared to be a Stone Age dildo. "Fertility objects," I think they're called in primitive-art nomenclature. But Muhammad Aidid was not merely a collector of paperweights; he sold ammunition to all of the longhouse communities between Marudi and the Kalimantan border, and from conversations with his far-ranging clients, he had the latest information on inland trade. Over the next few days we spent hours drinking tea and discussing obscure points of barter trade. Muhammad Aidid inspired confidence, and I quickly grew to trust his judgment. Months later I was still marveling at his vast knowledge of upriver trade values. I told him of my previous mistakes with trading and guides, and he laughed. Muhammad Aidid certainly had nothing to gain from revealing his knowledge, and I think he helped me because he felt I deserved a break. I amused him with my innocence, but he admired my determination. Few nontribal people (Malays, Chinese, or Indians) had attempted such a journey, so he went to great lengths to help me succeed. Meeting Muhammad Aidid provided me with the local knowledge I was lacking. Without his expertise I doubt my journey would have been possible. I owe him a great deal of thanks.

⮝ ⮝ ⮝

"No, no, you've got it all wrong again," said Muhammad Aidid one day. "Sixty *moks* of rice equal one large biscuit tin, not one *gantang*. Four *gantangs* equal one large biscuit tin."

After so many years of travel in Southeast Asia, bargaining

came naturally to me, but the upriver system of weights and measures had me baffled. An empty, eight-ounce tin of sweetened condensed milk is the standard unit of measure. It is called a *mok*. All other volumes are calculated in multiples of 1 *mok*. For example, when planning a trip overland there is a simple formula for calculating the amount of rice to carry. Three *moks* of dry rice equal one day's rice ration for one man. Therefore, a trip of ten days by four men would require 120 *moks* of rice, or eight *gantangs*, or two biscuit tins (3 *moks* × 4 men × 10 days = 120 *moks*).

I was a slow learner, but Muhammad Aidid was patient. After explaining my errors he sat down and again went over the relative trade values of the interior. I compiled a list that became increasingly more complicated and bizarre. Following, from my journal, is a partial guide to barter trade in central Borneo.

1 *mok* dry rice = 1 meal for 1 man.

15 *moks* = 1 *gantang* (5 days' rice for 1 man).

60 *moks* = 1 *kaling besar* (large biscuit tin).

1 *kaling besar* = 4 *gantangs*.

1 stick of *sugee* (Lombak chewing tobacco) = 4 *moks* rice.

5 sticks *sugee* = 1 bottle *arak*.

1 tablespoon *manik-manik* (seed beads — yellow, black, white, red, or blue — for decorating sun hats or cradle boards) = 1 day's wage for a woman in Kalimantan.

40 tablespoons (heaping) *manik-manik* = 1 old Indonesian head-hunting sword; these can be sold in Sarawak for 200 Malay dollars.

1 shotgun shell of buckshot (plastic cartridges only; cardboard ones swell from the humidity and get stuck in the breech) = 1 day's labor for a man in Kalimantan or a year in jail if caught by the police.

15 to 20 boxes of shotgun shells (25 per box) = either: 1 full-grown water buffalo, 2 to 4 Indonesian hunting dogs, 1 home-made shotgun, or a 10-horsepower Kubota Japanese diesel engine.

1 copper nose ring (for water buffalo or as ear weights) = 5 Malay dollars.

1 kilo edible swiftlet nests for soup (approximately 100 nests per kilo) = 200,000 Indonesian rupiahs in Kalimantan (650 ru-

piahs = 1 U.S. dollar in 1982). *Collocalia maxima* produces black nests; *Collocalia fuciphaga* produces white nests, the most valuable.

1 *batu bangat* (gallstone from black monkey with white face), a toe-size stone = 100,000 rupiahs in the forest and 300,000 rupiahs on the Kalimantan coast.

1 bird, Malay lorikeet (alive) = 1,500 rupiahs.

1 bird, yellow-crowned bulbul (dead), a food eaten by pregnant women so that their babies will have beautiful voices like the bird = 10 Malay dollars (2.4 Malay dollars = 1 U.S. dollar).

1 *kati* (1.33 pounds) *gaharu* (aloeswood) = 50 to 100 Malay dollars in the highlands; more than $350 in the upriver bazaars. *Gaharu* is a wood containing scattered concentrations of fragrant sap. This sap is found only in certain diseased species of *Aquilaria*. The best quality comes from *Aquilaria malaccensis* and is used in Chinese and Asian medicines. The lower grades (*A. gonystylus*, for example) are made into incense and perfume in the Middle East.

1 *tabok* (white ceramic jar covered with a pattern of polychrome floral designs; the lid is topped with a small, sculpted dragon handle) = 2,000 to 3,000 Malay dollars.

These apparently absurd values, explained Muhammad Aidid, were meaningless to most of the coastal population, but in the interior they contribute to an intricate barter trade system with Asia that began in the Stone Age. This trade — originally based on jungle products such as tree resins, edible bird nests, blue kingfisher feathers, rhinoceros horn (a Chinese aphrodisiac), and gold — reached its heights in the twelfth and thirteenth centuries during the Sung dynasty in China. Today this trade continues, although some of the items have changed. Rhinoceros are nearly extinct, and the aromatic wood *gaharu* has become the most important jungle product next to bird nests.

Muhammad Aidid was excited about my journey and thought out a number of complex trade situations where I could make a profit. One of his simpler schemes went like this: "Take three to five boxes of cartridges to the highlands of Indonesia just beyond the Sarawak border near the village of Long Bawang. Trade the cartridges for a young water buffalo. Then hire an Indonesian man who knows how to walk a water buffalo through virgin rain forest. Pay this man no more than 1,000 rupiahs ($1.50 U.S. per day). Then walk with the buffalo and man to Lawas on the coast. It will take you ten days. Food must be carried for the water buffalo because there is nothing for it to eat in the jungle. You must bathe the buffalo every day. For an investment of 100 Malay dollars plus personal food expenses, you would do very well."

"How well?" I asked with a tone of skepticism.

"When the buffalo is full grown, 1,000 to 1,200 Malay dollars, depending on the number of *piculs*."

"*Piculs*?" I asked.

"Sixteen *tahils* equal one *kati*," Muhammad Aidid explained. "One *kati* equals 1.33 pounds, and one hundred *katis* equal one *picul*."

"All right, let me try again," I said, making a quick calculation in my notebook. "A 2,000-pound water buffalo is equal in volume to about 4,000 tins of sweetened condensed milk . . . or 15 *piculs*."

"You will do fine, Mr. Eric," exclaimed my mentor. It was too silly, this talk about *moks* and *gantangs* and edible bird nests. I went for a walk to digest this new information. Returning to my hotel room that night, I calculated expenses and trade goods for a three-to-four-month journey.

It's not that I didn't have faith in the water buffalo project. Knowing Muhammad Aidid, I'm sure it would work, but I didn't have time to wait for a water buffalo to grow to maturity. I decided that shotgun shells, beads, and tobacco had the highest profit-to-size-and-weight ratio. Over the following days I purchased 250 rounds of 12-gauge shotgun shells from a Chinese ammunition dealer who didn't need to see my nonexistent gun license, four kilos of beads, and two kilos of tobacco. This put the weight of my supplies at just over fifty pounds. I would have to hire guides to carry my food, but this time I knew I had the correct merchandise.

♠   ♠   ♠

One of the greatest pastimes in Marudi was a morning cup of coffee and a copy of *The Borneo Post*. The headlines of this venerable paper were never disappointing. The local news was particularly stunning. One morning I picked up an old paper and read in bold print:

MONSTER CROC KILLS HEADMAN

It was while fishing on Batang Lupar tributary that Bangan anak Pali, 29, a recently appointed penghulu, was attacked and killed by a huge croc on June 26. . . . His brother, Kebir, 41, said he was paddling a perahu while Penghulu Bangan waded in the water scooping up prawns in a net basket held in one hand and using the other to grab a rope from the perahu. Encik Kebir said his brother suddenly shouted he was standing on top of a large object . . . a crocodile that swept Penghulu Bangan off his feet with its tail and grabbed him in its massive jaws.

I continued reading: *Parts of Penghulu Bangan's body were only found five days later by two men in a perahu on their way to hunt wild boar. Penghulu Bangan's head and upper chest were found nearby among some bushes. It is believed the 7-meter reptile had been feeding on the body after letting it decompose for a couple of days in typical crocodile fashion. . . . According to Iban belief, it is taboo for them to hunt crocodiles unless the animals attack first.*

The Borneo Post could always be counted on for a bit of sobering news. I could successfully indulge my romantic travel fantasies only if I didn't read the paper. *The Borneo Post* remained the most reliable indicator that the journey ahead was going to be anything but easy.

A few days before the crocodile incident, I had read another article that made me rethink my trading scheme. Twenty miles from where I was sitting with the morning paper, two smugglers had been found without their heads. One of the unofficial trade routes through the jungle that separates duty-free Brunei and Sarawak is called Asam Paya — Sour Fruit Trail — and that is where the two dead men were found. Their trade goods, probably portable items such as cameras, tobacco, and radios, were missing, and the police claimed it was a clear case of robbery and murder. Nothing unusual. All I could think about were the missing heads. Where had they gone? No American citizen could be unused to robbery with violence, but lopping off heads for cassette players and cigarettes made me feel very uncomfortable. Would I be safe with my goods? I had no way of knowing if the people in the highlands could be trusted when faced with temptation. On previous upriver journeys I had never been completely isolated with my guides, and soon I would be carrying the cash equivalent of six-months' salary in Malaysia. If I reached Kalimantan, the value of my trade goods alone would represent two years of manual labor. Certainly someone in the coming months would be tempted to rob me . . . or worse.

These concerns were perhaps a bit premature. I still hadn't left Marudi, and before worrying about the trustworthiness of guides I would first have to find some.

One morning I looked out the first-floor window of Muhammad Aidid's office and noticed a group of five men walking down the sidewalk in single file. They kept to the shadows of the arcaded shop fronts, and somehow they looked out of place. They wore shorts and T-shirts, but it was obvious from their light skin and powerfully muscled legs that they were from the forest. People were giving them discrete sideways glances.

Muhammad Aidid joined me at the window as the line of men continued slowly towards the market square.

"Who are those people?" I asked.

"They are Penan from Sungai Magoh near Long Seridan," said Muhammad Aidid. "They have bought shotgun shells from me before."

"Why are they in single file?"

"That's how they walk in the jungle. One behind the other. They don't know how to walk side by side. These people come down from the jungle to visit the government dispensary and to sell woven mats and blowpipes. They buy ammunition, tobacco, cooking pots, and old car springs and metal files to make jungle knives."

It occurred to me while standing at the window that maybe these men would guide me. In the market later that morning I tried to speak with the Penan, but they were shy, and I don't think they understood very much of my inadequate Malay. All I

53

could find out was that they would not be going upriver for a long time. I pressed the issue and clumsily asked whether they would take me with them. That was a big mistake. I had not yet learned the local technique of how to ask questions indirectly. By doing so, it allows the other person to save face or delicately probe what it is that is being asked for. For example, I should have said something like: I am Mr. Eric. I have been in Sarawak x number of days, and I have visited such-and-such rivers (travel credentials). I am collecting plants used in medicine, and I have heard that the rain forest between here and the Kelabit highlands has good hunting (exhibit modest amount of local knowledge). I don't know how to find my way through the jungle (be humble), and I am looking for someone who is clever and knows the trail (flattery). By phrasing my request like that the men could have responded as they wished. They might have talked about pig migration, the level of the water in a particular river, or whether certain trees were bearing fruit. General conversations allow time for everyone to get a feel for the situation. In this case, an opportunity for me to help them see that they might actually enjoy the company of a tall, white-skinned simpleton such as myself. By asking my question directly, and in front of the towns-people, I put the Penan men on public display, and they became tongue-tied. My approach was too confrontational and didn't allow them time to consider the idea. I must have seemed incredibly ill-mannered and abrupt.

The Penan's response was a simple, "*Kami takoot Tuan sesat dalam hutan*" (We are afraid you will get lost in the forest).

That was the end of the conversation. They saw me as a liability, excess baggage. Their comment wasn't meant to offend, but now I felt like a fool. In single file the men wandered off into the crowded market. I saw them over the next few days, making their careful purchases, but never spoke to them again. One day they vanished, and I guessed they had gone upriver, back to the forest.

After hearing my story Muhammad Aidid offered the suggestion that the Penan hadn't taken me because they would feel uneasy traveling with a stranger. If that was true, how was I going to make contact with the Penan and gain their confidence? Who would be willing to walk with me to the highlands? I saw a whole new crop of problems looming up.

Muhammad Aidid went on to suggest I try to meet the Penan in their own country. "They're always shy in town. They don't like direct sunlight or traffic or noise. They will be more relaxed in the forest." Muhammad Aidid recommended that I should travel to Long Seridan, beyond Gunong Mulu, above the big rapids on the Tutoh River.

"There is a new logging road between Long Lama and the Tutoh River," he told me. "Take the express to Long Lama, and from there catch a ride on a lumber company vehicle to the Tutoh River. Then find someone with a longboat. From the end of the road it is only five hours by river to Long Seridan."

This seemed like a good idea. From previous reading and conversations I knew Long Seridan was on the edge of an untouched forest reserve. This primary rain forest extended as far east as the Tama Abu Mountains. This was Penan country. Bordered on the north by the Limbang River and the south by the Tutoh, twelve different Penan groups roamed the forest. Occasionally they visited Long Seridan to trade. They knew the forest, and perhaps I could convince some of them to take me to the highlands. In the absence of any other option it seemed worth a try.

The day I said goodby to Muhammad Aidid and thanked him for his advice we joked that I would probably be back in two weeks, having flubbed my fourth attempt to reach the dividing range that blocked the way to Kalimantan. But I didn't see Marudi again, and five months passed before I returned to the South China Sea.

As I climbed aboard the morning river trader headed for Long Lama, my plan to cross the island by following the old footpaths, collecting jungle products and exchanging them for what I needed, still seemed like an elaborate daydream. Nothing from my first-hand experience gave me much cause for hope, but for some unknown reason I felt relaxed and confident as the riverboat churned upriver.

I had finally begun my journey into the rain forest.

CHAPTER THREE · ON FOOT TOWARDS THE HIGHLANDS

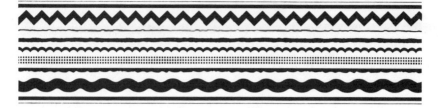

"I KAN! IKAN!" Maren Rajah pointed from the stern as he steered the dugout towards a series of concentric wavelets where the fish had jumped.

Maren Rajah was a 53-year-old Kelabit villager and with his teenage son Stanley had just finished nine months' work in a logging camp on the Baram River. They were returning to their tribal home — the lowland village Long Seridan. I had joined them as a paying passenger. Chain weights rustled in the bow as Stanley gathered the *jalla* over his shoulder. The circular net opened neatly in midair when cast then disappeared with a splash. Hand over hand Stanley slowly retrieved the net with his wrist rope until two fish, covered with large glistening scales, were pulled over the side of the boat. The fish lay entangled in the net, thumping the sides of the dugout as we moved on upstream.

This was to be the last day in the dugout before entering the rain forest. The river continued to narrow, and soon the tree branches from opposite banks met overhead, creating one long, green corridor. By early morning this twisting passageway was filled with warm, damp air that smelled of humus and still water; diffuse light filtered through the canopy, and all the jungle sounds were muted.

I stood in the middle of the dugout thinking about blisters. Hours earlier, as we had set off from the muddy riverbank at sunrise, Maren Rajah had protested when I stood up to help, convinced that I would fall out of the boat or cause us to capsize. But I insisted on sharing the labor because I wanted to establish a personal contact with the people rather than merely hire them as guides. This idealism wavered slightly whenever I glanced at my hands. After two hours of poling, the palms of my hands were covered with broken skin some of which stuck to the boat poles.

Poling our way along the inky green waterway, we glided upstream through quiet still-water bends in the river, where mats of fragrant white flowers had gathered, closing behind the stern of our 24-inch-wide dugout and concealing any sign of our passage. In bare feet I could feel the coolness of the river through the bottom of the smooth wooden hull, and I occasionally dipped my burning hands in the water to relieve the pain. As the ends of our 8-foot-long boat poles were lifted in unison, there was the sound of dripping water. With one foot placed in front of the other, we balanced, with our poles held the way tightrope walkers hold theirs. When the dugout lost momentum, we planted the steel-shod tips of the poles in the river bottom and gently propelled the boat farther upstream. We kept to the banks and followed the natural eddies and back currents. We were slipping into a timeless state where, I realized, I was forgetting the pain of my hands and becoming hypnotized by the rhythm of poling, gliding, and pausing.

Our movements were synchronized and repetitious, but no two motions were quite the same. Hands gripped the smooth hardwood shafts — knees flexed — and by crouching slightly we leaned into the poles. They bent like bows — a pause — and as the flex came out of the poles, we shoved off with our arms and upper bodies. We accelerated through the water, and I could feel the rush of bubbles softly vibrating the hull. In a series of gentle surging motions, we moved up the silent waterway.

Ahead of the longboat a brilliant blue kingfisher flashed its wings, dipped in flight, and glided from one branch to another. At the end of its territory, another bird took the lead. In this way we were led up the last few miles of river to the village of Long Seridan, beyond which lay the true Borneon jungle — a rain forest ecologically unchanged for millions of years.

I had learned that the Penan, small bands of nomadic hunters and gatherers, live in this damp, sunless world. Isolated from the coast by rapids and rough, broken country, these shy people have managed to retain their traditional lifestyle, thriving on the abundance of wild animals, sago flour, edible plants, fish, and jungle fruit. Living in a perfect symbiotic relationship with their environment, they carry few possessions and travel in groups of twenty-five to forty, changing camp every three to twelve weeks. From what I had read, and from what Maren Rajah had told me, these people are considered by all the inland tribes to be the true jungle experts. I had planned to make contact with them so that they could lead me into the interior, but the difficulties inherent in trying to contact a group of nomadic people that roams hundreds of square miles of virgin rain forest had not occurred to me until now.

We arrived in Long Seridan on a Sunday morning, and after explaining my plan to Balang Lemulung, the headman, I realized that I would have to hire guides to find the Penan. I soon discovered another problem: there were no guides available. The villagers practice swidden (slash-and-burn) agriculture, an intricate rice-growing technique that dominates nearly eight months of the year. The few villagers who knew the way to the highlands were busy making their *ladangs*, the dry rice fields that are cut from hilly secondary forest each year. I had arrived at one of the most critical periods of the rice cycle, just before the recently cut forest is burned. If the branches weren't dry enough or if the wind didn't blow in the right direction once the fire was lit or if the rains came early, the burn would be incomplete and all the previous effort would be wasted. No one could spare the time to come with me.

I could have waited until the burn was finished, but that might have taken weeks, and even then there was another problem that was explained by Balang Lemulung. The jungle paths to the highlands had disappeared years before because few people used them. A weekly 18-seater, twin-engine aircraft that flew between the highlands and the coastal markets has supplanted overland travel. What had traditionally been a two- or three-week journey on foot through the jungle can now be done in forty-five minutes by air. The fare was a reasonable fifty-five Malay dollars, so the old jungle trails have since grown over.

On these flights nearly every passenger from the highlands takes to the coast sacks of high-quality mountain rice or artifacts such as old headhunting swords, Chinese porcelain jars, and blowpipes. They sell or trade these items for hand tools, kerosene, and processed foods. With luck the passengers can cover the cost of a round-trip ticket and their purchases, and still end up with a profit.

The villages serviced by the plane are gradually becoming less self-sufficient and more dependent on the coastal economy. Because so few people now travel overland, the Penan have become even more isolated and enjoy primeval jungle conditions that haven't existed for generations.

During my first two months in Sarawak I flew over the interior numerous times collecting trade information and familiarizing myself with the terrain. To understand the local economy and to pay for the flights, I traded. My luggage ranged from plastic bags of live fish (to be released and fattened in the flooded upland rice padis) to vegetable seeds, live chickens, and boxes of copper nose rings to be inserted in the nostrils of water buffalo or in people's ears. Before departure from the coastal airstrips, I presented these items at the open-air "check-in" counters. They were weighed and then labeled with baggage tags. To comply with local flight regulations, I was told to immobilize my chickens. I tied their feet together with the baggage tags and stowed them under my seat as "carry-on" luggage.

I was stranded in Long Seridan because of the air service and the agricultural cycle. During the week most people lived in farm huts near the jungle clearings in order to avoid the long walk to the fields each day. For three days I stayed with Balang Lemulung in the nearly deserted longhouse, confined by the river on one side and by the towering wall of jungle on the other.

On the fourth day two Penan men in baseball caps, T-shirts, and British Army–style, flared, blue-cotton drill shorts, climbed the notched log steps of the longhouse porch. They had acquired their outfits by trading woven rattan baskets and the aromatic hardwood *gaharu* at the trading post in Long Seridan. Their clothing provided a dramatic contrast to the blue-black tattoos of flowers, leaves, and star shapes on their arms and legs. One wore a wristwatch on a stainless steel band. The watch was reliable — it was always precisely a quarter past four. Glancing at their lower legs, I was reminded of polished hardwood statuary. Their thickly calloused feet ended in powerful spatulated toes, which appeared to be quite capable of cracking walnuts. John Bong and Tingang Na had walked from their village, Long Lang, which was three hours away. They had somehow heard of my arrival and were interested in offering themselves as guides. I told them that to visit the rain forest I had come from my village (San Francisco), a 200-day journey by longboat with two engines. John and Tingang Na were familiar with the highland jungle and felt obligated to help me because of the distance I had traveled. They were also tempted by the illegal shotgun shells I was offering as wages.

Although my guides knew a few token phrases of English, we communicated in *bahasa pasar*, in which I was becoming more fluent.

John and Tingang Na arranged for workers to continue clearing their fields. They would pay those men from my guide fees. For each day I would provide fifteen Malay dollars, rice, tea, shotgun shells for hunting, plus forty shells as a fee, and rolling tobacco. In addition, if I were pleased with their services, they would receive a gift when we reached the highlands. In return, they agreed to hunt, cook, cut a path through the jungle, build the nightly sleeping shelters, and tell me stories about the forest.

Before I had left San Francisco I had purchased the most detailed map of Borneo I could find. Neatly folded in my pack — protected by a waterproof plastic envelope — was an ONC (Operational Navigation Chart) series map produced by the British Ministry of Defence. I had been particularly impressed by the technical details printed in the margins: "Scale 1:1,000,000,"

"Survey Based on Lambert Conformal Conic Projection Standard Parallels 1°20″ and 6°40″, (with a convergence factor of 06979)." There were topographical contours, aeronautical information, and terrain characteristics — all tinted in four colors. What more could I ask for?

What I hadn't realized was that the place names were forty years out of date and the few Malay, Indonesian, English, and Dutch surveyors who had managed to reach the center of the island and return had never agreed on their findings. The borders between Sarawak, Sabah, and Kalimantan didn't line up, and throughout the interior there were conspicuous white areas bordered by comments such as: "Map Sources Irreconcilable" and "Limits of Reliable Relief Information." To help fill in the blank spots the cartographers had added question marks beside unnamed rivers and indicated trail systems between villages that had since moved or were misnamed. It came as a shock when I located the fine print: *"Reliability warning:* Owing to inadequate source material there may be significant positional discrepancies in detail over areas of this chart."

I spread the big colored map on the ground in front of Tingang Na and John Bong and put my finger on Bario, the first major highland village. I told them this was our destination. From Bario I would take one of three mountain passes over the central dividing range and illegally enter Kalimantan across the open border. They crouched over the paper with puzzled expressions. Their hands seemed lost as they moved aimlessly over the entire island repeatedly smoothing out the paper. It hadn't occurred to me that they would never have seen a map.

"How do we get to Bario?" I asked.

Moving the map aside, Tingang Na smoothed a section of ground and laid out a series of sticks, grass stalks, leaves, and small stones. He drew a faint line in the dirt through these objects until his finger came to rest at the edge of a leaf.

"This," he said with a smile, "is the way to Bario."

"Right," I said, after a moment's hesitation. Then I moved closer.

"Now, what is this stick?"

"Tutoh River."

"The rock?"

"Mount Mulu."

"The leaf?"

"The Plains of Bah — Kelabit highlands."

I felt like a fool with my map. From memory they knew the terrain perfectly. Over the next few weeks they helped me realign the rivers and fill in the blank spaces.

We divided the weight of my trade goods: shotgun shells, beads, tobacco, salt, fabric, and nylon fishing line. Within an hour we were ready to leave. For the journey they brought two homemade 12-gauge shotguns. These marvels of Kalimantan ingenuity and jungle craftsmanship were created from reinforced water pipe, umbrella springs, bicycle inner tubes, metal from flattened oil drums, nails, a wild assortment of nuts and bolts, and hand-carved hardwood stocks and grips. On one of the guns the trigger return was fashioned with the elastic band from an ancient pair of underpants. Their kit also included two parangs (24-inch jungle knives), a 25-kilo sack of reddish hill rice, two badly chipped enamel bowls, checkered bedsheets, and yellow-brown woven rattan backpacks. My equipment consisted of a mosquito net, a blue-and-white cotton bedsheet, a small green ripstop nylon backpack, one change of clothes, malaria pills, a camera, and a pair of running shoes with camouflaged shoelaces that a friend in Baltimore had sent as a going-away present.

Leaving Long Seridan, I followed my guides through the new farm clearings. There we were confronted by the maze of newly felled trees and shattered branches. The trees were almost dry enough for the burn-off that would initiate the onset of the rice cycle; five or six months later the harvest would begin. A mile from the village we entered a stand of trees two hundred feet tall. This was the rain forest. It was cool and dark; except for occasional glimpses, I was not to see the sun for the next four weeks.

We didn't bring food other than rice and tea — no medicine, no compass, no radio to call for help. I was committed to the journey. There was no possibility of turning back or contacting the outside world if something went wrong. I placed all my trust in the jungle skills and goodwill of these two strangers. I had decided to go with Tingang Na and John Bong because I liked the way they laughed with raised and incredulous eyebrows when I told them where I wanted to go. I had explained I wanted to travel in the most traditional way possible — by hunting and gathering. This naive statement was received with polite, knowing nods and undisguised merriment. John Bong and Tingang Na knew from the moment I pulled out my map that I had very little idea what I was getting myself into.

They were right. Nothing had prepared me for the terrain through which we slowly traveled. The rain forest felt magical and enchanted as long as I was sitting still, but the moment I began walking it became an obstacle course of steep razorback ridges, muddy ravines, fallen trees, slippery buttressed tree roots, inpenetrable thickets of undergrowth, and a confusion of wildly twisting rivers running in every direction. All of this was in the shade of the interlocking branches of giant rain-forest trees. I became disoriented. Tributary streams filled with moss green boulders cascaded into space from unseen jungle precipices, creating an eerie rising mist that filled the rain forest and kept us damp all day. In this giant green house the air was saturated with the smell of damp earth and rotting vegetation. I exhausted myself trying to remain upright. It was futile.

Of the first few days in the jungle I remember the muddy slopes and river rocks coming up to meet my face with astonishing regularity. My fears concerning snakes, leeches, and the possibility of not being able to find food vanished within hours. This part of the trip became an exercise in relearning how to walk. I was reduced to a childlike state, totally lacking in coordination and the ability to anticipate the ground surfaces.

John and Tingang Na nursed me through the first miserable days with patience, gentle laughter, and a compassion that completely won me over. They cooked, set up camp, and did everything they possibly could to make things easier. Their sensitivity to the difficulties I was experiencing galvanized our friendship and transcended the need for words. After five days we settled into a fairly predictable routine.

One morning towards the end of the first week, the dawn chorus of female gibbon monkeys was just fading as the smoke from our fire drifted into the roof of the rain forest. A hundred feet overhead horizontal shafts of sunlight streamed through the canopy, illuminating the smoke and upper tree branches and casting a yellowish haze into the depths of the jungle. I was still dozing under the *pondok* we had constructed on a mountain ridge the night before. The *pondok* was a sapling-pole platform, lashed together with rattan vines and covered with a sloped roof of fan-shaped jungle leaves. For breakfast Tingang Na was steaming rice and pieces of wild pig inside a large section of bamboo. He had shot the pig the day before. I got up and added another section of bamboo, this one filled with tea and water.

While the water heated, I had another look at the map. We were somewhere near the headwaters of the Tutoh River, one of the most remote and rugged areas in Borneo. The Penan trails we were following in the rain forest were indistinguishable from the network of indefinite animal tracks that meandered in all directions through the jungle. Tingang Na smoothed a patch of ground to make another dirt map for me. Pointing to a forked twig, he announced, "This is where we are. We call this place Tocang Buduksiwan."

That morning I decided to put away my map. With maximum views of about fifty feet beneath the jungle canopy, it wasn't much use. In eight to ten hours of walking each day, we were covering fewer than four miles; on the map that was represented by about one-quarter inch. John Bong said he could tell direction by the network of streams, by where on the tree a certain vine grew, and from brief views of the sun. All the vines looked the same to me, and since I spent most of my time looking at the ground immediately in front of my feet, I simply followed as best I could.

The morning tea began to boil in its bamboo kettle. Seated by the fire, we could glimpse a rare, distant view between the trees.

Thick clouds of steam were rising from the jungle valleys five hundred feet below. Silhouetted against this sea of white billowing clouds a pair of black Brahminy kites (*Halastur indus*) circled briefly then drifted from sight. For a moment their shrill cries continued to hang in the air, then it was again silent. I finished mending a tear in my running shoes with nylon fishing line, removed two leeches and flicked them into the fire, and handed out shotgun shells for the day's hunting.

Our plan for this day, as with every other, was to walk for about eight hours; yet no one was in any hurry to get started. We joked about the previous night's rainstorm, which had left us cold and shivering throughout the night. By contrast, the early morning hours seemed especially pleasant. Our bedsheets were spread out to dry in three different patches of sunlight. Tingang Na cracked open the section of charred bamboo filled with a leaf-wrapped tube of rice and succulent morsels of fatty pig meat. He tapped this mixture onto a broad communal leaf, and we squatted in a circle, eating with our fingers.

The week we had spent in each other's company made me realize how helpless and dependent I was: I had no jungle skills, and as a result, my admiration for John and Tingang Na grew each day. Their uncanny and seemingly effortless ability to live off the jungle filled me with excitement and wonder. This was a feeling that would never leave me. A piece of thin bark placed between two small river rocks became a drinking fountain; a leaf plucked off a certain tree, folded double, and sucked on to create a vibrating sound, would call the inquisitive barking deer (*Muntiacus muntjak*) to within shotgun range; a vine known as *kulit elang*, when pounded and dipped in water and scrubbed on our ankles, would keep leeches from climbing up our legs. As we advanced through the rain forest, fruit trees laden with loquats, giant grapefruit, durians, mangosteens, guavas, rambutans, and jackfruit appeared at regular intervals, and it rarely took more than an hour to set up camp and collect food. It was so easy — in the company of experts. On my own I would have died of hunger.

The jungle was vibrant and dynamic with a pulse of its own.

66

For those who were sensitive to that rhythm, the jungle was bountiful and kind; for me, it remained a maze of obstacles for months. I didn't know how to blend in. I was charmed, but at the same time overwhelmed by the complex struggle of simply surviving on a day-to-day basis.

About an hour after sunrise we shouldered our packs and started off. The weight of the rice we had consumed was offset by the addition of dried fish, smoked meat, and a growing collection of plants. Certain varieties had medicinal value and could be used in trade. I was planning on paying for part of my journey by collecting these plants and selling them.

At midmorning, as we traversed a steep slope covered with waist-high brachiated ferns, John pointed to a jungle creeper that he called, in Penan, *tawan-turok*. Also, he referred to the vine as *obat ular*, Malay for "the snake medicine." When the vine was pounded to a pulp and applied to the bite, it acted as a general antivenin. Powdered gramophone records were another common remedy. For snakebites we carried a more popular cure, wooden matches, which could be ignited and plunged into the puncture wounds to "kill" the poison.

Climbing to the top of the slope, at about four thousand feet, we entered a fine example of moss forest. Gigantic epiphytes — clinging plants such as orchids, ferns, and mosses that attach themselves to other plants — had covered every branch and tree trunk with a thick, shaggy coat of green. John uprooted a plant and brought it to me. It was *gerangau mereh* (*Boesenbergia*, an unidentified species of grass), one of the most valuable medicinal plants in the rain forest. It is chewed or mashed and brewed into a sweet-smelling but bitter-tasting tea. A mild stimulant, it is used for upset stomach, nausea, headache, and lower-back pain. *Gerangau mereh* is collected mainly because it is the only known cure for a rice-wine hangover. During the two- to three-day nonstop rice-harvest parties, *gerangau mereh* becomes fantastically expensive: two finger lengths of dried root can be sold for a price equivalent to one day's labor. Where we were standing, the plant grew abundantly. We removed our packs and set about collecting twenty pounds of roots, roughly equivalent to six months' wages when sold by the piece.

We rinsed the roots in a narrow, leaf-choked stream and continued walking while John told me about *kayu hujan panas* (literally, hot rainwater wood). I was cautioned not to step over a fallen stick of this wood on the trail. When I asked why, John replied, "Your balls will become painfully swollen, and you won't be able to walk."

The antidote for swollen balls, I learned, was to drink a tea made from the scraped bark. There were other uses for the wood too: a piece of *kayu hujan panas* placed in the attic of a new longhouse would ward off evil spirits, and a small piece carried as a charm would keep poisonous snakes away. Until recently this wood was commonly used to prevent paralysis that comes as a result of being caught in a daylight rain shower during a rainbow. The tea is still given to Malay women after childbirth. To collect *kayu hujan panas*, you turn your back to the plant — being careful to shade it from the sun with your body — then grasp it with both hands and uproot it. Later that day I was handed a small piece of root, which I kept in my pack until I left the rain forest five months later.

Before Christian burials became common in the highlands at the end of World War II, the dead were placed in wooden coffins and allowed to rot on the longhouse porch. Holes were punched in the bottom of the coffins and bamboo poles inserted to allow for drainage. It was considered an expression of love and respect to put up with the stench of putrefying flesh. Each day at noon *kayu udjung panas* would be burned to scare away the spirit, the departed soul, and, it was hoped, some of the frightful smell.

We would often walk for hours without speaking, except to make brief comments on the terrain or the number of leeches. One day I removed more than one hundred leeches from my right leg; I didn't even bother to count those on my left. The best way I found to get rid of leeches was to pull them off and roll them between my fingertips for a few moments. They became disoriented, released their grip, and could be easily flicked off.

Otherwise they were like trying to get adhesive tape off my fingers.

When the walking became really rough, both John and Tingang Na would encourage me by repeating the words *hati, hati*. In my dictionary *hati* meant liver. What sort of message, I asked myself, were they trying to convey with the expression "liver, liver." Later I discovered that in Malaysia and Indonesia the liver is considered to be the emotional center of the body, as the heart is for Westerners. *"Hati, hati"* meant "Take courage, have a strong heart." There were other uses for the word *hati*. I once heard a woman referred to as *bagus dan murah hati* (good and inexpensive liver), which meant she gave of her emotions freely—a warm, generous person. If a person had *sakit hati* (sick liver), he or she was cruel and conniving. Practitioners of black magic have very sick livers.

Despite total concentration I managed to stumble and fall heavily on my face and backside at least ten times each day. My shins, knees, elbows, and shoulders soon became battered from many falls. Although I usually walked between my guides, watching their footsteps, it took weeks to recognize footholds properly. Innocent-looking river rocks were treacherously unstable and covered with a slippery invisible film. Eventually I assumed every step of the way was unsafe until proven otherwise. On the steep, clay slopes it was important to learn how to use the tangled, exposed tree roots to improve my footholds; edging my shoes and skidding down mud slopes was like skiing, except for the total lack of control. I slid down muddy trails, hands grabbing the air, as long trailing vines reached out to trip and choke me as well as to rip my clothing and skin with one-way barbs that acted like fishhooks. More than once I careened to a halt at the edge of the trail so entangled and bloodied by the rattan tendrils that John and Tingang Na had to come back and cut me loose. They treated the superficial cuts with *sakali-olo*, a leaf chewed to a paste and smeared on the skin to stanch the flow of blood and prevent infection. Sometimes moss was used. The deeper ragged cuts were treated with a root that was first roasted on the fire for five minutes then frayed with the edge of a knife. The resulting fibrous mass looked like grated ginger and had a similar smell. This preparation was placed on the cut with a leaf and held in place with thin strips of bark. These cuts healed quickly and left very little scar tissue.

The six-inch diameter, single-log bridges were the most trying obstacles of all: inclined, no handrails, slippery, and often rotten. They seemed to be designed to bear a maximum load of about 150 pounds. I weighed 175 without a pack, and at nearly two meters tall I was constantly confronted with a world designed for small people. Three times in the same day I watched my two guides with full packs safely file across one of those precarious affairs. In each case, when I arrived at midspan, the log gave way with a sharp crack, sending me headlong into the stinking mud and thorn bushes. Each time John and Tingang Na had to follow my cries as they cut a path to where they could extricate me from the network of bushes and snags.

"*Tiдak apa*" (it doesn't matter), they said, laughing at my predicament. As long as I wasn't hurting myself seriously, my poor balance and bad luck on the trail were a continual source of amusement to them. *Tiдak apa* is more than an expression. In a world filled with so many uncertainties and difficulties, *tiдak apa* has become a philosophy of life in Borneo — the universal "It's all right."

"*Tiдak apa*," I mumbled through clenched teeth as I got to my feet. Humility was the first jungle skill I acquired.

As consolation I conjured up the image of these two men seated behind the wheel of an automobile for the first time. With a line of honking vehicles backed up behind them, they were trying to merge into rush-hour traffic on the Santa Monica Freeway in Los Angeles. Also, I decided to grow a mustache to boost my self-esteem. It was one thing I could do that they could not. Compared to their hairless, baby-smooth complexions, I could grow the whiskers of a lifetime in a matter of weeks. I used the whiskers as a means of discovering what John and Tingang Na thought of me and my journey. Each morning they ran their fingers over the lengthening whiskers and asked if I used *obat* (med-icine/magic) to make them grow. They were always asking about my *obat*. What magic had I brought with me? White people are clever enough to build airplanes; surely they must have powerful potions or magic to help them? John and Tingang Na began to enjoy my company and sense of humor, but they were totally mystified by the amount of pain I was willing to endure for the sake of collecting plants, taking pictures of trees, and listening to their stories. Was I hiding some secret purpose, they won-dered? Why did I want to find the jungle Penan? Couldn't I just fly to the other side of the island? They would be terrified to travel alone into other tribal territory. Why wasn't I afraid of going into areas where I didn't know the spirits? We had become friends, but my journey remained a mystery to them.

At midday we heard the sounds of flapping wings somewhere above the green canopy of leaves and branches one hundred feet overhead. John and Tingang Na paused, smiled knowingly, and after identifying the unseen birds as *belingan* (*Buceros rhinoceros* — the rhinoceros hornbill), they asked whether I would like to try one for lunch. Feeling slightly incredulous, I said, "Yes, cer-tainly." We squatted comfortably, and Tingang Na began to call to the birds with a loud "Kock . . . kock . . . kock" sound. Within a few minutes two large, black birds were perched overhead.

There was a slight click as the thumb hammer of the shotgun was pulled back, followed by a pause just before the straining inner tube that ran the length of the barrel was finally unleashed to drive the firing pin home. There was a loud explosion, the smoke cleared, and one of the birds (last seen perched inquisi-tively on the branch), plummeted to earth not more than twenty feet away with a dull, feathery thump. We plucked the feathers from the warm bird, and a swarm of lice covered our hands and forearms. An hour later we were picking the last of the bones and finishing the steamed rice before setting off once again.

During this first foray into the rain forest, I learned to adapt my appetite and tastes to such foods as bee larvae and rice soup, roasted rattan shoots, boa constrictors, lizards, monkeys, bats, and the large animals — pigs and deer. I drank the river water and ate whatever my guides could find. I never got sick. I believed that by eating the local foods I would build up a natural resistance to the common jungle diseases: cholera, amoebic dysentery, typhoid fever, and malaria. My primary concern in this climate was septicemia. I was careful to treat every cut immediately. I knew from previous travels in Asia that even a small scratch could quickly develop into a festering tropical ulcer.

I began to learn about edible jungle plants. Many species of rattan can be eaten, but not all. After lunch one day I stopped to collect a large shoot for dinner. John and Tingang Na patiently watched as I avoided the barbed tendrils and removed the delicate yellow inner shoot with my knife the way they had shown me earlier.

"Not that one," they explained, "that is called *mato tagaro*, it will make your throat swell up, and you will die."

They conceded, however, that my knife work was improving. Later I pointed to some mushrooms and asked if they were edible. Tingang Na said they were, but the mushrooms would make me dream too much, and I would get lazy for many hours.

During the afternoons, as we tired from the river crossings, the terrain of the mountains, and the constant leech removal, our pace gradually slackened and more conversation developed. There were more frequent stops, and soon the talk turned to where we would camp for the night. This always depended on the availability of water and suitable fan palm leaves to make a watertight roof for the sleeping shelter in anticipation of the nightly downpour. Because of the winds, it was important not to sleep under trees with any deadwood or signs of termite activity. There are three types of wind to watch for in the jungle: storm winds, whirlwinds, and sudden direct blasts. The first two can bring down a lethal shower of dead branches and the occasional tree. The sudden blast of wind is much more dangerous. It can set off a chain reaction, toppling trees that may level a quarter square mile of rain forest. The only protection from the falling trees is to hide between the buttressed roots and hope your tree doesn't get pulled down. Falling branches and trees and a fuzzy red caterpillar are the most dangerous things in the jungle. John Bong was always chopping up caterpillars on the trail with his jungle knife, and when I asked him why, he showed me a hole in his foot where he had stepped on a red caterpillar ten months earlier. The invisible, fine hairs had painlessly entered the sole of his foot and had developed into a crippling septic wound that was just beginning to heal.

Once we found an ideal spot to set up camp, it took less than an hour to lash together a sturdy ten-foot-by-ten-foot sloped roof shelter with a triple layer of palm leaves on the roof.

The sunset and night air were filled with strange and thrilling insect sounds that variously buzzed, whistled, rasped, pulsated, and occasionally burst out in unison at such volume that conversation was barely possible. There were muffled animal screams in the distance, and one evening in the confusion of noises my ears deceived me and I was struck by a moment of nostalgia. I distinctly heard the ringing of my grammar school bell that had marked the end of playtime each afternoon.

Fireflies dotted the night like a blinking Milky Way punctuated with erratic miniature comets. Mushrooms (*Mycena cyanophos*) glowed in the dark, and splattered patches of yellow-green phosphorescence clung to the tree trunks. By early evening I would have completed my notes and we could enjoy some leisure time, which was always spent in the same way: storytelling.

One night we lay back on the irregular sapling floor, side by side beneath our blankets, adjusting our positions for greater comfort. The smell of smoke from the fire lingered as the first heavy raindrops began to fall, marking the steady patter of rain that would often continue throughout the night. Flashes of lightning briefly lit up the jungle, and I listened to traditional Borneo animal fables. Tingang Na and John often talked about the clever mouse deer, *plandok*, and the strange and frightening spirit *Pehnako*, who lives in the jungle. We could hear his cry: a loud "Kong-ka-ka . . . EEE-gut-gut!" I never discovered what made

73

the sound. With only the dying fire to illuminate the scene, their stories created a very haunting mood.

Tingang Na would sit up to add sticks of green wood to the fire to keep the mosquitoes away. When I asked where the first Penan came from, John told me the story of "The Hole in the Tree."

There was a tree in the deep jungle that had a big hole in the trunk far above the ground. Nearby was another tree that had a thick branch that grew at the same height as the hole and pointed towards it. In the same part of the jungle were a man and a woman who lived alone and didn't know about reproduction or sex. During a big storm the man and woman watched as the two trees were blown about by the wind. Eventually the two trees were blown against each other, and the branch entered the hole. The force of the wind made the branch move in and out of the hole for a long time, and this gave the man an idea. The man and the woman imitated the trees, and their children were the beginning of the Penan people.

Delighted with their story, I asked them whether they believed it. They were uncertain, but said it was common to joke about the groaning sounds of trees rubbing against each other.

One of the most popular stories I told was my special abridged version of *Cinderella*, with Cinderella working hard for her big, ugly, unmarried sisters — washing clothes in the river, cutting up tapioca for the pigs, and chopping firewood in the jungle. Along came the headman's son, who met her at an all-night rice-wine party and dance. Unfortunately Cinderella had to return to her village before midnight; otherwise her exquisitely carved and painted longboat would turn back into a banana (I didn't know the Malay word for pumpkin). The headman's son married Cinderella and took her away to the mouth of the river, where there were lots of fish and fat pigs. They lived happily ever after, of course. *Little Red Riding Hood* and *The Three Little Pigs* were told in similar fashion to my captive audience. As I developed fluency, my evening stories became more animated and absurd. The storytelling helped me remain optimistic during this first walk in the jungle. If I could fall asleep laughing, I would be fine for the next day. I could do without a map, but a sense of humor was essential.

The morning of the tenth day we waded through a thick ground mist that carpeted the surrounding fern forest. The air was damp, and each time we brushed against any of the giant ferns we were deluged by a shower of cold water. Before our morning tea stop we came across two freshly whittled Penan message sticks. They were four feet long and stuck obliquely into the ground. Notches and clefts along the sticks were embellished with pieces of rattan, leaves, and twigs. Message sticks usually give hunting or trail directions. Tingang Na "read" the sticks for me. One of them said, "We are hungry. Went hunting with blow-pipe for pig. This way." The second stick (known as *Bata'Oro*) said in Penan, "There are three strangers in the forest."

These sticks were placed where we could see them. This was the first time the nomadic Penan had acknowledged our presence. Where were they? We continued to see their message sticks for the rest of the day, but they would not answer our calls. Tingang Na said that they were shy and probably suspicious of me. He called out like an owl — "OOOOH-OOOOH!" — but there was no answer. We suspected the Penan were watching and sat down to wait. To encourage them we made it obvious that we had brought tobacco, tea, ammunition, and guns.

Jungle talk — similar to bird and insect calls of the area — is used by the Penan to avoid scaring the wildlife and to conceal messages from strangers. Here in the montane faunal area (four thousand feet) my lowland guides were unfamiliar with many of the natural sounds that could have been people talking to one another. I had been taught to use a soft, high-pitched "oooh" call or a quiet whistle if I wanted to attract someone's attention when we were hunting or walking. The tremor set off by a human voice quickly disrupts the tranquillity of the rain forest. A ripple of warning by the wildlife, inaudible to the untrained ear, radiates for hundreds of yards in all directions.

By sunset no one had responded to our calls, so after dinner

John announced that he was going out to shoot a mouse deer. He walked into the pitch-black night with a tree-resin torch and his gun. Five minutes later there was the sound of a distant shot. John returned with what looked like an overgrown rat with long legs and tiny cloven hooves. The body was riddled with pellet holes.

"*Planðok*" (mouse deer), he said.

Without disemboweling it he threw the carcass onto the fire, and the fur began to burn. It smelled horrible. He scraped off most of the hair and left the singed body on the wooden drying rack above the fire for the night. By morning the mouse deer was black and bloated, and the eyes were bulging in their sockets. We chopped up the body and boiled it in a pot with river water and salt. My anxiety mounted as the stench from the bubbling pot increased. Our morning's repast was dumped onto a bed of steamed white rice, and we began to eat. Tingang Na pointed out the delicacies — the stomach, lungs, liver, head, and what looked like the aorta. He handed me the head and told me how to eat it, "First the lips, then the tongue, then the eyes . . ."

My appetite faltered as I looked into the mouse deer's eyes. They had glazed over, and there were singed whiskers around the mouth. A meal with stubble was too much for me. I politely returned the avocado-size head to Tingang Na, who was touched by the generosity of my offer. He split the skull neatly in two with his parang and handed half to John. They scooped out the brains with their index fingers as I attempted to savor the aroma of burnt fur. I tried a lung; it was the texture of an old sink sponge.

As we were packing up, a hornbill's raucous call broke the jungle silence then drifted off into the surrounding vegetation. I was unconcerned and hoped only that we were creating enough interest for the forest people to show themselves.

That morning we finally got a response to our calls.

"OOOOH-OOOOH," someone called back.

We replied with the customary, "*My ke put koo*" (don't shoot us with your blowpipe).

In a sing-song manner the voice said, *"Tek-kenay?"* (who are you).

"Ak-O ee-to" (it is I), I responded. *"Jee-an ako ee-too"* (I am a good person), I added.

"Ma-hat ku koo-ee" (let us know where you are), called out Tingang Na.

The response was a vague, "I am here."

The exchanges continued until finally, and silently, a powerfully built jungle man appeared beside a nearby wall of leaves. I was startled by how close he was to us. His earlobes were distended, and he wore his hair in a ponytail that hung to his waist. The hair on his forehead was cut in a perfectly straight line, and there wasn't a trace of facial hair on his copper-colored cheeks. He was dressed in a loincloth and a very worn Western T-shirt that read, "Sgt. Pepper's Lonely Hearts Club Band." The incongruity of his T-shirt didn't detract a bit from his mesmerizing presence. Half-concealed by the undergrowth, he stood perfectly still, staring at us cautiously. In his hand was a seven-foot-long blowpipe. A spear tip was attached to the end with thin strips of carefully knotted rattan. At his waist was a bamboo quiver of poison darts and a 24-inch-long parang in a hardwood sheath. He continued gazing at us, and for the first few moments we returned his wordless stare. Tingang Na spoke a few words; then the Penan turned and motioned us to follow. As we walked, he removed the dart from his blowpipe and replaced it in his quiver. He was the first nomadic Penan I had met. Walking in this man's scent trail, I picked up a very distinct acrid smell of smoke and unwashed skin. The man's body odor wasn't unpleasant — it was animallike, a primeval, natural smell.

The camp was so well hidden that we arrived before I had any idea we were even getting close. There were five open-air sapling shelters laid out a random on a low ridge between two small streams. The shelters were similar to our nightly *pondoks*, but had permanent cooking areas and slat shelves for overhead storage. A special raised platform bed near the fire was for the favorite hunting dogs. The sapling floors were built two or more feet off the ground, to provide ventilation and to avoid snakes, leeches, and fire ants. Woven mats helped make sitting and sleeping more comfortable.

Two dozen people lived in Ba 'Talun camp, but there were only two old women and a few children in sight when we arrived. They looked ready to bolt for the jungle at a moment's notice. Jangang, the man who had met us, was watching the camp while the other men and women were out collecting sago shoots, gathering firewood, or hunting.

I handed Jangang and the women large pinches of powerful red Thai tobacco. They rolled four-inch-long conical cigarettes with pieces of dried banana leaf and put the rest in waterproof bamboo containers where they stored their flint and steel.

The children were terrified of me, and the women feigned disinterest. In typical Borneo fashion everyone waited for "the mood to be right." There were no frantic handshaking introductions, nor was there an urgency to establish who we were or why we were in the jungle. Eventually Tingang Na told Jangang that I had come to collect plants and stories from the forest. He emphasized the fact that I had plenty of tobacco and ammunition with me. This comment was followed by an hour of "sharing news" about our journey from Long Seridan. Tingang Na and John spoke a Penan dialect that I didn't understand, but by following their movements and excited patterns of speech I knew what they were talking about. Watching them, I was amazed by how they remembered every incident in detail. In great dramatic style they took extreme pleasure in embellishing their favorite moments. They took turns performing merciless imitations of my falling off the log bridges.

Satisfied with the stories and the tobacco, Jangang pointed to an area of ground next to a small clearing and said, "You can build your shelter there, but first we will eat."

We were served a dish that was described as "Penan cake," which consisted of smoked wild sago flour moistened in pig blood then dumped into a great cast-iron wok of sizzling pig fat.

Stirred constantly over high heat, the mixture eventually attained a chewy granular texture. The cake had a pleasant nutty, animal taste and wasn't nearly as greasy as I had expected. We ate with our hands, and before we were through the ever-present camp flies were thick on our fingers. We wiped our hands on the trees to get rid of the flies; then John Bong, Tingang Na, and I went into the jungle to collect poles and rattan for our sleeping shelter. For the sake of the Penan, Tingang Na and John displayed their skill by spending more time than usual on the construction. The vine lashings were more decorative, and every sapling that pointed towards the clearing was neatly cut to a four-cornered point.

People began returning to camp in the late afternoon, and introductions were made. I handed out more tobacco to the adults and some brightly colored balloons to the children. Abat, a diminutive childlike mother of five children, was without doubt the most beautiful and graceful woman I met in the rain forest. Her husband, Tevaoun, I soon learned, was the most skilled hunter. They lived in the shelter next to ours.

At first the men were shy, but the prospect of borrowing a shotgun helped them get over their hesitation. The next morning I lent one of the guns to Tevaoun and offered him a handful of shotgun shells. He took one and disappeared into the jungle.

Three hours later Tevaoun's whistle call was picked up by people in the surrounding forest. His message was quickly relayed to camp by more excited whistles. The message was: "Tevaoun returning with pig . . . *big pig!*"

Tevaoun must still have been half a mile away when the first ripple of excitement passed through Ba'Talun camp. By the time he arrived everyone was waiting. Tevaoun stepped out of the forest with a wild pig lashed to his back. The dead animal was beautifully trussed up on a five-foot stick and supported with a tumpline and shoulder straps of fibrous bark that passed through the carcass. The pig must have weighed well over three hundred pounds. The rump hung down below Tevaoun's knees, and the snout was at least eighteen inches above his head. I tried to lift

79

the pig off the ground by grasping it around the midsection with both arms and lifting with my legs. I strained—nothing happened—and there were a few snickers. Attempt number two was more successful, and I managed to budge the pig slightly. Tevaoun looked ill. He had carried the pig for hours and was utterly exhausted. He climbed into his shelter and fell asleep immediately.

The animal was butchered, and equal portions were given to each of the six family groups. The liver was placed directly on the coals and consumed immediately. The families took turns receiving the head. That night I helped cube the meat and force it onto 18-inch skewers that were smoked over the fire. The women rendered the fat in a wok 2½ feet wide. The fat was more valuable than the meat because it could be used in trade. It would be carried to Bario in sealed, 3-foot lengths of bamboo 5 inches in diameter and traded for salt and shotgun shells.

The Penan do not practice any form of meat preservation other than heat smoking. When there is food, they eat; when there is none, they search for it.

Every family brought leaf bundle after leaf bundle of barbecued, boiled, burned, fried, mashed, and skewered pig meat to us. It was an amount impossible to consume, but since we had provided the gun we kept receiving a large share of the meat. Every man wanted to use the gun, so for the next week we continued to eat, cook, tell stories, sleep, and eat again. Ba'Talun camp took on a holiday spirit.

Sago is the Penan's staple food, and one day I went to the river with Tevaoun and Abat to learn how to make sago flour. We had no language in common. They handed me a tool that looked like a croquet mallet, and I tried to imitate their effortless movements. Straddling the logs that Tevaoun had split with a short-handled ax, we worked our way forward—striking rhythmically at the soft inner pith with our sago mallets. The damp fibrous pulp fluffed up between my ankles as the sweat ran down my nose. I hit my toes a few times. The pulp was placed in a low 4-foot-by-4-foot sapling frame that held two finely woven rattan mats—

one above the other. The sago pulp was mixed with water in the top mat and kneaded by Abat's bare feet. This action extracted a fine brown sludge, which was caught in the lower mat. The pulp was discarded and the process repeated. The sludge in the lower mat was allowed to drain. Back at camp it would be smoked to remove excess moisture and would become sago flour. In one day we made enough sago flour to last four or five days.

We relaxed on the gravel beach after we finished the last of the logs, and I washed the blood off my toes where I had walloped them twice with the sago mallet. Tevaoun waded into the stream and rinsed out his shorts. Abat sat on a discarded sago log and began to sing a quiet song. She stopped occasionally and then continued. Her song was sung very sweetly to no one in particular. Then Tevaoun began to sing back. I watched the two of them in their totally natural and spontaneous interaction. They stopped to tease each other then sat at the water's edge. They continued singing until Abat reached between her husband's legs and gave him a friendly squeeze and a tug. It was her way of telling him it was time to get the sago back to camp.

After dinner that evening a small *damar* (tree resin) fire flickered to life in the clearing in front of our shelter. As I relaxed in the shelter, I began to notice rapidly moving orange-red bars of light in the darkness. They came from different directions. As the lights grew closer, people appeared from between trees waving small bundles of glowing sticks in front of their feet to find the way. They placed the sticks on the *damar* fire and sat down at the edge of the firelight. The men and women sat separately. A dulcimerlike three-stringed *sapeh* was quietly tuned as people warmed up with bamboo nose flutes and a bamboo's Jew's harp. A bright half moon cast an eerie glow on the clearing through the opening in the forest canopy. Jangang stood up and performed a solo dance —*ngajat* (traditional dancing). Tevaoun got up next; then one by one the other men took their turns. Each dancer changed into a special red-white-and-blue loincloth. The dances began with blood-curdling screams into the night, hot-blooded challenges to imaginary foes. Those were followed by

81

rhythmic circling and twisting movements of arms, legs, and hands. Some of the better dancers used a parang in mock combat; others danced just for fun. Every man did his best to impress the women, who watched carefully out of the corners of their eyes. After some good-natured urging and serious tugging by strong girlish hands, I was persuaded to put on the loincloth. As Jangang helped adjust the back, I let out a scream (in imitation of their war cry), as if he were trying to goose me.

Dressed in the loincloth with a headhunting sword in my hand, I stepped into the moonlight at the edge of the clearing. I wasn't quite sure what I would do. The women were far less uncertain; they took one look at me and collapsed in laughter.

I let out a savage cry as the music started then stepped back and caught my heel on a root. A terrific crunching and snapping of twigs followed as I lost my balance and disappeared backwards into the darkness. There were more shrieks of laughter as I reentered the *damar*-lit dancing ground. I performed a sword dance, pretending I couldn't get the blade out of the sheath as an imaginary foe pursued me around the clearing. Flapping the loincloth at the women and waving the now unsheathed sword over their heads, I sang out one of my few Penan phrases: *"My ke medai, my ke medai"* (don't be afraid, don't be afraid). They remained unconvinced until I was safely seated with sword in sheath. We were all laughing, and from behind me I could hear Tingang Na giggling uncontrollably, "They are liking too much . . . they are really liking too much!"

The women began to dance. They got up one at a time. It was a basic side-to-side step — arms waving alternately in front and back. Compared to the sinuous movements of the men, these dances were quite plain. The women danced with their backs to the fire out of shyness, and all that I could see from the men's side of the fire was the dancer's black hair against a brown back and swaying hips. Then one of the younger unmarried women — bare breasted and dressed in a brand-new sarong (with paper label still attached) — performed an astonishing dance. Keeping time to the music, she turned to face the fire and the men. She began rubbing her hips, crotch, and thighs in such a blatant manner that I was uncertain how to interpret her gestures. When I asked the man next to me what her dance meant, he nearly rolled over backwards in amusement before he said mockingly in Malay, "Well, what do you think it means?"

Some of the later dances were even more graphic. One older man did an absurdly exaggerated version of lovemaking. He leapt about trying to copulate with an imaginary, elusive lover. First he pretended his penis was too small, then too soft, then much too big — he staggered around the fire under the weight of it. Men, women, and children were laid out on the ground shaking with laughter.

The dancing continued until the moon was lost in the trees. We danced in groups, and in the end the best mimics got up and improvised variations on recent events: Tevaoun's big pig, a child chased by tiger hornets, Jangang's being bit on the end of his penis by a deerfly, and a white man pounding his toes with a sago mallet. The dancing served as a catharsis; it helped people shed their burdens and reinforced the fact that life in the jungle was good — the very best.

The music finally stopped, and people began to leave the dance ground. Singly and in small groups people took glowing sticks from the fire to find the way back to their shelters. As I lay beneath my mosquito net, my sides were sore from laughing. I fell asleep feeling euphoric.

At dawn I was awakened by the thud of a parang blade and the splitting of firewood. Rain had fallen lightly for most of the night, and fine droplets of water still clung to each leaf tip and spider web. Snug under my bedsheet in a sarong and sweater, I woke up realizing that all my doubts and misgivings about being in the jungle had vanished. I felt accepted. By making a complete fool of myself the night before I had shown trust in the good nature of these people. I had made myself vulnerable to ridicule, and they had loved it. The only white men these people knew were either Christian missionaries or European geologists. I was something else.

One of the men had an ancient transistor radio. He warmed the batteries by the fire to strengthen them, and, using a shotgun barrel as an antenna, we tuned in to a "Voice of America" broadcast from Singapore. Over the static we listened to the Beach Boys singing "In My Room." There was some twangy Don Ho–type Hawaiian ukelele music, and finally "This Old Man" was sung by a group of Australian preschoolers. Then the radio went dead. When I was asked about the songs I said that they were for traditional dancing in my village in America.

Ten days had passed since we had arrived in Ba 'Talun camp. On the other side of the Tamabo Mountains was the Kelabit highland community of Bario, my destination. I was fascinated by this first group of jungle people. I felt like one of the family and had a difficult time deciding when I should leave. John Bong and Tingang Na were happy to stay as long as I wanted. They were delighted with how the journey was developing, and they continued to earn their wage each day. There were some practical considerations. We had run out of our own food days before, but when I asked my guides to mention this to Tevaoun, he replied; "We have food, and therefore we can share."

While I was trying to think of a way to repay them for their hospitality, I came upon a shredded *jala* (cast net). Ten years earlier I had worked on an Australian prawn trawler off the coast of Arnhem Land patching the shark holes in the nets. I could remember the sequence of knots and diamond patterns, so I spent an afternoon repairing their net with nylon fishing line and a hardwood mending needle.

As I worked on the net, Abat sang a song for me as Tevaoun and his sister played a nose flute and bamboo Jew's harp. Abat sang about my arrival in the camp, what had happened during my stay, and how I would be leaving them soon to "go to the mouth of the river." "You will be leaving us in the jungle and will fly through the sky like a bird to your home. We would like to go with you, but we are lower people. We have no money and must stay here in the forest. Be careful at the mouth of the river." The

84

mouth of the river is the farthest point in the Penan universe. No one at Ba'Talun had ever seen the ocean.

The next day I left the camp. The Ba'Talun Penan walked with me as far as the river, stroking the hair on my arms and holding my hands warmly. They loaded us up with skewers of smoked pig meat and a large sack of sago flour. I gave them tobacco and five shotgun shells — for the next time they borrowed a gun. I crossed the shallow, slow-moving river with a walking staff that Tevaoun had cut for me. Before reentering the jungle on the far side of the river, I turned to wave. Everyone was lined up holding their children and smiling. As long as we were within calling distance I could hear their sing-song voices:

"*Dawai-ðawai* . . . *ðawai-ðawai*" (go slow, be careful . . . don't fall down, don't cut yourself with your parang).

That day we joined a major highland footpath and passed abandoned longhouses and old fields that had been reclaimed by the jungle. On the third day we stopped to rest at a pass called Punga Pawan. The clouds to the east parted, and for the first time we could see the Plains of Bah in Kelabit country. We descended the eastern slope of the Tamabo Mountains through heavy rain forest and emerged onto a wide plain of shimmering emerald green rice padis. I could see the great dividing range that marked Indonesian Borneo ten miles to the east. It was thrilling to be out of the jungle. I could see the sky, clouds, people working in the distance; and the ground was flat. The trails were three feet wide and seemed like super expressways. I could walk with my head up and stretch out with a normal stride. I was beaming as we approached Bario longhouse just before midday. We had been in the rain forest nearly a month.

CHAPTER FOUR · RAJAH KUMIS

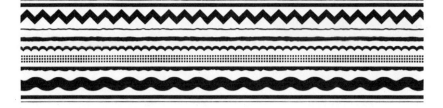

THE DRAGON jar of Chief Lawai Bisari had been making
strange roaring and booming sounds at infrequent intervals for many weeks. The people of Bario longhouse were so
concerned by this strange new noise that they took the big, ceramic, rice-wine jar out to the fields and tied it to a buffalo teth-
ering post. The people then waited cautiously for a sign, an omen
to guide them. One foggy morning it arrived with a splat as British paratrooper Tom Harrisson landed on his backside in the
middle of a Bario swamp. Seven other parachutists floated to
earth, followed by a large quantity of supplies. The terrible roaring sounds gradually receded until a great silence descended on
the Plains of Bah. The year was 1945, and the soldiers had
dropped behind the lines in Japanese-occupied Sarawak. The
roaring sounds over the previous weeks had come not from the
dragon jar, as suspected, but from the four-engine Liberator
Bomber on earlier reconnaissance flights. The occupants of the
big plane had been looking for a gap in the cloud cover and a
suitable drop zone.

At the first sound of the aircraft, invisible above the morning
clouds, the men of Bario had stationed themselves across the
valley to keep a lookout. It took the Kelabit warriors less than
an hour to respond to the invasion of their homeland. With only
spears and blowguns these men rounded up the heavily armed
soldiers and took them back to the longhouse. According to Harrisson's account of the incident, the first thing the Kelabit people
wanted to know was whether the eight white men were humans.
This established, work on the Plains of Bah came to a standstill.
Out came the rice wine, and the party began.

In the highlands today people refer to Tom Harrisson as *Tuan Major* (Sir Major), the name given to him when he returned to Bario during Sukarno's Konfrontasi Campaign in the early 1960s. I had studied Harrisson's route over the mountains to Long Nawang and down the Kayan River to Tarakan at the end of World War II and was planning to follow his route as closely as possible. Harrisson, who stayed on in the highlands for many years after World War II and who later became curator of the Sarawak Museum, described his journey in *World Within*, a book I discovered in the Sarawak Museum reference library. People in many of the villages where I later stayed wanted news of *Tuan Major*. Because there are so few white men in the world (from the perspective of people who live in central Borneo), many people assumed that we would know each other. Forty years had elapsed since he had passed through these villages, yet many of the older men and women remembered him well. Black-and-white photographs of a trim young man gazing intently into the camera were still displayed on the longhouse walls. Once again the *Sarawak Museum Journal* had come in handy: in it I had read Tom Harrisson's obituary and could tell many people of his death in a tourist-bus collision between Chiengmai and Bangkok in 1978. The effect on the people was startling. This man had obviously touched them deeply. Some of the people wept at the news while others reminisced about how much rice wine he could drink. Eyes glazed over as the great rice-wine parties in the highlands were recalled, parties that are no longer held since the arrival of the mission. Bario has become a good, clean, upstanding, sober, hard-working Christian community. What a loss for these fun-loving and generous people.

There may be considerably less alcohol in the Kelabit highlands today than in Tom Harrisson's day — thanks to the continuing diligence of the Borneo Evangelical Mission — but the hospitality has certainly not diminished. In all of Borneo there are no people more generous with their time and skills and information than the people from Bario. They are trustworthy, intelligent, and delightful. Tom Harrisson and his companions couldn't have fallen into better hands.

♣   ♣   ♣

The best way to arrive in Bario is on foot. It gives one a true sense of the extreme isolation that the highland people lived in until the end of World War II, so isolated that a head had not been taken from the Kelabit highlands for eighty years prior to the war. Considering their downriver neighbors' propensity for gathering heads, that fact is even more remarkable. After a month in the rain forest, Bario was the perfect place for me to rest and plan the next phase of my journey. I stayed in the Kelabit highlands for two weeks.

It felt good to be out of the shade, but to my surprise Tingang Na and John Bong did not share this excitement. The direct sunlight gave them headaches, and they tried to stay out of it as much as possible. To them the rain forest was home, and they returned to it before nightfall. I paid them with ammunition and Malay dollars, as agreed, and added a few extra cartridges as a thank you. We waved goodby, but after all of our intimate and humorous experiences their departure seemed rather abrupt. It was not their intention to be thoughtless — the problem was that I was still judging people's actions by sentimental Western standards. Lingering farewells and elaborate thanks aren't part of Penan behavior.

♣   ♣   ♣

Ara Dalan and Bario are two of the ten longhouse communities to be found in the Kelabit highlands. The slightly undulating terrain of this valley is ringed by giant, green mountains and fed by innumerable small streams that originate in the mountain forests. These streams are diverted into an ingenious maze of hand-dug irrigation canals that are capable of reaching every square inch of fertile soil. This skill of harnessing water has allowed the Kelabits to practice wet-rice agriculture rather than the more common slash-and-burn, hill-rice techniques used in the lowlands. The rice fields dominate the landscape by carpeting the valley floor in a patchwork design of colors ranging from brilliant lime green to yellow to mud brown and finally to shimmering blue-green, depending on the phase of the agricultural cycle. Access to the longhouse communities is confined to the narrow, packed-mud trails between the rice fields.

During my two months of reconnaissance I had made a short visit to Bario by light aircraft to talk to the people about the feasibility of walking into the uncharted parts of Kalimantan. At the time I made some enduring friendships with the people of Ara Dalan, a small community at the western edge of the valley just below Punga Pawan Pass. On this second visit I was taken in by my friend Stanley Massy, who lived in Ara Dalan. Stanley gave me a large room in his four-room house and provided me with everything, even a bed. Nights were cold and damp in this highland valley, and I was given extra blankets.

Of the many memories I have of Ara Dalan and the Kelabit highlands, the one that stands out is the skillful cooking of Stanley's beautiful wife. I'm ashamed that I have forgotten her name, but the meals I will never forget. Who would think that the small, conical, rice-padi snails were edible, let alone a culinary treat? Or that grated tapioca root slightly sweetened and deep fried in pig fat would be anything but gray, gummy muck tasting of rancid bacon drippings? The resulting warm, golden brown, light, fragrant, chewy, sweet morsels served with morning coffee have made me rethink my feelings toward the humble tapioca root.

In the weeks I stayed in Ara Dalan I was treated not only to the best food on the entire island, but to some of the best regional cooking I have had anywhere in the world. Considering the limited ingredients, this is quite astonishing. Most of the food was stir-fried in a wok over a floor-level wood fire in the center of the kitchen. There was no chimney. Food from the jungle, such as sago shoots, tapioca leaves, succulent fern tendrils, wild mushrooms, and certain rattan shoots were lightly sautéed and served as side dishes with the fine, long-grain Bario rice. The most common meat was wild boar, but there were small fish from the rice padis, jungle deer, snakes, and the occasional monkey. The fruit was plentiful, and there was always a new variety coming into season: guavas, pomelos, small sweet bananas, papayas, jackfruit, wild durians, pineapples, mangos, and passion fruit.

One of the most unusual dishes I had was called *Telluh Babi* — sour preserved pork, aged without cooking or refrigeration in a section of a giant bamboo. It is prepared in the following way. Mix one-half small water glass of salt and one plate (three double handfuls) of fatty wild pig meat cut into 1-inch-by-2-inch-by-3-inch pieces and adjust seasoning with pepper — or chillies, if available. Add one double handful of steamed rice (cooled) and mix with a clean wooden paddle (if you touch the mixture with your hands, it will go rotten). Store in a new bamboo container, tightly sealed, for at least one month, but preferably for six months.

I had come across a description of *Telluh Babi* in my reading, and the author had described it as putrefied pork laced with maggots. It sounded revolting. Uncooked, the mixture does have an almost overpowering odor of sour fermented rice, but the pieces of coated meat become transformed into something altogether different when laid directly on the coals for five minutes. The fat flames up until one would think the meat was burned to a cinder, but when slightly cooled it is absolutely delicious. Crispy and sweet on the outside from the carmelized, tangy, fermented rice and juicy on the inside — full of complex and unexpected flavors. Each bite brought forth a new taste sensation. What a spectrum of flavors: piquant, sour, fragrant, and sweet! When sliced across the grain, the meat revealed an iridescent shimmer similar to corned beef or pastrami.

♠　♠　♠

In addition to the two longhouses in Ara Dalan, there were many single-family houses. Three houses down from Stanley lived Pedera Ulun, his wife, and two grandsons. This man was one of the few remaining great hunters in the Kelabit highlands. He was thought to be in his midseventies, and he still hunted in the jungle mountains west of Bario. He spoke Kelabit only, and it was his twenty-year-old grandson Petrus who translated his stories into

English for me. Petrus had inherited his grandfather's jungle skills and love of the rain forest people. He was one of the few young men in the community who took delight in living in the jungle and had once spent four months with the Penan. He took me on many short trips into the forest and was an invaluable source of information.

His grandfather, Pedera Ulun, was not yet twenty years old when he joined his first rhinoceros hunt. It was sometime in the 1920s, and Pedera Ulun's mother had forbidden her son to join the hunt because it was too dangerous. After all, he had only a spear to defend himself while the older men would be hunting with a gun. Like dutiful young men elsewhere around the world, Pedera Ulun assured his mother he wouldn't go and then slipped out of the village with the small hunting party. They disappeared into the jungle and followed tracks for many days before they found their quarry—one of the last Bornean rhinoceros. They brought it to bay, and the great beast snorted and threw up great clods of damp earth with its powerful feet. Pedera Ulun convincingly imitated the sounds during the telling of the story. The maddened rhinoceros charged through the undergrowth like a locomotive, flattening everything in its path as the men with the gun ducked behind trees attempting to get into position for a clean shot. Finally a great cloud of gray smoke shot out of the barrel of the ancient muzzle-loading relic. The smoke cleared, and the rhinoceros was still on its feet. Apart from a minor flesh wound to its neck, the animal was uninjured. There was no time to reload as the rhinoceros charge again and again. The men scattered into the maze of trees. All of them, that is, except Pedera Ulun. He had been waiting for his moment. He stepped from the protective cover of the big trees and faced the wounded animal, killing it with his spear, thus becoming one of the greatest hunters of his generation.

Later that night Petrus told me of another great hunt that his grandfather had made, which was quite different from the first. Petrus's father had died from leukemia when Petrus was about six years old. His grandfather had to provide for the entire family, and there was little money. Petrus's mother eventually re-married, but the new husband would not provide money for Pe-trus's school books. Petrus sat in the open-air classroom day after day feeling foolish and alone while the other children teased him because his family was poor. At night he cried for his stepfather to help, but the man saw no value in school. Petrus began to fail his classes because he couldn't study. He had only two books, English and math. One morning Petrus could bear the humilia-tion no longer. He sent word with the Penan for his grandfather to come help. Pedera Ulun was hunting near Pa Tik and arrived with his hunting dogs after a three-day walk through the jungle. He listened to Petrus's story and then cried with his grandson. "I have no money to give you for your books," he said. "There is only one thing I can do to help you—tomorrow we will hunt in the jungle."

The next day they shot a wild pig, and Petrus took the gutted carcass to Bario longhouse. He sold the meat to the parents of the boys who had teased him. When the situation of the school books was revealed, there was much discussion. Why didn't the stepfather help? And why couldn't the clever schoolboys hunt for their own families? Had they—the descendants of hunters— forgotten those skills? The people were ashamed. They bought the meat, and Petrus purchased his books. Pedera Ulun, having made his point, walked back to Pa Tik the next morning.

♠   ♠   ♠

During my stay in Bario an *irau* was put on by Nicol to celebrate the birth (six years earlier) of his first grandchild. An *irau* is a big party, and more than a thousand people were fed. Some of the guests had walked all day to attend. The idea behind an *irau* is to show unlimited hospitality. It is an economic occasion, where one settles old debts and creates new ones. Understand-ably, one person or one family could never afford to throw such a grand party without help, so contributions in labor and food are made by many people on a payback basis. Prior to the morn-ing slaughter (ten pigs for this one), each animal is carefully weighed on a huge balance-beam scale supported by a tripod stand. The weights are recorded in people's minds and remembered for years. Your contribution today will be your gift in later years. You must calculate for future births and work out a satisfactory network of debt relationships to avoid huge costs later on. At Nicol's *irau* for his granddaughter, more than a thousand folded-leaf packets of steamed rice and skewers of meat were served. There were cups of sweet coffee and soda crackers for everyone. In former times there would have been unlimited jars of rice wine to encourage dancing and game playing, which would last for two or three days. Now, because of the mission and changing values, an *irau* will usually end before midnight on the first day.

Irau debts are passed on from one generation to the next. The deceased grandfather of the air-traffic controller at the Bario airstrip (grass runway, wheelbarrow-toting porters, with the baggage hauled to the longhouse by water-buffalo sled) owed a jungle deer. The air-traffic controller was asked to honor the debt that he knew nothing about. His ancient aunt was consulted, and she confirmed the debt. The grandson was not a hunter, and the particular type of deer owed was no longer easily found near Bario, so a money settlement was agreed upon by both parties on a per-pound basis of the original deer.

Substitutes can also be made, depending on mood. For example, Peter Ibu, a shopkeeper, decided to provide ten tins of soda crackers rather than his promised pig. He calculated his "gift" crackers on Bario retail prices rather than on the 50 percent lower coastal wholesale price he paid. In return he will hope to get a pig, but even if he receives crackers, he can sell them in his store for a good profit. This illustrates a relatively simple debt relationship. The idea is to become economically entangled, socially bound for years to come.

An *irau* is also a time for name changing. The Kelabits have official names for their National Identity Cards, but they change their names frequently and are allowed many aliases. A common name change takes place on the birth of a first child. Perhaps the child's name is Bulan (The Moon, a girl's name); the father would change his name to Tama Bulan, Father of Moon. Names are also chosen to suit the individual's mood or situation in life. Young men often select names to project their future aspirations: Balang Nakrau (Tiger Roar), or Bayah Punga (The True Crocodile). In later years people may change their names to sum up their life experiences. Petrus's grandfather, for example, had lost his favorite son. He had also found a lost patrol of half-starved and dying Japanese soldiers and led them out of the jungle to the safety of Bario, where they could surrender. On this walk he had seen many men fall down and die from exhaustion. Pedera Ulun means Life of Many Sadnesses.

To join in the name changing at an *irau* one is expected to make a contribution. The offering is made earlier, and when everyone is assembled on the longhouse porch, individuals stand up to announce their new names. What is one to think of someone who calls himself Inandiu (A Place to Take a Bath) or Inantudu (A Place to Sit Down)? These two names required some explanation. A Place to Take a Bath meant Refresh Yourself in My Company; A Place to Sit Down meant Visitors Always Welcome.

The meanings of other names were clear:

Matala Ulun	Chose Life
Mulun Balang	Live Tiger
Seribu Munung	Many Faces
Ta Low (Penan)	Short Penis
Do-Eelah	Very Clever
Nap-an Aran	Hidden Honor
Siron Lemalun	Look at Me

Stanley's father-in-law had one of the best—Mulun Kadangan, Eternal Light. This name had two meanings: ever watchful throughout the night or sexually active the whole night. Eternal Light was about seventy years old, but he refused to update his name.

The people seated around me said that I should select a new name. Nothing appropriate came to mind, so I asked for a suggestion. The men and women conferred briefly, and I was given

95

my Kelabit name: Rajah Kumis, King of the Mustaches. Over
the previous six weeks my mustache had quickly out-paced all
contenders.

➚ ➚ ➚

The Borneo Evangelical Mission experienced a vigorous revival
in the Kelabit highlands in 1973 when two young schoolboys,
under duress of examinations, stopped their studies and began
to pray. They continued for days, and spontaneously the mood
caught on. This miracle had many repercussions. Fellowship
meetings were no longer confined to Sundays; they were held
one to three times daily starting at 5:30 A.M. The call to worship
would be sounded by rhythmic beats on a bamboo or hardwood
drum. I attended the predawn service once to listen to the singing, but the most interesting aspect of the service was the offering. People brought leaf packets of garden or jungle produce —
such as field mushrooms, green beans, edible ferns, and bitter
melon. These were auctioned by the pastor for twenty cents to
fifty cents per bundle. The man of God would encourage the
congregation with pleas of: *"Lima puluh sen! Lima puluh sen!"*
(fifty cents! fifty cents!)

It is claimed that no one smokes tobacco or drinks in Bario,
but, of course, the cynics claim that the revival has only driven
the tobacco smokers and *borak* drinkers to the isolated farm huts.

➚ ➚ ➚

With Petrus I took many short trips into the jungle near Bario to
collect medicinal plants for trade, and on one occasion to look at
old burial sites hidden in the cliff faces. Along a rock-strewn
ridge I was shown half a dozen priceless *tabok* ceramic jars partially filled with bones that had literally turned to dust. If I was
ever to be a grave robber, this was my opportunity. The jars were
as fine as any I had seen in the Kuching Museum. But the jars,
the hidden setting, and the atmosphere of the place were mesmerizing. I wasn't even tempted by these treasures.

One day I learned of a group of Kelabit and Murut men who
were going to introduce Christianity to the Penan of Ba'Talun. I
had heard of these first contacts and had seen re-creations of

missionary encounters in the movies many times, but I had never seen such an event firsthand. I couldn't resist the opportunity, so I returned to Pa Tik, the abandoned longhouse near Ba'Talun camp, with one native pastor, four Kelabit men, and nineteen hunting dogs. The first night I sat cross-legged with the other men knee to knee around our banana-leaf picnic dinner blanket stacked high with boiled pig meat and steamed white rice. The technique of bone disposal was tricky. We threw the bones over our shoulders to the dogs prowling around in the dark. Like a school of piranhas they would fall upon each morsel with a ferocity that I found alarming. A mere arm's length away the sounds of snarling and snapping jaws was unnerving. Occasionally one of the men would pick up a stick and drive the dogs back a few feet, but they would return within moments. They savaged each other, and tufts of unwashed dog hair wafted across the dimly lit dinner scene. Not exactly my idea of a floor show.

The next morning, as we walked in single file, the dogs developed an irritating habit of threading their way through everyone's legs before ranging far out into the jungle to pick up the scent of wild game. They would then circle back to the end of the procession, pass through and around our legs, and repeat the procedure *ad nauseam*. With nineteen dogs performing this maneuver it was very difficult to walk, and I started to lose my temper. The dogs were constantly underfoot at the most inopportune moments. I eventually made the mistake of getting impatient and learned a painful lesson — don't touch the dogs. One of them had been tripping me up for a few minutes in his attempt to pass me on the steep, narrow trail. Each time I stepped to the side to allow him to pass, he hesitated. This continued until I was in the middle of a muddy traverse, and once again the dog was making me stumble. On impulse I grabbed the dog by the scruff of the neck, intending to shove him ahead. Instantly I received a mouthful of teeth to the back of my hand. Four nasty puncture wounds covered with dog slobber. I never made that mistake again; it was two weeks before I could make a fist without pain.

Two days later we arrived at the ruins of Pa Tik, and arrangements were soon made for an evening service. The floor and roof of the longhouse were still intact, but there were no walls. As far as I could determine, the purpose of the journey was to distribute songbooks that had been translated into the Penan language. This was curious because the Penan can't read. They love to sing, and I think the aim was to get them to learn theology by memorizing European church songs about flocks of sheep and green pastures.

After dinner about a dozen of the Ba'Talun Penan arrived. We acknowledged each other with nods of recognition. The service began with a sermon in Kelabit and Malay, which I doubt the congregation could follow. I couldn't follow what was being said, but soon it was time for individual prayers. The Kelabits have a peculiar habit of praying out loud and together — not in unison, but rather in a jumble — a pandemonium of beseeching voices one overlaying the next. An older lady began clapping her hands together and crying out, *"Terima kasih, Tuhan!"* (Thank you, Lord!) She repeated the words again and again, gradually increasing the volume until she was half-singing, half-shouting. *"Terima kasih, Tuhan! Terima kasih, Tuhan!"*

The clapping became more frantic, and I began to wonder if this were one of the "Holy Spirit" experiences that I had been told about on the Baram River. When the concept of the Holy Spirit was first explained to the longhouse people and the Penan, they were told that through trance the Holy Spirit could give them direct access to God. The woman was obviously experiencing something very intense, but it seemed to me that she was also trying to please the pastor, perhaps to show him the depth of her religious conviction. The volume and length of personal prayers are important indicators of one's faith. At first, no one took special notice of the woman, but as the other prayers faded, the woman continued at a more feverish pitch. We all sat and waited to see what would happen. She broke out in a heavy sweat, and her eyes filled with tears.

"Terima kasih, Tuhan! Terima Kasih, Tuhan!" she was screaming.

The pastor began to look worried. The service had fizzled out, and we all stared at the woman. Then, without warning, she suddenly flopped on her back directly in front of where I was sitting, her hands held in prayer above her chest. She began babbling, and it occurred to me that she might be speaking in tongues. This was an exciting new possibility. I leaned forward and placed my ear close to her mouth in hopes of picking up snatched phrases of French or Serbo-Croatian, maybe a few liturgical invocations in Latin or the soulful patter of a southern Baptist minister.

My mind wandered back to an early-morning drive into New York City with my friends David and Carolyn. On the radio was Manhattan's very own Reverend Wade, broadcasting live to his radioland congregation from The Prayer Room. He was inviting us all to come up and get our straight money blessings. "Put down your work, stop what you're doin'," he entreated us as we crossed the George Washington Bridge and entered the city. "Come up, come straight on up to The Prayer Room and get your straight . . . straight money . . . straight money blessings!"

I listened to the woman on the floor and could make no more sense of her continuous string of unintelligible words than I had the words of Reverend Wade. The woman's daughter put her ear to the woman's mouth, but she couldn't understand the sounds either. What happened next was totally spontaneous and it was the only touching incident of the entire evening service. We all moved in to sit as close as possible to the woman. Some of the people sang quietly while others prayed. Most of us touched the woman. I placed my hands on her forearm and squeezed softly and stroked her skin in an attempt to calm her down. The woman continued screaming for another five minutes, until finally she lay silent — totally spent from her efforts. An audible sigh of relief came from the pastor as he wiped his brow. "Not like church services in your country," he confided to me in English.

♣   ♣   ♣

Near Long Banga I had heard stories about "Holy Spirit meetings." They are particularly popular with the settled Penan communities. It is believed that people possessed by the Holy Spirit can not only speak in tongues, but can also perform faith healing. The Holy Spirit meetings are becoming very popular. Holy Spirit cassette tapes are available from Indonesia, Brunei, and Miri. February and June are the most common months for these meetings because they correspond with free time in the agricultural calendar.

Holy Spirit meetings can be spontaneous, but are sometimes organized when it is felt that the longhouse is "getting cold" (lacking in spirit). This is a direct carryover from older times. To "warm up" a house traditionally, one would need fresh human heads. Now that the longhouse people can no longer collect heads, they substitute with Holy Spirit meetings. If the longhouse is only a "little bit cold," the people simply slip a Holy Spirit cassette into their portable tape players.

After two days of religious instruction, we returned to Bario. During the journey the minister's electronic wristwatch malfunctioned and began to emit "Oh! Susanna" on its musical alarm with increasing regularity.

⁂

During my stay in the Kelabit highlands, I looked across the wide, green valley to study the mountains that marked the border of Kalimantan. They were only a few miles away, and I knew that this time I would reach them. A few nights before I left, Pedera Ulan gave me some travel advice for the land beyond the mountains. Petrus translated: "You must obtain a *surat jalan* (walking letter). Get one from the headman in Bario longhouse and show this letter to the headman in the first village you reach in Kalimantan. It is your letter of introduction. For your safety always travel from one headman to another. Each headman will write you a new letter. If you travel as a stranger, you will leave yourself open to suspicion."

I was warned to take only guides who had been arranged by the headman. This was because a guide who is answerable to the head of his village will take care of you. He is responsible for your safety and well-being. People in the center of Borneo have long memories, and any local who violates the code of village hospitality can expect his family and their descendants to bear the guilt of his actions.

"Never select your own guides," emphasized Pedera Ulan. "If there are no guides available, it is better to wait. With the exception of the Penan, the people in Indonesia are different."

He went on to explain *elmu hitam*—the practice of black magic. Certain people with *sakit hati* (sick livers/bad hearts) can cause illness by sending a *pisau* (knife), through the air over any distance. It enters the victim's body, and he or she gradually weakens over several months and dies. People from the upper Mahakam River, he warned me, can send a *djarum* (needle), splinter of wood from the ironwood tree, or a *tulang* (bone) through the air. These objects can also be hidden on the footpaths. They painlessly enter the foot, and a lingering illness and death follow. Pedera Ulan told me that only a parang forged from the local iron ore (*batu besi*) can kill a practitioner of *elmu hitam*. I thanked Pedera Ulan for the thoughtful advice, but I was a fool and didn't take it seriously. I always traveled with a *surat jalan*, but I didn't heed the warning about black magic and jungle spirits.

When it came time for me to leave Ara Dalan, Pedera Ulun made a short, formal speech about my time spent in the Kelabit highlands. He spoke of my long journey and finished with, "When you go, please remember the Kelabit people. Safe journey Rajah Kumis."

CHAPTER FIVE · THE ROAD
TO PAYE RUNGAN

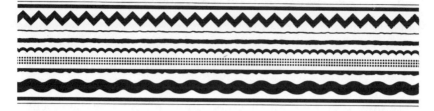

TRAVELING EAST from the Kelabit highlands there are three major mountain passes leading into Kalimantan. Sarawak and Kalimantan share a common border of more than seven hundred miles, and in that distance there are perhaps fewer than five controlled crossings. It seemed like madness to my friends in Bario that without a permit or visa for Kalimantan I should choose to cross the border at Long Bawang, one of the official checkposts.

I decided on Long Bawang because I had heard that a group of Japanese ethnobotanists was working in the area, looking for native plants that might contain anticancer compounds similar to those found in the rosy periwinkle, a native to the rain forests of Madagascar. The drugs vincristine and vinblastine are used in the treatment of cancer of the lymph system (Hodgkin's disease, as well as acute lymphoblastic leukemia). Both of these pharmaceuticals are derived from the rosy periwinkle. I wanted to talk with the botanists about rain forest plants and hoped that they would be able to identify some of those I had collected while with the Penan. These plants were stored in plastic bags and kept at the bottom of my pack.

I asked my friends in Bario what would happen if I were apprehended with my shotgun shells in Long Bawang. "Don't get caught!" was their emphatic reply. At the very least, they warned me, the shells would be confiscated, leaving me with no way of paying for guides. At worst, I could receive up to one year in jail for each shotgun shell. This second possibility was highly unlikely because the police and army border guards would be much more interested in keeping the ammunition for themselves, rather than confiscating it and turning me over to the coastal authorities. Either way, I ran the risk of being turned back at the border. I decided to test my luck.

As I was preparing to leave Bario, Ray and Janet, two English friends I had met during my stay in Kuching, unexpectedly arrived by light aircraft from the coast. I told them what my plans were, and they asked if they could join me for five days. They wanted to walk over the border and then return to Bario on one of the established trails. It would be an easy walk for the first week; they were experienced, so I agreed.

The walk to Long Bawang was along a clear track over a surprisingly low pass. A guide wasn't necessary, and the journey took three days. We stayed in longhouses at night and didn't need to carry more than a small amount of food. On the morning of the second day we heard a helicopter overhead and caught a fleeting glimpse of it through the forest canopy. The helicopter had military markings, but it disappeared before I could determine whether it was Malaysian or Indonesian. I wasn't sure which country we were in. We emerged from the rain forest a few hours later and began walking through a checkerboard maze of rice padis. We stopped in Parupai — the first small community in Kalimantan — to ask directions. A shopkeeper invited us in for tea. There were several men already seated inside his store, and they greeted us with smiles and nods of welcome as we entered the cool, dark room.

Soon after we sat down, one of the men got up and left. I was taking my first sip of tea when the man returned — dressed in his border-guard uniform. No one in Bario had mentioned a checkpost in this little village, and my immediate response was to panic. With the unlimited power bestowed on border officials throughout the world, the man collected our passports and disappeared out the door. I was nervous about the shotgun shells in my pack, but my main concern was for Ray and Janet. They had no idea what I was carrying, and it didn't seem fair that they might have to share the guilt. When the guard returned five minutes later he was carrying a freshly sliced pineapple. This gave me some relief. He informed us that he must keep the passports overnight, and my nervousness returned. I suspected he simply wanted some company for the evening, which would have been fine under normal circumstances, and he seemed like a nice man, but I wanted to get away from all officials as soon as possible. All I could try to do was bluff him.

"Thank you for the pineapple," I said. "Did it come from your garden?"

"No," he replied, "It came from my father-in-law's garden."

"I think it was one of the most delicious pineapples I've ever had. Well, now that you're finished with the passports, we can take them back now. We've got to get going."

To my amazement he agreed. We were free to go.

Wouldn't it be wonderful, we said to each other later as we continued through the rice fields, if all border guards served pineapples from their fathers-in-law's gardens and handed back travel documents upon request.

The inevitable visit to the immigration office at Long Bawang the following morning didn't go quite as well. At the office I handed over my *surat jalan* and mentioned we would be doing a quick loop back to Bario. None of us had Indonesian visas, but then this border guard didn't have the bad manners to point that out to us while examining our passports. He had other interests.

"What's in your bag?" asked the officer in Indonesian.

A 200-year prison sentence, I thought to myself. Ray and Janet sat next to me, smiling, unaware of what was happening. I looked at my double reflection in the man's mirrored, neo-Nazi sunglasses and felt short of breath.

"Do you have a pistol?" the officer asked, gesturing towards my bag with his chin.

This was getting serious. What was I to do?

"Yes," I blurted out, "I have a pistol . . . and," I smiled, "I also have bombs. *Saya orang jahat*" (I am a bad man).

The officer looked at me carefully for a few seconds; then a smile appeared on his face. He sat back in his chair, and I relaxed. We joked in Indonesian about the unlikelihood of terrorists coming to Long Bawang. It was a quiet outpost, he explained. He spent most of his time watching water buffalo and relatives crossing from either side of the border. He didn't bother going through our belongings, but insisted on typing us an official letter to accompany our *surat jalan*. When he was finished typing and had stamped, signed, and placed the letter in its envelope, he asked for ten Malay dollars each. This, I explained to Ray and Janet, with a tone of resignation, was the "unofficial" Kalimantan entry fee. We were given permission to stay in the Long Bawang area for one week. Then we were to return to Sarawak.

I asked the border guard about the Japanese researchers, but to my surprise he told me they had left a month earlier. I was sorry to have taken the risk of coming to Long Bawang, and also I felt disappointed because I had missed the opportunity to talk to these people about their work.

We soon discovered there were other amusements in Long Bawang. The evening was spent with Samuel and Genever. Samuel was a local schoolteacher, and Genever, at 38 proof, was the brand name of his favorite drink—more commonly known as Dutch gin. For the evening's entertainment Ray, Janet, and I instructed Samuel and two of his friends in English conversation. Their grammar and pronunciation were very good, considering they had so few opportunities to speak the language. It was their vocabulary that had us confused. Many of the words they used I had never heard of, and when we questioned them on these words, they responded with, "But that word is in the dictionary!" When we accused them of making up words, they became indignant and impatient with our ignorance of our own language. We continued to drink Genever, and then someone used the expression *niddle-noddle* in a sentence.

"And what, may I ask, is *niddle-noddle*?"

"It is in the dictionary," came the now-familiar reply.

"Very well," I said, "I would like to see this dictionary."

Samuel walked into an adjoining room and soon returned with

a dog-eared copy of *Kamus Lengkap—Inggeris/Indonesia* (The Complete Dictionary—English/Indonesian) by S. Wojowasito W. J. S. Poerwadarminta. Inside the front cover I found my first clue to Samuel's odd vocabulary: "The selection of the entry words is based upon the author's subjective experience for a knowledge on a basic level."

Samuel thumbed through the *n*'s and, yes, *niddle-noddle* was one of the entries. The dictionary gave the Indonesian equivalent, but no English definition. Turning to the Indonesian/English section, I found only the word *niddle-noddle*, so I was unable to discover its meaning. For Samuel, the precise meaning was of minor importance. The word was in the dictionary, and that was all that mattered.

Intrigued by this dictionary, I looked through the pages at random and discovered other words that I was unaware of. Words such as *unchastity*, *unblunt*, *unborrow*, *niminy-piminy*, and *irreligion*. I suggested a new game. We would take turns selecting English words from the *Kamus Lengkap*, and the others would have to guess the meanings. After several unsuccessful rounds Ray claimed to know the meaning of the word *wordle*.

"It is a colloquial English speleological term," he explained in a marked Welsh accent. "*To have a wordle* means 'to take a pee in a cave.'" No one could dispute that, and Samuel penciled the definition into his dictionary.

With the help of the unabridged *Oxford English Dictionary* I have since discovered that *niddle-noddle* means "to nod unsteadily to and fro, to nod the head rapidly." Why this archaic term should be included in an Indonesian dictionary of no more than twenty thousand words was a mystery to me. I also located *niminy-piminy*. It means "mincing, affected, trifling, lacking in force or spirit."

The word *wordle* continued to bother me for years. Until quite recently the closest I came to discovering its meaning was in Thomas Wright's *Dictionary of Obsolete and Provincial English*. There I found *whorle*, the verb "to rumble." I knew that wasn't correct, but it was better than "a pee in a cave." I have finally located *wordle*. It is listed in the Oxford English Dictionary as one of six alternate spellings for *wortle*: "An implement used in drawing of wire or lead pipe . . . a perforated steel plate through which pipe or wire is drawn to reduce its diameter."

My only explanation for Dr. S. Wojowasito W. J. S. Poerwadarminta's dictionary is this. The Indonesian language, based on modern Malay, was created soon after World War II when Dutch Colonial rule came to an end. An English/Indonesian dictionary was needed at once, and to fill the required number of pages, prefixes and suffixes were added to nearly every word; hence, irreligion and unblunt. The anachronistic nineteenth-century words must have been selected at random from other dictionaries, with little regard to their suitability in Southeast Asia. Imagine trying to learn a language with a dictionary like Samuel's. I promised my hosts a real dictionary, but the years have gone by, and I never took the time to send them one. I regret not doing so, but I regret even more not having bought their dictionary. I doubt if a dictionary has ever provided such amusement for a group of people for an entire evening. Ray, Janet, and I still sign our letters: With best wishes and niddle-noodle.

�;   �;   �;

I said goodby to Ray and Janet at Tanjung Keria, a small village one-and-a-half-days' walk from Bario, and they returned to Bario as they had promised the border officials. They had been wonderful traveling companions, but after a week I was glad to be on my own once again. I continued south through settled countryside for three more days before reaching the primary rain forest of Kalimantan. From that point there would be no more border checks or police. Cut off from the coast by long hazardous overland journeys, the communities in this area followed their own laws, with little interference from the coastal authorities.

Approaching the village of Long Lieyu late on my second day of solo walking, I met an old woman on the trail bent double beneath a tremendous load of firewood. She gave me directions to the headman's house, and in return I offered to take her bundle of neatly split sticks. "I'm not so old I can't help myself," she laughed and insisted on carrying the wood.

As I had hoped, I was invited to stay with Pa Lee Wee Galah, the headman. After an evening bath in the river and a dinner of steamed rice and fresh river fish, Pa Lee Wee was summoned to the door by a distraught woman. I couldn't understand what she said, but Pa Lee Wee went with her immediately, and he didn't return until dawn. Pa Lee Wee was the *kepala adat*, the man responsible for administering *adat* (customary law). He had been called by the woman to settle a dispute over an accidental spearing. At sunset that day a 14-year-old boy with a spear was being chased around the longhouse by his friends. One of his pursuers decided to run in the opposite direction to surprise him. They met at a corner and collided with near-fatal results. The spear went through the boy's hip, and he was carried to his family house. The wound was examined, and when it seemed likely the boy would live, an argument erupted over compensation. Pa Lee Wee negotiated with the fathers of the two boys, and by dawn a settlement had been agreed upon. Quite sensibly, people believe that if a decision is not reached quickly, bad feelings will escalate and the situation will get worse. The *kepala adat* does not get paid for his services. In this case, Pa Lee Wee decided that because the spearing was accidental, the compensation would be reduced. Nonetheless, the agreed-upon payment seemed astronomical to me. It was one large female buffalo worth 200,000 rupiahs (300 U.S. dollars), which represent a two-year wage for a laborer; one large boar, worth 35,000 rupiahs; one bolt of fabric (forty yards), worth 35,000 rupiahs; one blowpipe; plus all future medical expenses.

A minor flesh wound would have required a small pig; an eye, much more. At Pa Lee Wee's invitation, I went to visit the boy that morning. The father gently lifted his son's sarong to show me the wound. I was prepared for something ghastly, but the wound had been cleaned and neatly stitched up (without the use of anesthetic) by a skilled neighbor. I asked about local medicines, and this made Pa Lee Wee chuckle. "What medicine can you put on a wound like this?" he wanted to know. "We use Western medicines when we can get them, but people have flown from the coast looking for jungle medicines. We sell the plants to these people. Especially the Chinese."

The practice of settling disputes on a compensation basis with a respected mediator works so well that the Indonesian government, rather than trying to impose a set of modern laws, encourages that all problems on the village level be brought to the *kepala adat*. Only when traditional methods fail will the government step in to make a decision. This happens very infrequently.

I wanted to get started that morning, so Pa Lee Wee described the eight-hour walk to the next village, Pow-O-Pan. Again without a guide I left the village at midmorning and for the first hour walked through an eerie devastated landscape. The jungle had been burned only the day before to clear a new field for the approaching rice-planting season.

The trail wound through low hills blanketed in warm, black ashes. Large charred tree stumps, still smouldering, lay in all directions. There was no shade, not even a leaf in sight for much of the way, and the heat from the sky and ground was intense. Wind-blown grit stirred up by my feet stuck in my nose and mouth and made my eyes sting. There were no birds or other animal life noticeable, and I became acutely aware of the cinders and ashes crunching beneath my feet. I had to hurry through some areas because the ground was still hot to the touch. By the time I reentered the cool, green shade of the jungle, I was plastered in perspiration and abrasive black ash. It rubbed the skin raw around my neck as well as where my pack straps fitted over my shoulders. I soon came upon a stream and decided to rinse myself. I took off all my clothes and lay down in the water between smooth greenish brown river rocks. The quick-moving, clear water was just deep enough to float in. I lay on my stomach and put my head in the water. My fingers discovered handholds between the rocks, and I let my body trail in the bubbling current. After a few minutes I turned onto my back and wedged my heels between other rocks to brace myself as the surge of water ran from the top of my head over my naked body and past my feet. With eyes closed I imagined the water was stationary and I was moving through it like a great white fish. Then suddenly I sat up, thinking I had heard someone coming. But of course that was absurd; I was utterly alone. There was only the hum of insects and the sound of water trickling over and between the river rocks. I felt foolish, then laughed about my self-conscious reaction, my conditioned fear of being caught without my clothes on. I lay back in the water until my fingers and toes ached from the cold; then I stood up and walked to the gravel beach to wash the ash from my shorts and T-shirt. When my clothes had dried on the big river rocks, I dressed and continued into the forest.

Later that day I came to a wide valley surrounded by big trees and covered in tall Imperata grass. I approached the edge of the inviting pale green wall of waving grass, and as I did so the trail became indistinct. I was surprised when I realized that the grass was taller than I. Without thinking I walked into the field and within minutes had lost all sense of direction. I turned to retrace my steps, but to my alarm the tall, green curtain had closed neatly behind me. The hot sun was directly overhead and gave no clues as to which way I was facing. The grass was only inches from my face, and when I spread my arms I could see no more than a couple of feet. I began to panic. I *knew* I couldn't be more than a hundred yards from where I had entered the valley, but it was now impossible to know from which direction I had come. I flattened a small area so that I didn't feel so claustrophobic and sat down to try to come up with a plan to find my way out.

I needed to get a distant view, so, beginning from my little clearing, I matted down the grass for about ten yards in one direction. I returned to the clearing and looked down the laneway, hoping to catch a glimpse of nearby trees. I couldn't see anything but the sky and very distant hillsides. I continued trampling down grass laneways, but it wasn't easy work. The edges of the grass cut my hands and ankles until they bled. I did manage to maintain a sense of humor during the hour or more that it took me to get out by imagining the tabloid headlines that might have described this bizarre incident: Man Taken by Killer Grass . . . Search Called Off.

Eventually I spotted trees nearby and walked towards them and soon emerged from the green labyrinth near where I had entered. Following the edge of the jungle, I discovered a two-foot-wide trail across the valley. It was unnerving to realize how easily I could get lost, and Tom Harrisson's words came back to me: "Take two steps off the trail, get disoriented, and that's the last anyone sees of you."

I felt good about one thing. I had become lost, had thought out a sensible plan, and had found my way again. That gave me a very small, yet gratifying taste of confidence. It was still a long way to Pow-O-Pan, the next village, so I hurried on, hoping to arrive before dark. I made it with just half an hour of light remaining.

Pow-O-Pan marked the end of the agricultural land and the beginning of primary rain forest. There were no trails beyond this village, and I needed someone to take me cross-country. I presented myself to the *kepala kampong*, Pa Thomas Gueer, and showed him my letters of introduction. I let him know that I wanted to go to the headwaters of the Bahau River, a distance of twenty-five miles, which by my estimation represented a leisurely five-day walk. Pa Thomas let the community know my plans; then all I could do was wait. I stayed in Pow-O-Pan for three days, and the highlight of my peaceful time there was watching Pa Thomas make a blowpipe.

Pa Thomas selected a roughed-out, slightly tapered shaft of hardwood. It was 4 inches thick and 6½ feet long. He had let the wood season for six months. To bore the hole he set up an adjustable tripod to a height of approximately 2½ feet. The narrower end of the blank was clamped to the tripod; the other end was shoved against the base of the wall to provide resistance during the drilling of the long hole. For a cutting tool Pa Thomas used a length of steel rod hammered and sharpened into a spade bit. It drilled a hole the width of the first digit of a small finger.

Pa Thomas sat on the floor facing the tripod. Some of the hand-hewn floorboards were four feet wide and a hundred feet long; covered in thousands of evenly patterned slightly concave adz marks, they were beautifully polished by five generations of bare feet. Pa Thomas held his hands at chest level with his palms together, grasping the tapered handle attached to the bit. He quickly rotated his hands back and forth, and the bit slowly disappeared into the wood. As he did this a light dusting of powder-fine orange sawdust began to appear on the floor. Pa Thomas spit on his palms at regular intervals to maintain proper friction with the handle. To prevent blisters he spread a thin coating of cooked rice on the wooden handle. As the hole slowly deepened, he removed the drill from one wooden holder and attached it to one which was slightly longer. The bit was held in place with a brittle tree resin that released its grip with a sharp tap from a metal tool. When it was time to fit a new handle to the bit, the glue was made pliable by heating it slightly with a candle flame. The blowpipe was frequently released from the tripod holder and tapped on the floor, hole end down, to remove the impacted sawdust. This procedure went on for hours. I had worked as a jeweller and production woodworker for seven years and was eager to record each step. When I asked Pa Thomas what he would do with the blowpipe when he was finished, he told me he would sell it in Sarawak, where it would be used for hunting, or to one of the American Mission Aviation Fellowship (MAF) pilots in Kalimantan. They bought the blowpipes to decorate their walls or as gifts for friends back home. A good blowpipe in Kalimantan is worth fifteen thousand rupiahs, five thousand rupiahs extra with a spear tip.

Pa Thomas finished drilling the six-and-a-half-foot-long hole after five hours of continuous work. I inspected the hole, and to my astonishment it was perfectly straight. This was a remarkable feat considering that most people can't bore a straight 3-inch hole into a piece of softwood with a power drill. Some observers attribute the making of a good blowpipe to the special wood and straightness of the grain. Others say it is the tools. My opinion, after watching the procedure, is that it requires an intuitive feel for the material and tools that few people possess. Once the hole is completed, another day is spent smoothing the bore with two different grades of abrasive "sandpaper leaves," medium and fine grit. These are attached to the end of a flexible rattan ramrod similar to a gun cleaner that is repeatedly shoved in and pulled out of the blowpipe. The final, mirrorlike polish is achieved with another length of rattan, the shaft of which has been shaved into a series of bushy clusters with a sharp knife.

When Pa Thomas had completed the work and I had finished my last photograph, he asked whether I would like a picture of myself with the blowpipe.

"Sure," I replied. "Let me just set up the camera for you. You stand here. I'll show you how to press the shutter, and I'll stand right over . . ."

"No, no," interrupted Pa Thomas, "I have Kodak."

"Huh?" I responded dumbly.

He rummaged through a trunk full of fishing nets and old tins and excavated a serviceable-looking Kodak Colorburst 50 camera. He showed it to me, and all I could think was: Where did he find that thing? Had some unlucky traveler been knocked over the head? Surely he didn't have film?

"This Kodak makes photo quickly," he explained. "You don't have to wait to have the film developed."

"Ohhh?" I replied, trying my best to look surprised.

Then he produced a box of film. "You put the film in here. There's not enough light, so we'll use the flash."

This scene was seriously eroding my primitive jungle experience. I felt like telling him not to take my picture, because he would steal my spirit. I posed. He told me to smile. "Click . . . flash . . . sparkle . . . whir . . . zip . . . slip . . . rip," spoke the camera.

Pa Thomas held the blank photo in front of me and said something like, "Now wait until you see what happens next!"

The film performed its magic, and a color image of me holding the blowpipe at my side slowly materialized. Pa Thomas beamed with pride.

"My Kodak!" he cried with excitement.

"Fantastic," I replied, in all sincerity.

I had spent the entire day thinking how privileged I had been to watch the making of a blowpipe by this master craftsman using early Iron Age technology. But no sooner had Pa Thomas brought out his camera than, poof, daydreams had been obliterated. I felt both amused and disappointed. Different versions of this situation continued to occur throughout my journey to surprise me when I was least expecting them.

Pa Thomas had arranged for two Penan men from the ulu Sungai Malineau (upper Malineau River) to accompany me on the next stage of my journey, to the Bahau River. Bo 'Hok and Weng spoke Indonesian with the same fluency as I now did, and we could converse quite easily. They were in their late twenties and were obviously keen to earn one shotgun shell per day for what we estimated would be a two-week journey. We worked out how many *moks* of rice and how much salt and tea we should take. Little did we realize that nearly two months would pass before we parted company, having crisscrossed hundreds of miles of uninhabited rain forest. Pa Thomas's trail instructions gave a good indication of what was to come.

I wanted to walk to a remote hunting area known as *padang rusa* (the deer field), also known as the Bahau grasslands. This area lay between Pow-O-Pan and my nearest destination, the Bahau River. *Padang rusa* was covered in many square miles of grass, similar to the grass I had become lost in a few days earlier. Large herds of wild cattle, deer, and pigs roamed the grasslands. There were no villages within a week's walk, so game was plentiful.

The most direct route on my map from Pow-O-Pan to *padang rusa* was down a small unnamed valley. I estimated the journey would take four or five days. Pa Thomas claimed the walk would take at least ten days and Bo 'Hok and Weng nodded in agreement with him.

"How could it possibly take ten days? It's only twenty-five miles in a straight line?" I began to suspect that they were conspiring to lengthen the trip in order to increase the number of days I had to pay them. I wanted an explanation.

"We cannot walk down that valley," said Bo 'Hok. He then described a route that went well to the east of the trail I had suggested. It was true that the indirect route would require about twice as long to walk.

"Why can't we walk down the valley?" I asked. From their evasive replies, it was obvious they were withholding some important information.

"We can't go to that valley because it passes close to Paye Rungan," said Weng. *Paye* in the Krayan language means "place where the ground is sandy and not fertile."

"What is at Paye Rungan?"

The three of them looked uncomfortable, and there was a brief pause before Pa Thomas spoke. "Ular Naga . . ." (the big dragon), he mumbled.

This was something I hadn't anticipated.

"What is the Ular Naga?" I asked. There was a hesitation on their part to explain; perhaps they thought I might make fun of them. It was Weng who told the story of the Ular Naga. Weng was a natural storyteller. He spoke slowly and with much deliberation, pausing frequently to allow listeners to digest significant thoughts before elaborating on them or moving on to a new aspect of the narrative. Here is a fair translation from the Indonesian:

THE STORY OF THE DRAGON

From the Kampong of Long Rungan, walking in a southwesterly direction, you will arrive at a place called Paye Rungan.

Perhaps thirty years ago near Paye Rungan, Iban and Krayan people hunted for rhinoceros. They sold the rhinoceros horn in Malaysia to the Chinese. It was very valuable and was usually traded for gold. According to the Penan living on the Tabu River and at Long Pulau, a long time ago a person had a dream one night. In the dream an old man came to him and said, "Hey, you Penan people, if you want to live happily, look in the mountains and the valleys around here and you will find the Ular Naga. Kill it and eat its meat."

After this, the Penan woke up and collected his friends and told them about his dream. When they had listened to this dream, the Penan people agreed to look for the Ular Naga and kill it and eat it, because they wanted to live happily.

The next day all the men departed to the jungle. Some carried parangs, some blowpipes and spears. After looking around in the jungle for some time, they found the dragon and killed it.

The Ular Naga was about as big around as an oil drum and very long. They cut it up and took it home. After cooking it, many Penan people ate the meat. Only a few people did not eat it.

After they had eaten the meat, a big wind and hailstorm came. All of the Penan who had eaten the meat died, and they went to the place of the spirits, where they lived happily. The Penan who didn't eat the meat didn't die, and their descendants still survive. Up to this time the Penan are afraid to go to Paye Rungan because another dragon is still living there in a cave by a lake that is found in the middle of the Paye, the sandy ground.

My initial response to this story was to go to Paye Rungan for a look. There was one problem with this plan: no one would take me. I offered what I knew to be an irresistible daily wage (five cartridges) in order to tempt someone, but there was not a single person in Pow-O-Pan who would even consider making such a foolish trip.

In the following months I asked many people about the Ular Naga, and the most interesting comments came from Eric Michaels, an American teacher at the KINGMI Theological School at Long Bia near the mouth of the Kayan River in East Kalimantan. KINGMI is an acronym for Kemah Injil Gereja Masehi Indonesia, which means Gospel Tabernacle Christian Church of Indonesia, an American mission.

In his letter of 11 June 1983, he wrote to me in San Francisco: *The other day I was in an area where I met a pastor who lives in the area of the reported dragon. He claims that pilot Marvin Ellington [Mission Aviation Fellowship] saw two dragons wrapped around each other and reaching upwards from the ground. The area all around them was burned. He says no one has ever dared go near the area, which is about two days' walk from Long Bawang. . . . The pastor said Marvin Ellington reported the incident to Chuck Smith [another MAF pilot].*

Eric gave me addresses for Chuck Smith and Marvin Ellington in the United States. I wrote to Marvin three times asking him to comment on the story, but he never replied. Chuck Smith wrote back promptly with the following information: "I am sorry to say the Ular Naga story has not the remotest connection to fact or experience on my part. . . . I was always interested in the local animal life and talked often with people about what there was around, but never did I see anything of consequence from the air, or did I ever hear of anything strange or unusual while living there."

For this last sentence to be true, Pilot Smith either never spoke to a single person during his tour of duty or maintained a permanent holding pattern with his aircraft over the jungle and never actually landed in Kalimantan.

I'm not suggesting there are dragons in central Borneo, because their physical existence is unimportant. What was of utmost importance for me to recognize was that dragons existed in people's minds. It would have been grossly arrogant of me to disregard those beliefs or to trivialize the people's fears. What did I know, anyway? I had been in the area two days; these people had lived there for generations. I soon came to realize how foolish it was for me to try to prove or disprove the existence of the dragon. I decided to respect their fears and stopped asking to be taken to Paye Rungan.

The environment was evidently beginning to work its spell on me. The signs were there. I was losing my appetite for truth based on rational, Western thought processes or even on the spoken word. My habit of judging situations by methodically and logically sorting through events was a hindrance when I was dealing with the people in the highlands. I gradually learned that it was more important to understand a situation by sensing the mood or spirit. Until I got better at "feeling the mood," I continued to make embarrassing social blunders. It just wouldn't do for me to go around telling people there was nothing to worry about. It was as absurd as if they had landed in New York City and had told me on their second day that a night ride on the subway through the South Bronx was safe.

And, anyway, I liked the idea of giant dragons copulating for missionary pilots. And if I had to walk miles out of my way to avoid being eaten by a dragon, so much the better. I marked the appropriate spot on my map with an X and penciled a notation in the margin: "Caution: valley closed — dragon cave ahead."

Bo 'Hok, Weng, and I assembled our food and equipment on the floor of Pa Thomas's room. Included were a large sack of hill rice; leaf tea; brown sugar flavored with chillies, cloves, and cinnamon (a local concoction); a cooking pot; a block of purple-black Bario salt wrapped in leaves; three parangs; a two-day supply of dried pig meat; two homemade shotguns; our bedsheets; my beads and shotgun shells; and three woven backpacks. Not exactly high tech.

Late that night a news report came over Pa Thomas's radio: An MAF pilot, Paul, had been attacked in his home on the coast by as many as six intruders wielding knives. He had suffered deep lacerations to his arms, legs, and back and was slashed across the face so viciously that he had lost two teeth and part of his tongue. Despite his terrible wounds Pilot Paul had defended his wife and two young Krayan schoolgirls by grabbing a spear-tipped blowpipe off the wall and ramming it into one of the intruders. The men fled, carrying their companion, and it was rumored that the man died of his wounds. Police were still investigating, and no arrests had been made. Pilot Paul had been flown to Singapore for emergency surgery and would be sent to the United States to recuperate.

With this news my feelings about the trip once again shifted. Fantasy met reality, and I realized I could no longer afford to be careless. If missionary pilots were open to such dangers, what might happen to me? I was infinitely more vulnerable. The walk from Long Seridan to Bario had been a Sunday afternoon stroll in comparison to what was ahead. I was committing myself to a very long, very difficult journey to the east coast, and I wasn't sure that I was ready. It wasn't too late to change my mind, but once we left Pow-O-Pan the next morning, there would be no turning back. I didn't sleep well that night. My mind was troubled with thoughts of Pilot Paul on the operating table, and I lay awake for hours examining aspects of the foolishness that had brought me to this lonely place.

CHAPTER SIX · GREAT FOREST

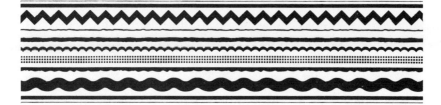

A WARM, moist wind blew from the south down a valley lost in green folds of undulating rain forest. Carried on the wind were thick earthy smells of sweet-scented plants and decomposing leaf litter that carpeted the jungle floor. This enticing fragrance conveyed the first hints of what life would be like within the 120,000 square miles of rain forest that separated me from the coast by more than 400 miles.

Bo 'Hok, Weng, and I left Pow-O-Pan before the sun had reached the valley floor. Roosters crowed intermittently, but few people were about as we shouldered our rattan packs and started towards the formidable-looking wall of big trees. Bo 'Hok and Weng walked ahead. We crossed a few hundred yards of garden plots, and then, as I watched, they nonchalantly stepped into the forest and disappeared from the world of settled village life. Moments later I, too, entered the forest. At first it seemed as if my guides had vanished, but then I caught sight of them. The moved silently, nearly obscured by the patterns of light and shade that rippled through the forest understory. I hurried ahead to catch up with them. The sunlight soon dimmed and with it the last familiar traces of my own culture. Bo 'Hok and Weng were having quite the opposite experience. They disliked populated areas and direct sunlight, and it came as a relief to return to a familiar place where in the cool darkness no movement, sound, or scent held a mystery. This jungle, so foreign to me, was their home; yet within minutes of entering it I felt myself willingly moving into a timeless world of natural rhythms.

The rain forest on this southeast side of the dividing range seemed drier and less slippery, but this may have been due to my improved balance and sure-footedness. The terrain was certainly flatter, but the most significant difference in the *feeling* of this portion of the jungle was its immense size. Whereas, when I left Long Seridan I knew I would be in the rain forest three or four weeks before arriving in a familiar place, I now had only a vague idea of where I was going and for how long. This uncertainty made me feel very vulnerable, but more important I had a very distinct physical reaction to the jungle. I could feel my body becoming tense and alert. I felt tight. The only similar sensation I can relate this to is the experience of swimming in the middle of the ocean where you *know* the water is many miles deep. The Kalimantan rain forest was like an uncharted, fathomless, green ocean, and I continued to nurture a healthy fear of the place.

We had entered a community of plants, insects, and animals that has remained ecologically undisturbed for millions of years. The interwoven tangle of branches, lianas, ferns, and orchids found in the Borneo rain forest sustains one of the world's most complex and least-studied ecosystems. The diversity of tree species alone is estimated at a staggering twenty-five hundred. In one ten-hectare sample plot of Borneo jungle, the Royal Geographical Society has identified nearly eight hundred species of trees. This is more than twenty times the total number of native tree species in all of Britain. This forest would be my home for the next eight weeks.

We moved through the damp jungle air, and the first sensation that returned to me was the mad, erratic, echoing cacophony of sounds, seemingly played by a group of quirky, invisible musicians. I'm referring to the insect hum, bird warble, animal cry, wind rush, tree-branch sigh, and the incessant patter of water droplets on broad jungle leaves. In this 24-hour, 7-day-a-week, primordial music hall a deranged orchestra played on laconically without need for a conductor or audience. At unexpected moments a succession of incongruent single notes would come to me from all sides, producing incomprehensible musical phrases. Discordant harmonies blared from high up in the jungle canopy only to be obliterated by staccato bursts of nearby insect sounds. The ground was alive with the rustling sounds, inaudible to the human ear, of millions of foraging insects (up to two thousand termites per square yard). The quietest activity of all came from the bacterial fungi, which steadily munch away at fallen leaves, gradually reducing them to perfect gauzelike skeletons.

I was spellbound by the dramatic interplay of shifting light and mysterious noises. One of the few bird sounds I could identify from the bewildering jumble of chitter-chatter, hoots, and whistles was a babbler (genus *Malacoptera*) known as the Beethoven bird because it sings the familiar four opening notes of Beethoven's Fifth Symphony. Apart from this bird, and the by-now-familiar, frantic electronic buzzing of twenty species of cicadas, the origins of the sounds were a mystery to my untrained ear. There were literally hundreds of them, and I was to learn that each one held a special message for Bo 'Hok and Weng.

Perhaps it is too fanciful to compare the natural sounds of the jungle to structured music. In the rain forest there was certainly little to remind one of musical conventions, but the feelings evoked by these strange sounds had the same disturbing effects as music can have. I was hearing courtship calls, declarations of feeding territories, threats, warnings, and startled shrieks of terror as unseen prey was torn to pieces by silent predators.

We were only a few hours' walk from Pow-O-Pan when we happened upon a living example of Kipling's giant red rock python from my childhood bedtime stories. The snake lay coiled on a river rock, iridescent and shimmering like a sinuous gem until

Weng drew his parang and hacked the creature's head off during its midday nap. Weng fastened the writhing, headless, ten-foot-long snake to his pack, and we continued into the jungle — a place so bountiful and lush, yet so unforgiving of the slightest human weakness. We moved farther into this steaming, fetid world of great horrors and indescribable beauties whose elements were impossible to separate one from the other; and, as I learned, there was little sense in making simplistic distinctions of "good" and "bad." As a visitor to the jungle, I was privileged to be allowed a brief glimpse of the natural patterns of plant and animal life on earth as they must have existed before the arrival of human beings. We were frail and insignificant creatures, and at any moment we could be swallowed up by the forest. When a plant, animal, or human dies in the rain forest, it soon becomes a part of the forest. Flesh is digested, nutrients recycled, and body moisture reclaimed. The realization that the rain forest was a living, breathing organism capable of consuming and digesting me was disconcerting, but also rather exciting. I made me feel as if we were traveling through the intestinal flora of some giant leafy creature.

Any fears that I may have entertained concerning my safety with Bo 'Hok and Weng were soon proved to be unjustified. Like Tingang Na and John Bong a month earlier, Bo 'Hok and Weng did their utmost to make me as comfortable as possible by anticipating my every need. Although they had had almost no contact with Westerners, they had a highly developed intuitive sense of what I was experiencing, and this gave me a strong sense of trust and safety. In Pow-O-Pan, Bo 'Hok and Weng had treated me with excessive formality. They had called me *Tuan*, which means "Sir"; and, like *Bwana* in Swahili, the title carries the suggestion of "white master," which made me feel uncomfortable. Fortunately, Bo 'Hok and Weng became more relaxed in the jungle. I always made a point of praising them on their extraordinary knowledge of the jungle, and soon the last traces of the white explorer–native guide relationship dissolved. This allowed me to start to develop our friendship. They called me Mister Eric and, less frequently, Rajah Kumis.

When we were sitting by the campfire the first night, I asked what they thought about the knife attack on Pilot Paul. From their expressions it was obvious that they were confused and troubled by the incident, and they admitted they did not know why people downriver did such things. We discussed acts of violence and crime beyond the jungle. Theft they could understand, but rape, mugging, suicide, and murder were completely foreign to their way of living. Neither one of them could remember a Penan committing any of these acts.

"What would be a serious crime in the Penan community?" I asked.

They conversed for a minute, as though they were having difficulty thinking of any crime. Then Weng explained the concept of *see-hun*, which means to be stingy or not to share. An accusation of stinginess, I was told, could cause arguments and very bad feelings. Both Bo 'Hok and Weng expressed great surprise by clicking their tongues when I told them there were no laws in America regarding stinginess and that, in fact, stinginess or hoarding for oneself is esteemed and rewarded.

Social behavior, from the Penan perspective, is judged in terms of what sorts of feelings result from different acts. Considering how close together these people live, it is not surprising that the feelings of others are of the greatest importance. As in traditional village law, certain offenses in the jungle communities require compensation. Adultery was given as an example."Adultery," Weng told me, "can create bad feelings, and the offenders must pay a fine." The payment for adultery varied, but it was never less than one cooking pot, a blowpipe, and a parang. In special circumstances an additional payment of one good hunting dog and a spear might be required.

Whereas Tingang Na and John Bong, my two Penan guides in Sarawak, had settled with a few other families on the Magoh River to cultivate hill rice and tapioca, Bo 'Hok and Weng were still seminomadic. They spent three months of the year in a village cultivating crops, and the rest of the time they lived in the jungle and depended exclusively on forest resources. This more traditional lifestyle was reflected in their attitude towards the jungle. Their attitude was partially expressed in their manner of speech. For days their conversational style had me confused. They never spoke directly about anything, especially hunting. Also, they seemed extremely reluctant to refer to any kind of subsistence activity. Initially, I wondered if they were using a secret language to confuse me, but that was unlikely—if they had wanted to discuss something privately, they could have spoken Penan rather than Indonesian, our common second language.

Through observation and discussion I eventually discovered the purpose of their intentional vagueness. They frequently used the Penan expression *tie neet-neet*, which, roughly translated, means "we're going to go to the jungle and pull our foreskins back." I assumed this was a rather crude way of announcing they were going to have a pee. After these announcements, however, they would often take their shotguns and disappear for hours, returning later with game they had shot. *Tie neet-neet*, I discovered, actually indicated "we're going hunting." I questioned them further about their indirect manner of speaking, and they explained that it came from their great fear of forest spirits. Not necessarily a fear of personal harm, although that was a consideration, but fear that if the spirits were forewarned they would hide the game or food. Before hunting men will therefore not talk directly about guns, dogs, or spears.

In certain circumstances both men and women use expressions that they consider to be disgusting or dirty. They do this hoping that the forest spirits will be equally disgusted and will keep away. One expression I frequently heard the Penan women in Sarawak use was explained to me by Weng. *Muee-loto*, the women would say. The expression means "to go and wipe our rear ends." At the time, I assumed they were simply very open about their bodily functions, but Bo 'Hok and Weng laughed at this interpretation and said that it was the women's way of indicating they were going fishing. Like fishing, *muee-loto* is an activity done in the river.

These guides were vague for other reasons. It used to frustrate me when they couldn't tell me how long it would take to arrive at a particular place that they knew well. The confusion arose from the fact that I was thinking in terms of miles and hours and they were thinking in terms of hunting. If there was a lot of game, a short distance could take a long time to cover because they would hunt. Equally, we could travel long distances quickly if there were no animals about or if they wanted to reach a place where they felt the hunting would be better. Their concept of distance was also dependent on mood or need. A destination "not too far away" could mean a five-day walk through difficult terrain to a friendly village where they could buy tobacco. A "long journey" might turn out to be a four-hour walk in the hated sunlight through flat farmland.

It was equally as difficult for them to undestand my idea of time as it was for me to understand theirs. They took little interest in days and minutes and seconds. They were led by their moods and circumstances, whereas I was still controlled by my expectations.

We usually didn't speak during the day for fear of alerting animals to our presense. Bo 'Hok and Weng moved through the tangle of undergrowth in near-perfect silence, while, try as I might, twigs crunched beneath my feet and branches rustled, making my presense painfully obvious to all. Early in the morning before breakfast and late at night were the best times for discussion. I asked them about the moon and stars, but they had no stories or explanations of the celestial bodies. This should have been obvious to me because the forest canopy effectively blocks out the sky. Again and again I was startled to look up and find the leafy green ceiling one hundred feet overhead. It was like and unlike being indoors, as if we were in a huge hemispherical greenhouse with the air and light coming from all sides. Bo 'Hok and Weng, like all other Penan, had never seen the ocean, and it became apparent that their whole cognitive view of the world was in terms of the forest and rivers. Every place was referred to as "upriver" or "downriver." When we talked about "Amureeka," they referred to it as "downriver." Likewise, "Australee" and "Ingalan" were both "downriver." The rivers are their reference points in the forest. In the jungle, where the visibility is so low (you can see only a few hundred feet because of the undergrowth), the rivers form the whole organizational skeleton. At any given time the Penan will know where they are relative to rivers and even the smallest streams.

Bo 'Hok and Weng used to play a game with me that I called Where Are We? At random times during the day, when we weren't hunting and when they felt like amusing themselves, they would ask me from which direction we had come that day, or a question such as "Which way is Sarawak?" I would nearly always point in the wrong direction, and that would elicit great hoots of laughter from them. They couldn't imagine being so disoriented. I didn't mind being laughed at, but it was disconcerting to realize how easily and totally lost I was. We usually walked on the forested ridges, passing from one river system to another. The rivers wind back and forth in such a way that I would often forget in which direction I was going or which river valley we were following. We might cross the same river five times in a day, and I would assume these were five rivers flowing in different directions. When checking with Bo 'Hok and Weng, I would often discover I was walking in the opposite direction to what I had thought.

The Penan are capable of going into an area where they've never been, making a great circuit, and coming back to camp without prior knowledge of the river and ridge systems they have been traveling. They like to expand their knowledge of the landscape by occasionally going into new areas. They are extremely observant, and I found their sense of direction uncanny.

It was still dark when a loud "Ho-hummmm!" from Bo 'Hok startled me from my dreams. The bird and insect sounds told me that first light was still two to three hours away, so I closed my eyes, hoping to go back to sleep. When I found myself unable to drift back into dreaming, I joined Bo 'Hok by the fire, where he was deftly coaxing the embers back to life. The fire had kept us sufficiently warm when the temperature dropped to the relative cool of the mid-70s Fahrenheit. The night air seemed colder than usual partly because we hadn't taken the time to build a proper shelter and partly because we had slept on the damp ground upon a bed of leaves covered with pandanus leaf raincovers and woven rattan mats. Moonlight filtered into the green-black darkness, and an occasional star could be seen through gaps in the forest canopy.

The fire came to life, bathing us in yellow flickering light. We sat there quietly, feeling the warmth of the flames on our bare skin. After a few minutes of companionable silence, I asked Bo 'Hok why the Penan wander. I had assumed, from reading and from my brief observations in Sarawak, that the Penan followed pig migrations that corresponded with regular cycles of fruiting jungle trees. This was not so. Bo 'Hok pointed out that Penan migration is dependent on the availability of hill sago, from which they extract their staple food, sago flour. Hill sago is found in the headwater areas of large mountains at higher elevations. The Penan know the precise location of sago in their areas and carefully gauge their exploitation of this important food resource by moving from one area to another. They might avoid returning to a particular stand of sago for up to twenty years so that it can fully regenerate.

Traditionally the nomadic Penan have two sorts of settlements. There is the base camp, which can be occupied for several weeks to several months. This base camp is for the very young and the very old people. Forty is old for a Penan. Penan age is difficult to gauge because they rarely know the year of their birth. They age quickly because of the harsh environment, and few live to reach fifty. The second type of settlement is the sago camp in the forest, usually with about three shelters for men and women from different households. Sago is processed there, and every three to five days they take sago flour from the forest camp to the base camp. Even today, in settled Penan villages, the two-camp system hasn't changed much. The settled or semisettled village is still a place for the older people and children.

Bo 'Hok explained that wild pigs are virtually everywhere in the rain forest, so it doesn't really matter where the Penan move in terms of pig migration. During the soft-fruit season the pigs will be fatter, but not necessarily more numerous. Soft-fruit trees, as it turns out, have little if anything to do with pig migration. The tendency is for the pigs to move to fruiting trees within the same general area. The trees at lower elevations usually bear fruit first, with the trees at higher elevations gradually ripening later. If at the beginning of the fruit season the Penan, who characteristically range from about five hundred to two thousand feet, were at the higher elevations, they would not move camp downriver in order to pursue the pigs. More likely, they would just wait for the fruiting to move up in elevation and let the pigs come to them.

Jules and Serena Caldecott, consultants for the National Parks and Wildlife office in Kuching, pointed out to me that the mass pig migrations depend on the infrequent heavy crops of edible seeds from two tree families: the Dipterocarpaceae and the Fagaceae (oaks). These seeds, commonly known as illipe nuts, contain up to 70 percent oil and are collected for export. One commercial use of Dipterocarp seed oil is in the manufacture of chocolate. The wild pigs in Borneo (*Sus barbatus barbatus*) migrate infrequently, and when they do, it is over hundreds of miles. During a migration up to a million fat pigs may move through the forest for more than a year in search of these edible seeds. It is inconceivable, therefore, that any one Penan group would follow a particular migration. Some of the migrations occur only once in twenty-five years. During a migration the Penan men in the area might devote all their time to hunting, but that would last only a few weeks. The men would not pursue the pigs as they moved on because the Penan prefer to stay within the boundaries of their recognized forest area.

Bo 'Hok finished talking, and dawn was approaching as Weng joined us by the fire. We boiled a pot of water and were soon sipping hot black tea sweetened with the spiced brown cane sugar. The jungle was coming to life, and after the hours of conversation we fell silent to shift our attention to the gathering sounds. At sunset the night before, a troop of gibbon monkeys had settled in the tree-tops just on the other side of the stream from where we were camped. As the first rays of orange sunlight touched the uppermost branches, the monkeys, many carrying their young, began to stir. It was some while before I spotted the first one. A shimmer of rustling leaves and the occasional black silhouette were all that betrayed their passage through the forest canopy 150 feet above us. Not long after the monkeys left we could hear their ascending "whoop-whoop-whoop-whoop-whoop-whoop-whoop" cries as they claimed their feeding area.

Bo 'Hok, Weng, and I ate a breakfast of boiled white rice and leftover smoked fish that we lay in the coals to warm up. When we had finished our morning meal, we were soon moving through the jungle again.

Towards the end of the first week we reconsidered our original destination and decided that the hunting was so good in the jungle that there was little point in visiting the Bahau grasslands. I had already seen wild cattle, and the open grasslands held little interest for me. It was the jungle I wanted to experience. I surprised Weng and Bo 'Hok by asking them where *they* would like to go. They were taken aback because it is common knowledge throughout Borneo that white people live in cities and do not wander. They walk from one place to another, are foolishly obsessed with time and distance regardless of terrain, weather, mood, hunting, or unexpected situations that constantly present themselves in the jungle. These bad habits account for the Penan

131

hesitation in working as guides for geological survey teams, scientific expeditions, or, in one extreme case, a group of carabiner-slinging professional adventurers (sponsored by an American cigarette company) who set out to cross the island from west to east in a more-or-less straight line. That is not the Penan way.

People who are used to living in cities, where the streets and highways are set out in orderly fashion, have little regard for the proper pace of jungle travel. They are renowned for their lack of patience when it becomes impossible to walk in a straight line. I had been guilty of that straight-line mentality during my two-month reconnaissance, but after the dragon-cave incident, I began to learn that the only way to enjoy jungle travel was by relaxing and remaining as flexible as possible in the face of the unavoidable, changing circumstances.

With Bo 'Hok and Weng leading the decision-making process, we eventually decided to head west towards the headwaters of Sungai Iwan and Sungai Lurah. Neither Bo 'Hok nor Weng had been to the area, and they were keen to visit a new place, and to get paid a wage at the same time. This change of plan would extend the trip to the lower Bahau River by at least two weeks, but I was now enjoying myself and didn't feel any sense of urgency to reach the river communities that were only a few days' walk to the south of where we were camped.

My ultimate destination was the east coast, but we turned west to follow Sungai Bahau upstream as far as Sungai Atang, a small tributary. Here the going became very difficult. We veered to the southwest for two days before continuing west across the Sungai Iwan watershed. This 250-square-mile area, bordered by unidentified peaks and valleys, was indicated on my map by a now-familiar notation: "Relief Data Incomplete." The only feature on the whited-out section was a thin, dotted, blue line indicating the approximate course of the upper Sungai Iwan. For two weeks we traversed a perilously rough area of thickly forested hills crisscrossed by countless unnamed waterways. During the time we were in this area I was completely lost. No sun, no distant views, and no clues on the map to give me even the illusion that I knew where we were. But what did it matter if I was lost? I was in a beautiful, untouched forest where there was plenty of game, and I was content to relish the company of my two companions. I have always been a compulsive map reader and have always had an overwhelming fear of being lost, needing the printed map, however inaccurate, to give me confidence. So this ease I felt in what was potentially an extraordinarily vulnerable situation came as a very real pleasure to me. It was a relief to unburden myself from the problems of destination, time, and direction. Bo 'Hok and Weng would sort out these things, if they could be bothered to do so. By relinquishing this element of imaginary control over my surroundings, I suddenly found the immediacy of my experiences greatly intensified. I became blissfully preoccupied with the present tense. It was at about this time I finally came to accept the fact that the rain forest was not a chaotic wilderness to be battled and conquered. There was nothing to conquer, and the chaos was entirely due to my inexperience.

Our daily routine was devoted to hunting, searching for *gaharu*, hunting, gathering medicinal herbs for my collection, and hunting. We usually moved camp each night, but on two occasions large pigs were shot, and both times it took the three of us two days to consume most of the meat. Bo 'Hok and Weng were tremendous eaters, and I found it difficult to adjust to the copious amounts they ate. The main problem we faced while hunting, apart from the noise I made while walking, was finding an animal small enough, one we could eat in a reasonably short time. The hunting was good, too good, and in our wake we left a meandering trail of evenly spaced, half-eaten carcasses.

Bo 'Hok and Weng were incorrigible. They could not resist hunting, and one morning I decided not to give them ammunition for the day because we were already loaded down with smoked pig and deer meat. Smoked meat will stay good for about five to seven days, so there was little reason that I could see to continue the slaughter. Silly me. My one-man crusade to conserve the local fauna was totally inappropriate because I was depriving them of their greatest joy, hunting. They sulked for two days, and I relented. I gave them ammunition again, and the resulting carnage was considerable.

It came as a relief when, after two weeks of excellent hunting, the animals became scarce and the eating orgy abated. We were running out of rice by this time, and with no available game we soon found ourselves two weeks from the nearest settlement with enough food to last only two days. Bo 'Hok and Weng appeared unconcerned by this dilemma. How could people live with such uncertainty, I wondered? I felt foolish about not letting them hunt earlier on. Then I began to worry about the lack of food. Of course, Bo 'Hok and Weng collected edible plants and wild fruit until the hunting improved.

Government observers, keen on getting the Penan out of the valuable hardwood forests, have claimed that Penan health is poor and that they are malnourished. This is a ploy to get them settled so that they can be controlled. Also, it is a source of embarrassment to the governments of Malaysia and Indonesia that in the 1980s nomadic hunters are still roaming the jungles. This doesn't help the national image of a modern, developing country. Yet the only Penan I have seen who were not in superb physical condition were from Sungai Ubong on the ulu Tutoh River in Sarawak. I attribute their health problems to the fact that their traditional hunting grounds were squeezed between Mulu National Park and a huge timber concession.

Our lack of food came as a relief in some ways. Instead of devoting all our time to hacking up animals and discussing the hunt, we found time to talk about other subjects. I was curious about a story I had heard downriver, that the Penan women still practice public childbirth. Bo 'Hok said it was so. He also said that sometimes the child would be born in a small screened-off area of the family shelter. Some Penan groups construct special platforms for the exclusive use of women in labor. Not unlike gynecological examination tables, these low platforms have an inclined back as well as a place for the woman to place her feet as she draws up her knees. Behind the inclined back is an upright pole that the woman can grasp with her hands during contractions and while bearing down during the birth.

Bo 'Hok also described the husband's role during childbirth. He vigorously massages his wife's stomach. Bo 'Hok imitated the pushing and rubbing of a pregnant woman's belly and explained that it was intended to ease the delivery and to comfort the wife. Medical services for the nomadic Penan are virtually nonexistent, but they have songs to ease childbirth, one of which was recorded by Carol Rubenstein and is included in her book *Poems of the Indigenous People of Sarawak*.

PENAN PRAYER TO SPEED CHILDBIRTH

I release, I throw out, I set free
this child from her stomach,
from the stomach of the mother of Lai —
so that she will quickly come to deliver,
soon again to be holding the ax to pound sago pith,
holding the parang knife to collect rattan,
making mats for the floor,
making sitting mats for men to wear.
Come released, come with smoothness,
come so that you can be seen,
so that you go out and reach your people,
you who are now so weak.
Quickly release this child!
Why has this child become stuck?
Perhaps because of tying the shelf for firewood too tightly,
binding together the beams too tightly,
binding the roof, binding the joints of the shelter;
perhaps because a tree, felled,
caught on the way down and hung, not touching the ground.
Probably a leaf monkey, shot,

clung to the treetop, stuck there, and did not drop.
Probably an animal was trapped inside a hollow log.
One, two, three, four —
come out from inside her stomach,
this child red all over its skin.
Move freed along a clear path.
One, two —
go clear of any obstacle,
fall all the way down to the bottom, drop.
Come child, come out
from within the soul of the mother.

There were many things I learned from these two men, but the most difficult lesson of all was how to void my bowels in front of them. My habit of squatting far away was unsociable by local standards and definitely bordered on suspicious behavior. Bo 'Hok and Weng, who had no sense of modesty apart from covering their genitals with one hand while bathing or washing their clothes, would perform their morning ablutions side by side as they chatted to each other. Meanwhile I would have taken up my position seventy-five yards up- or downstream. Visible but distant. I soon sensed this wasn't altogether proper, but what could I do? I had been brought up on white vitreous enamelware behind locked doors. It was with great trepidation on my part that I began to decrease the distance. Each day I moved closer — sixty yards . . . fifty . . . forty . . . then a giant leap to twenty. It took three days to break the twenty-yard barrier, but soon I was within hearing distance. The experience was similar to that of working up to a high-diving platform from the standard springboard. At ten yards I asked myself, "Can I actually speak to people while taking a shit?" I tried, and I could. It was another breakthrough. I doubt that my altered toilet habits made a very significant contribution to the brotherhood of man, but my gesture helped us all to relax.

One of the reasons Bo 'Hok and Weng wanted to travel to the

Sungai Lurah area was so that they could look for jungle produce to sell to the villagers on the Bahau River. Back in Marudi, Muhammad Aidid had explained the relative trade values of goods in the interior, but I still didn't understand how the Penan fitted into the larger picture of island trade. What was their connection with the coastal economy and the overseas markets in the Middle East and China?

The Penan are regarded by all the inland villagers as *ahli hutan*, the forest experts. There is no denying this. To the Penan the jungle is a self-maintaining garden/warehouse from which they collect food as well as certain saleable items such as *damar* (tree resin), beozar stones, edible swiftlet nests, and *gaharu*. The problem for the Penan is not collecting items for sale, but rather the sale itself. They are childlike in their attitudes towards trade, and most of them lack the ability to protect themselves while doing business mainly because of their shyness with strangers. They much prefer to let their settled neighbors in the longhouse communities (usually Kayan or Kenyah) play the part of middlemen with the Chinese traders from the coast, who make periodic buying and selling trips to the interior. This arrangement, of course, leaves the Penan wide open to being cheated. For example, in Sarawak one *kati* (1.33 pound) of super grade A *gaharu* is purchased from the Penan for 50 to 100 Malay dollars. The Penan hold the money briefly; then the longhouse traders bring out cheap bazaar merchandise such as red fabric, sugar, plastic shoes, tobacco, and candies. The end result is that the longhouse people get the *gaharu* and their money back. *Gaharu* sells for 350 to 400 Malay dollars in the upriver bazaars such as Belaga. In Kuching and Singapore the price again increases, and one can only guess at the final price in China and the Middle East, where the aromatic wood is turned into medicine and incense.

The Penan will resist the temptation to spend immediately what they earn if they are saving towards a major purchase such as a shotgun or a cassette player, but they are mainly interested in tobacco and fabric, ammunition if they have access to a shotgun. Until the Penan learn to deal directly and skillfully with the Chinese merchants on the coast, their trade situation is unlikely to improve.

🔺   🔺   🔺

One day while fishing with the gill net in the ulu Sungai Iwan, we discovered the derelict remains of a longboat. We were ready to head downstream and therefore made the decision to rebuild the boat. It was in dreadful condition. The rotting hull was split longitudinally in many places, and the caulking had deteriorated in all the seams. After several hours' labor we managed to float the longboat, but none of us had much confidence in the boat or our repairs. We could have walked, but for a change we decided to take the longboat down this unknown river.

For two harrowing days we traveled downstream through sunlight and shade, and the longboat proved to be so battered that we had to make constant repairs in order to remain afloat. I spent most of my time bailing with my dinner plate, while Bo 'Hok and Weng, who were not very skilled with the paddles, kept running us into the rocks. Frequently we would stop to strip bark from river trees. We pounded the bark between rocks to make a sticky, fibrous pulp, which we then hammered into the cracks in the hull, using stubby wooden wedges and rocks. The cracks in the hull got wider, so we removed the bark caulking and with the tips of our small jungle knives slowly drilled sets of holes on either side of the larger cracks. Through these holes we threaded narrow strips of rattan and clinched the gaps closed. This worked for a while, but the boat continued to spring new leaks. We would make repairs for an hour, travel for twenty to thirty minutes, then stop to make more repairs. After a couple of spectacular and comical collisions with river rocks, some of which spun us around stern first, we holed the longboat so badly that it sank before we could move from our seats. We saved our packs, but in the effort I was carried fifty yards downstream. Struggling to shore without my shoes on, I smashed my feet and ankles on sharp rocks. At the time I was concerned about the bruises and didn't give much attention to the numerous small superficial cuts. Since I hadn't had any infections so far, the cuts didn't worry me; I assumed they would heal by themselves.

Without remembering the consequences of tropical infections, I relaxed my guard. I had forgotten what happened to Bruce Sandilands when his feet became infected in similar circumstances and his guides abandoned him in the rain forest. I would soon regret my nonchalance because within ten days those "insignificant little cuts" crippled me so terribly that I was left speechless with pain and fever.

CHAPTER SEVEN · PA LAMPUNG
PADAN'S SEWING MACHINE

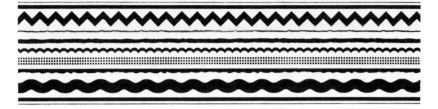

THREE HUNDRED miles from the east coast and two days' walk from where the longboat sank, I climbed to the top of a mountain ridge smothered in giant trees. It was the morning of my 115th day in the jungle. Like an island, the ridge sat half-submerged in a sea of blue-white valley mist. Each day before noon those cool rising mists would submerge the jungle mountains like an ocean tide.

My two guides and I slashed a small clearing in the dense undergrowth with our parangs and sat down to make tea. After collecting wood and splitting it, Bo 'Hok showed me how fire was made before the Penan discovered Bic lighters. He cut a two-foot length of green bamboo with his parang and from his tin tobacco box produced a smallish flake of flint. He called it *batu api*, the fire rock. Holding the flint and a thin mat of tinder between his thumb and first two finger-tips, Bo 'Hok vigorously struck the smooth surface of the bamboo at an oblique angle. To my astonishment sparks appeared. The tinder soon glowed red in patches and was then placed into a prepared handful of dried fibrous sago bark mixed with ash from burned leaves. This mixture, he explained, was *tiðak takoot angin*, not afraid of the wind. Bo 'Hok added wood shavings, blew two or three times, and within seconds we had fire. Flames danced around the base of the blackened cooking pot, and we brought out our enameled mugs and a plastic bag of Lipton tea.

As the water heated, I watched the column of smoke meandering up through the twisted network of branches. Three swallows appeared briefly against a patch of blue sky to dart across the one small opening in the jungle canopy. Far off, black cicadas intermittently droned their predictable phrases.

I tried to wash daily, but hadn't been able to the previous afternoon; the streams on the steep slopes were too small to bathe in, so by morning I smelled of stale sweat and mosquito repellent. Living in the perpetual shade was beginning to make me feel confined and irritable. The sunlight was only 150 feet above my head, but there was no way of getting to it. My inclination was to climb hand over hand up through the layers of the forest canopy to poke my head above the highest branches and feel the sun's warmth on my face and forearms. I imagined that the rolling expanse of closely clustered tree crowns would look like a densely planted garden of giant broccoli. Bo' Hok and Weng could have managed the climb, but they didn't feel the need. For me, it was an impossible feat. I had to abandon the thought.

It was during moments of relative inactivity such as this that I would start thinking about how completely alone I felt. The sounds, the smells, and especially the terrain were still unfamiliar. I had chosen to come, wanted to come, but that did not dissipate the sense that I was isolated in a place that wasn't my own. I was completely restricted to a pace dictated by circumstances beyond my control: the weather, the moods of Bo 'Hok and Weng, and the availability of wild game. I felt I had become fluent enough in Indonesian, but the cultural gap between my Western middle-class background and that of these two nomadic hunters had come to feel like a sociological Grand Canyon. The three of us had experienced so many intimate, humorous, touching moments, but I knew I didn't really matter to them. We were physically together, but separated by our histories, thoughts, perceptions, and expectations. To them I was a slightly amusing stranger who had some shotgun shells that they needed. One day soon we would say goodby, and they would return to the forest without me. The likelihood that I would be forgotten troubled me because I knew that the memory of these months in the rain forest would stay with me forever. I needed someone to reflect the intensity of my experience in order to validate it. Bo 'Hok and Weng didn't think in such terms. They had a much more immediate sense of the world, based primarily on survival. I spent much of my time thinking; they spent theirs looking for food and a place to sleep.

Few outsiders had ventured into this part of the rain forest. None had come as alone and vulnerable as I was. Nieuwenhuis had brought 110 porters and bodyguards this way in 1898; then there was the story of poor George Muller. In 1824, as a representative of the Dutch Colonial government, he had set out to cross the island from east to west. He wanted to be the first white man to accomplish the journey. Traveling up the Mahakam River from Samarinda with twelve Javanese soldiers, he succeeded in negotiating the maze of smaller rivers that led into the rugged central mountains that now bear his name. He crossed the watershed, and with his goal seemingly possible, yet still months away, he set up his last camp on Sungai Bungan at the headwaters of the Kapuas River. The next morning the longboats were loaded, but as Muller made final preparations to leave he and his soldiers were attacked and cut down by a band of marauding natives. One of the Javanese men managed to escape and somehow found his way through hundreds of miles of unknown rain forest to reach Pontianak with news of Muller's death.

Even with this knowledge, I felt comfortable that I would not share Muller's fate. I gradually came to realize that by traveling as a total novice — ignorant of even the basics of jungle survival — the highland people gave me special treatment. I was viewed as being either very brave or very mad, and I don't think anyone was quite sure which. I wasn't certain myself. It was clear that I was doing something they would never consider — traveling without tribal companions beyond the boundaries of their land. There was a practical reason for my traveling this way. I wanted to avoid intimidating anyone. Having white skin, long feet, and standing nearly twelve inches above most people were provocative enough. Had I traveled with a group (of Westerners), the community response would have been completely different. They would have been inhibited. On my own I was in the minority, always off balance, completely vulnerable. I was the stranger, and the people treated me exactly as they saw fit. The quickest and most accurate way of judging a community, it seems to me, is to observe how its members react to strangers. Traveling on my own was the only way to see what the people were like. I had consciously put myself in a position where I was the one who had to adapt — both to the people and to the environment. It was my ability to adapt to change in response to what was going on around me that ensured my continuing survival. By living in their leaf huts, eating their food, learning their language, joining the hunt, and dancing with them at night, I let the people know I accepted them and wished to be accepted by them in return. I felt comfortable making a fool of myself, and the people responded to my openness with hospitality and good humor. Their sympathy and friendship surrounded me with an aura of safety that no passport, weapon, map, or radio could ever have provided.

I hadn't slept well the previous night because of the damp, so I held the teacup close to my face and blew the steam into my eyes to help clear them. Over the rim of the cup I could see Bo 'Hok and Weng sitting on the other side of the fire. They were preoccupied with the task of oiling their gun barrels with stomach fat from an eight-foot snake they had hacked to pieces the day before.

A nearby rustling and crunching of twigs caught my attention. Something large was moving towards us on the trail. Bo 'Hok and Weng instinctively slipped cartridges into their shotguns, eased the breaches shut, and waited quietly. Staggering into view, a man suddenly appeared on the narrow game trail. He was bent double beneath the weight of what looked like a large hardwood box. His arrival came as a surprise because we hadn't seen any other human being in six weeks.

The man was dressed in blue satin jogging shorts, black high-top tennis shoes without socks, and a red T-shirt. It wasn't until he got closer that I recognized what he was carrying. It was an old-fashioned treadle sewing machine mounted on a cast-iron frame within a hardwood cabinet. I knew there wasn't a village for more than eighty miles in the direction from which he was walking. I stared at him in disbelief. He walked up to us and with a half-smile, raised his eyebrows slightly in greeting, then lowered himself to his haunches, gently placing the heavy machine upright on the ground. Cast into the metal base I read the word "Singer."

I had absolutely no idea what this man and his sewing machine could be doing in the jungle. It seemed unlikely that he was a mad nomadic tailor, but no other possibility presented itself. The timing of this man's arrival was perfect. For the previous few days I had been congratulating myself on my great adventure, and now I was confronted with serious competition. There is a perverse sort of one-upmanship that obliges travelers all over the world to outdo one another with stories. This man didn't have to utter a single word. One glance at his sewing machine and I felt my journey fade into insignificance.

I later learned his name was Pa Lampung Padan. I offered him *sugee*, but before our conversation began I was distracted by a metallic clanking sound. The commotion grew louder, and soon a second man appeared on the trail. His rattan pack was filled with a mass of shiny aluminum rice-cooking pots. Dozens more were attached by their handles to the sides of the pack. His footsteps were accentuated by the sound of many pots striking one another. The pot man sat down next to the sewing machine with a resounding crash of metal. Immediately another man arrived carrying a 25-horsepower Johnson outboard motor and a brace of rainbow-colored golfing umbrellas. The group continued to grow as three more men appeared. The pile of booty was impressive. There were tape recorders manufactured in Java, Stihl chain saws from Sweden, a battered World War II British Commando Special Z Unit jerry can full of gasoline, red and blue plastic buckets, and four large tins of Huntley and Palmer's Superior Reading Biscuits. I was unfamiliar with this brand name and incorrectly assumed the biscuits were to be eaten while reading. I imagined myself seated comfortably in an armchair by a fireplace — a bone china teacup and saucer on the polished mahogany side table, the fragrance of bergamot, a small dish of reading biscuits, and P. G. Wodehouse in hand.

The men sat on the jungle floor surrounded by their remarkable loads with expressions of total nonchalance. They might have been simply returning from the corner store with a bottle of milk and the newspaper. I caught sight of Bo 'Hok covetously admiring the umbrella man's right forearm. It displayed three identical stainless steel Seiko 5 wristwatches. The three of us were very impressed by this caravan of coastal goods.

Pa Lampung Padan told me that for the previous four weeks they had been shuttling this tremendous amount of newly purchased tools and gifts over the mountains from Sarawak. According to his story, there must have been two or three thousand pounds of the stuff stacked on the banks of a nearby stream. There is no air service between Sarawak and central Kalimantan, and the only way to transport these goods is by longboat and on foot.

For generations men have left the isolation of the highland communities to travel out into the world. It is considered "good" to travel far. This practice is called *peselai* (the long journey) by the Kenyah, and *bejelai* (to walk) by the Iban. This tradition goes back to headhunting days. The fact that the men are now returning with sewing machines and tape recorders rather than with heads has not significantly changed the purpose of the journey or the rituals of spirit worship. Before World War II a man's wealth was calculated in terms of ceramic rice-wine jars, brass gongs, salt, and cloth. Today the items of consequence are radios, batteries, medicines, chain saws, outboard motors, and front teeth sheathed in gold by Chinese dentists on the coast.

The coastal boomtown economy — created by the timber, oil, and natural-gas industries — was evident in the selection of the goods the men had brought. These products of modern technology made me reflect upon how one culture measures what is of value in another culture. When the Kalimantan Kenyah go to the coast, they return with utilitarian objects such as tools, kerosene, and cooking pots. Other items, such as sunglasses, Milo (a health drink similar to Ovaltine or Horlicks), plastic toys, printed T-shirts, and plastic dinnerware sets, are purchased primarily for social status. Back in the upriver longhouses some of these products of Western industry become ritual power objects.

146

During my two-month reconnaissance through Iban country in Sarawak, I once saw a lurid pink plastic suitcase used as a portable shrine. Instead of neatly folded clothes and a shaving kit, the suitcase contained steaming fresh pig livers for divining the future. In another Iban village chain saws and famous headhunting swords were lashed to the upright roof supports and draped with red hibiscus flowers. People danced around these temporary displays during *Gawai*, the June rice-harvest celebrations. We might laugh at the notion of plastic tea sets in the jungle, but it is a time-honored ritual for Western travelers to collect preindustrial artifacts to use as home decorations. A woven rattan sago mat on a living-room wall creates a lifestyle image with that ethnic touch. Possession of primitive artifacts suggests worldly knowledge, just as in the highland communities of Borneo an electronic wristwatch that plays "Happy Birthday" is the mark of a great traveler. Funny thing how travel can narrow the mind.

The man with the Seiko watches asked me what I was doing in the jungle. I told him I was collecting plants and trading shotgun shells and beads for stories. I'm afraid this explanation didn't make much of an impression.

"How far is your home, *Tuan?*" asked Pa Lampung Padan.

"From the coast, two hundred days by longboat with two 40-horsepower outboard engines," I answered with my standard reply.

I could see the men measuring this distance in their minds. How many tins of gasoline? How many *gantangs* of rice? Would the fishing be good? This great distance was "too far" for them to imagine. How could all the supplies for two hundred days be carried in the boat?

The men were more impressed by the Borneo rivers I had traveled and the names of the villages where I had stayed. They nodded and occasionally conferred privately as I correctly recited the succession of headmen who had passed me from one tribal area to another. The list stretched from the coast to the last village in Kalimantan Pow-O-Pan. When I finished, Pa Lampung Padan exclaimed, "*Tuan*, you are not just collecting leaves and tree bark. You have come far from your home. You, too, are on *peselai*. You are the same as us." I agreed, to help them make sense of what I was doing, but I felt that in no way did my wanderings compare with their stupendous journey.

The purpose of *peselai* is to acquire wealth and social status. In many ways these trips are also spiritual journeys and provide an opportunity for young men to establish or enhance their sense of self. It is a time for the men (and some women, too, these days) to test themselves in new places. A successful trip will add prestige to the individual and his or her community. *Peselai* serves other practical purposes as well. Young women put considerable pressure on eligible bachelors by asking them pointedly, "Have you gone on *peselai*? What is your story? What have you done?"

In a lifetime there are few opportunities that allow men the time to leave their villages and farms to go on these long journeys. It is also unusual to meet a man who has not made at least one extended trip to the coast. There is an expression in the highlands of Kalimantan: Four trips to the coast and you are an old man.

Traditionally, before leaving on *peselai*, the men must first receive proper omens from the jungle. One waits for the first call of the *isit* bird (the spider hunter, *Arachnothera chrysogenys*). Then the *elang* bird (white-headed hawk, *Haliaster intermedius*) must be seen flying from right to left. The men also wait for the call of the crested rain bird (*Platylophus porphyromelas*) and finally for the deceptive doglike sound of the barking deer (*Cervulus muntjak*). Waiting for the omens and preparing the proper food offerings can take a minimum of two weeks, usually much longer.

"How long did it take for you to receive the omens?" I asked Pa Lampung.

"Oh, I don't consult the birds now. I am a Christian. I pray to the forest spirits with help from Jesus and God. One quick prayer is enough."

"As well it should be," I agreed.

Pa Lampung Padan had said goodby to his wife and children two years earlier. He left his village, Long Peliran, one morning with two friends. Carrying parangs and light packs, the three men wandered for weeks through the giant forest. They traversed the great dividing range to the north and eventually located a river flowing through Sarawak towards the South China Sea. They lived off the jungle and traveled downstream for another five days before arriving in the twentieth century. Their longboat was beached at the Holly Stene Quarry on the banks of the Baram River. The local people called the place Batu Gading (The Ivory Rock), named for the tremendous bread-loaf-shaped white stone monolith that rises dramatically out of the green jungle at a tight bend in the river. Pa Lampung Padan and his two friends found work at the quarry. For twenty months he drilled holes in Batu Gading, set explosive charges, and blew up the dense blue-gray rock. The stone rubble was reduced to gravel and sent downriver on barges to pave the coastal roads of Brunei and Sarawak.

As illegal workers in Sarawak, the Indonesians are taken advantage of by the Chinese camp manager. They are paid less and sleep on the floors of corregated metal hovels, twenty men to a room. The toilet facilities are unspeakable, and most workers prefer the river. The starting wage for Indonesians was less than three U.S. dollars per day. This was two-thirds the local wage, but twice what they could earn in Indonesia. Consequently, the coastal Malays and nearby longhouse workers looked down on the Indonesians because they represented cheap imported labor that deprived them of jobs.

Pa Lampung Padan persevered and eventually became a relatively highly paid laborer. He did well for himself and never lost sight of how his efforts would benefit his family.

"In a month I could save 400 Malay dollars [175 U.S. dollars] from my 500-dollar wage," he told me. "The other 100 dollars went for rice, sugar, canned drinks, biscuits, soup, salt, and soap. We made kerosene lamps out of old soft-drink cans. The wicks were made from twisted cloth and stuck into the tops. We bought our own food, also fuel for cooking, work clothes, and made our own entertainment. There was the river for swimming and one dirt badminton court. We bought the nets, racquets, and shuttlecock. Everything we bought [at inflated prices] from the company store."

The combined pressures of hard labor, nowhere to go after work, and the loneliness of being separated from their families and land caused some men to grow despondent and to squander their meager wages on petty luxuries from the company store. They also spent their money on card games, alcohol, and the camp prostitutes. For the two hundred workers the Chinese shop owner had contracted six women from the coast. A new group of women came each month. For twenty dollars (one to two days' wages) a man could spend an hour with one of these women, as others waited their turn.

Credit was readily extended by the company store, so that some of the workers were laboring merely to service their debts and to feed themselves. I was told that one Indonesian man had been at the stone quarry for nineteen years and hadn't saved any money. He had lost contact with his family, and the shame of returning to his village empty-handed kept him at Batu Gading.

After twenty months of this life, Pa Lampung Padan had saved enough money. He left the blasting pits of Batu Gading and traveled downstream to the Marudi bazaar. There, after testing the weight of several models, he bought a sewing machine for his wife — the best one he could find. There are other sewing machines in the highlands, but such a marvelous new machine had never been seen by the people of Long Peliran.

From Marudi Pa Lampung Padan joined five other Kenyah men for the return journey to Kalimantan. They traveled upstream to the village of Long Moh near the border then hacked a longboat out of a single tree trunk with short-handled axes and an adz. The longboat was loaded and poled upstream to the headwaters of Sungai Janan, the last river in Sarawak. From there Pa Lampang Padan carried the sewing machine over the precipitous mountain ridges to the first stream in Kalimantan. Another longboat was built of hand-hewn planks lashed together with rattan vines. Pa Lampung described the half-submerged bamboo raft piled high with the sewing machine and other precious cargo, slowly floating along quiet jungle waterways. Pa Lampung had traveled more than seven hundred miles roundtrip in the previous two years and was now within four days of his home village. He had risked blowing his body to pieces in a dust-filled quarry where no one cared about him and had lived among strangers in a miserable shack eating cheap tinned food for both those years. The loneliness must have been unbearable. His wife had been through her own ordeal. She had not heard from her husband since he had left and had continued to take care of the farm and the children while he was gone, with no idea that her husband would be home in a matter of days.

Pa Lampung finished the story of his journey, and I was speechless. There was something almost too touching about his efforts. What more was there to be said about "man, the loving, thoughtful provider," or "woman, the faithful home keeper"? These values had long ago been reduced to clichés in modern culture, but listening to Pa Lampung, I was moved by his sense of devotion to his family, exemplified by his sacrifice and the incredible physical strain to return with his gifts.

The cooking pot with the tea had gone cold for the third time, and the steady rising valley mist was now creeping through the trees. It was time to start walking again. The men began stripping the bark from freshly cut six-foot-long saplings. With steady strokes of their knife blades, they decorated the ends of the poles with long spiral ribbons of wood shavings. The six poles were placed in the ground at the edge of our clearing to thank the spirit of the omens as well as *balai utung*, the spirit of each man, for the successful journey. This was the final ritual for their *peselai*, as they were now entering their own country.

Pa Lampung Padan squatted in front of the sewing machine. He adjusted his shoulder straps and placed a pounded, bark-fiber tumpline across his forehead before struggling to his feet. Bo 'Hok, Weng, and I watched them go. One by one the men lifted their packs and in single file disappeared into the jungle. The sound of clanking pots was eventually replaced by the bird and insect sounds of the forest.

CHAPTER EIGHT · ARRIVAL IN LONG BIA

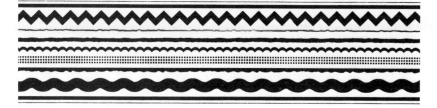

D AYS AFTER my meeting with Pa Lampung Padan, a hunting party of five Penan men and their dogs surprised us during our midday meal. The men, armed with six-foot-long spears, were hunting for wild pigs. They appeared unexpectedly, but after a moment of tension they sat down for an hour to "share news." One of the men told me that three hundred miles downriver there were two white missionaries living in the village of Long Bia. By coincidence, Long Bia was where I was headed.

I wanted to buy more supplies in Long Bia and send a telegram to my family to let them know that I was safe. No one had heard from me since I left Kuching. More important, I wanted to get out of the jungle. I had become physically exhausted and was rapidly losing my patience. The sense of magic and wonder that had sustained my spirits this far was disappearing. In the jungle, time usually seemed to stand still. There was no sense of urgency or destination. The journey was an end in itself. But now, having crossed the last mountains and with the possibility of speaking English for the first time in months, a destination became implanted in my mind. I began thinking about arriving in Long Bia.

Long Bia became an obsession. I assumed that the missionaries were isolated from the outside world, that they would be fluent in the local dialects, and that they would be sympathetic towards the local people. I assumed many things, even that they would enjoy my company.

Three narrow trade routes cross the great dividing range between the Kelabit highlands and Kalimantan, but because Bo 'Hok and Weng, like all Penan, preferred the deep shadows of the forest, we meandered through a maze of game trails that had no beginning or end. I had been with Bo 'Hok and Weng for nearly two months. This was new country for them, and our route zigzagged through the forest in an aimless fashion as we traversed the mountain forests looking for food. Bo 'Hok and Weng wanted to explore this new landscape, and they laughed at my frustration about how little progress we made some days.

"*Dawai, dawai*" (slowly, slowly), they would say. They had a point. Why should they rush? There might be *gaharu* or stands of sago nearby. I didn't know where I was and had finally learned to keep my suggestions to myself. Bo 'Hok and Weng were the pathfinders, so we continued to meander through the rain forest. During this phase of the trip I remained thoroughly disoriented. I knew we were headed in a generally southeasterly direction and stopped asking, "How far?" or "How many days?" The questions were meaningless.

"If you haven't been to this part of the forest before," I asked Bo 'Hok, "how do you know where we're going?"

"*Mal-cun-uk*" (we follow our feelings), came the reply.

He made it sound easy. It wasn't.

My anxiety about wanting to get "somewhere else" was partially due to the fact that I knew too many "other places" in the world. For Bo 'Hok and Weng there was no "other place" apart from the jungle, and I grew to envy their sense of place, their contentment with where they were. When I became anxious, I would embark upon extraordinary journeys in my mind. When, for example, a steep, muddy trail became impossible because of the leeches, I might imagine myself on a pair of cross-country skis, gliding across expanses of unmarked snow, a picnic lunch and a bottle of wine in my pack. The sight of bee-larvae soup could send me around the world to the Empress Hotel in Victoria, British Colombia, for afternoon tea and scones with freshly whipped cream and thick strawberry jam. Outside, a light snow would be falling on the passing traffic.

Even during this relatively difficult period, there were some days in the rain forest that were effortless and full of new discoveries. We saw tree-climbing pigs and flying snakes and lizards, and one day Weng brought me a leaf in the palm of his hand. When I touched the leaf, it stood up and walked around looking for a place to hide. The leaf was actually a cleverly disguised insect that blended in perfectly with the leaf litter on the jungle floor.

Also, Weng told me the story of a diving ant that launches itself from the rim of Lowes pitcher plant (*Nepenthes lowii*) and plunges into the insect-eating reservoir of digestive fluid contained within the body of the plant. The diving ant rescues some of the insects by "swimming" them to the edge of the reservoir like a miniature lifesaver. Then the ant eats the insect.

There were also times when nothing went right. One particularly nasty evening I lay sleepless alongside Bo 'Hok and Weng, shivering beneath a damp bedsheet. In the darkness I got up to pee and, without realizing it, walked over a column of fire ants (*Leptogenys processionalis*). I couldn't see the little monsters, but I knew straight away what they were. After swatting at my ankles and toes with my free hand, my fingers were covered with enraged biting ants. Then I made the mistake of switching hands, and a fire ant sunk its mandibles into the head of my penis. That got me moving. "Ohhhhh, shit!" I yelled in a panic. The bite was like a wasp sting, and the pain shot up the sides of my body like an electrical shock and made my scalp tingle. Swatting and dancing about, I remembered an Australian remedy for neutralizing jellyfish stings. You simply pee on the affected area. I was desperate; I peed on my hands and feet to get rid of the ants, and that seemed to help. I brushed the survivors away and washed myself in a small stream. Much relieved, I lay down in the mist-sodden *pondok*, but soon became aware of a strange vibration shaking the sleeping platform. A moment later I heard a sudden snort, like someone gasping for air, followed by a series of muffled cackling noises. I propped myself on one elbow and discovered Bo 'Hok and Weng weren't asleep at all. The bastards were convulsed with laughter at my performance.

I wasn't the only one who suffered that night. Bo 'Hok and

Weng didn't have mosquito nets, so they nursed a smoky fire with damp wood to keep away sand flies and mosquitoes. The blinding cloud of hot, choking smoke kept us hacking and sneezing until dawn.

To add to the miserable scene, my feet and ankles were battered and painfully swollen from the sharp river rocks. Lying on the sapling-pole platform, I could feel my feet throbbing from small infections that had erupted on my ankles.

Bo 'Hok had many talents, the least endearing of which was his ability to fart. He had been at it all night, and by morning it seemed as if his reserves were truly without measure. With each purposeful blast he seemed to be bugling the sleepy jungle to life. Under his onslaught the sounds of the night-hunting creatures and insects gradually yielded to the chorus of monkeys, followed by the lilting song of the yellow-crowned bulbul (*Pycnonotus zeylanicus*). Months later, an ornithologist at the Sarawak Museum would tell me that the nightingale really had a much better range, but as I sat up in the predawn chill with arms clasped around my legs, chin on my knees, and eyes still closed, I became even more convinced that there couldn't be a more lovely or peaceful sound in the world. I was being blissfully carried along by the bulbul's song when the jungle harmony was suddenly shattered by one last tremendous fart from Bo 'Hok, who then got up to start the morning fire.

We had definitely been reduced to basics, and I was beginning to wonder, after 127 days in the jungle, how much more I could take. I was becoming numbed and seriously disoriented by the never-ending search for food and a place to set up camp. I was also constantly aware of the closeness of the jungle. Distant views were no more than one hundred feet, and I spent long hours on the trail watching where I placed each foot while scanning my legs for leeches. The experience of jungle travel had become stupefying. But, worst of all, I was now becoming increasingly conscious of time. My feet were infected as a result the wreck of the longboat, and it was painful to walk. I had been in the interior long enough; I wanted out. I wanted a rest from the jungle, to sink back into the comforts of my own culture, if only for a day. I convinced myself that all I really needed was to be able to catch a glimpse of my own people. They would help me remember who I was and where I had come from. I figured the missionaries in Long Bia would restore my fading spirits. I might be offered a bed with crisp, sun-dried cotton sheets, perhaps a pillow. My mind reeled at the thought of such luxuries.

For the next four days we cut our way cross-country towards the village of A Pau Peng. Below that village the Bahau River became navigable for long stretches between the rapids. Those days were wonderful. The jungle, in contrast to what we had so recently passed through, was spectacular. Two-hundred-foot hardwood trees were draped with orchids, ferns, and moss-covered vines. Bright orange bracket fungus grew in fan-shaped steps on dead logs, and the buttressed tree roots grabbed the steaming earth like giant webbed fingers. Occasionally we could catch glimpses between the trees of long, green valleys and sheer rock walls. The air was thick with brightly colored butterflies, and at one point we stopped to watch hundreds of large flying foxes settling in the mass of overhead branches. Flapping and wheeling with leathery wing beats, their chattering shrieks finally subsided as each creature found the right branch from which to hang. In the air they looked prehistoric. Bo 'Hok brought one down with a round of bird shot, and we ate it for lunch. It tasted awful. The meat was full of sinew and lead pellets, and the unpleasant smoky flavor lingered in my mouth for several hours.

Bo 'Hok and Weng were not river people, and once we left the river they began to take a renewed interest in the journey. We started talking about the plants again and would stop whenever we saw something interesting. Weng pulled up an aromatic root called *lung*. "It's used to prevent ghosts from making babies cry," he told me. Later that day we collected *akar korek*, the "matches vine." Once lit, the dried vine smoulders for days and is a convenient way to transport fire. To keep leeches from climbing up our shorts, we pounded the vine *akar sukilang* to a pulp and rubbed the resulting white mash on our legs. *Akar sukilang* could also be used for fishing. Like the *tuba* root the Iban use, *akar sukilang* can be pounded and mixed with water then poured into the river to stupefy the fish and make them float to the surface.

We decided to stop walking at noon one day, and Weng showed me how to catch birds with the sap of the *talun* tree. We smeared the sap on thin sticks 18 inches long and wedged them into parang cuts at the tops of fruit trees. Malay lorikeets (*Loriculus galgulus*) arriving at dawn to feed in the treetops became harmlessly glued to the sticky perches. We then climbed up the trees to collect the birds. They showed little fear and became tame very quickly. We made bamboo cages for the birds and carried them on top of our packs. The birds were friendly, affectionate little creatures, and we fed them cooked rice and bananas. The original idea had been to sell the birds downriver to the timber-camp workers for 1,000 rupiahs each ($1.60 U.S., a day's wage), but after collecting twenty we opened the cages and let the birds go. Unperturbed by their captivity, they flew back into the jungle. There was no clear reason why we did this. I guess I felt I had enjoyed traveling with the little birds and no longer had the urge to sell them.

We gauged time by the light and temperature as well as by animal and insect activity. A couple of hours before dusk every evening, swarms of sweat bees would cluster on our lower legs and start daubing the rivulets of perspiration with their little black proboscises. They didn't bite or sting, but they tickled to distraction. They also lacked even a basic knowledge of insect survival. They refused to fly away. In a single swat I could kill dozens, and those were immediately replaced by others. When the sweat bees arrived, it was time to start setting up camp. From earlier walks in Sarawak, I knew that at precisely 6:00 P.M. black cicadas would start their evening chorus to let us know that nightfall was near.

One evening as the bees swarmed over my legs, I pulled off my pack and felt the relief of a cool breeze blowing against my damp T-shirt. The swelling of my feet was getting worse, and I estimated I had another three or four days before it would be too painful to walk. The first thing we did was light a fire to keep the sand flies away. We had stopped at the site of a former longhouse. I knew this because along the riverbank there were fruiting pomelo trees that had outlived the last traces of the village. Within the thick, pale green skins of these giant grapefruit were pinkish yellow segments of cool, sweet fruit. After walking all day they were irresistible. I ate one after another until the corners of my mouth stung from the zest of the peel. We sat on a flat-topped knoll peeling our pomelos and soon noticed the movement of fish in the stream. Weng finished eating, stripped off his shorts and T-shirt, and walked naked across the gravel riverbank with the gill net slung over his brown shoulders and buttocks. Keeping his genitals modestly covered with one hand, he stepped into the narrow stream and waded across to a partially submerged log. I could see him suck in his stomach as the cold water reached his waist. He attached one end of the net to the log and let the other end drift free. The line of evenly spaced white plastic floats attached to the end of the net drifted in a lazy, undulating motion before settling in a straight line with the gentle current.

At a familiar sound of leaves rustling, my ears flattened and the back of my neck tingled with excitement. I turned my head slowly and spotted the wild pig. Bo 'Hok had already seen it. We froze as the huge boar wandered out of the undergrowth one hundred feet from where we sat. The pig paused at the base of a thick stand of bamboo and suspiciously sniffed the air. Standing upwind, he was confused by our presence and stood there long enough for me to locate a shotgun shell in the bottom of my bag. Without taking his eyes off the pig, Bo 'Hok—who was closer to the shotgun—held out his hand for the cartridge.

Before the smoke of the shotgun had cleared, we were upon the animal with our parangs. The back of the neck and the hind legs were slashed deeply, and we stood back as the thrashing animal bled to death. No more than two minutes had passed from the moment of first sighting the pig until it was lying motionless at the edge of the clearing. After the blast of the shotgun, all sounds in the jungle ceased. There was only the trickling sound of the river and the smell of gunpowder and blood. Three-inch, curved, yellow tusks were visible from between the lips, and the thick, wiry bristles that stuck out from the snout continued to twitch for a few more minutes. It was a big pig. What we couldn't eat or smoke that night we would have to leave behind. The flesh would putrefy within a day. The instinct to kill and eat was growing on me. It was the natural response of the hunter and something I had never felt before. We forgot about fishing. Weng gathered up the net and rejoined us as we began the task of butchering the pig.

On a bed of wide leaves we cut back the skin with our small-bladed, long-handled knives. We carried these knives in a folded-bark sheath attached to the parang sheath. These smaller knives are called *anak* parang (child of the jungle knife) and are used for delicate work. The warm skin was spread out like a blanket. Setting aside favorite pieces such as the liver, tongue, and the twin muscles found inside the lower rib cage, we jointed, boned, cubed, then shoved the meat onto 18-inch wooden skewers. These would be hot-smoked over the fire during the night. We wrapped the brains in a leaf and steamed them on top of a potful of backbones. The local people would usually have rendered the skin and fatty tissue into cooking oil, but we didn't have a large enough pot to do the job. Locals rated pigs in terms of how many finger widths of fat they have in cross section on their backs. One finger width is not so good; four widths is excellent. For trading, the oil has a much greater value than the flesh because it's easy to preserve and transport and because there is a big demand for it in the villages. The pig we had just killed had three finger widths of fat.

We recovered four of the nine shotgun pellets from the carcass and put them away for later use. The spent plastic cartridge would be reloaded another ten times, at least, before being discarded. The firing caps would be poked out of the casing with a thin iron rod, hammered flat, and reprimed with a match head. Black powder is poured into the cartridge, followed by cloth wadding and the recycled lead shot. The cartridge is topped up with melted beeswax to make it waterproof.

I took half a side of ribs and forced it onto two sharpened green sticks that had been shoved into the loose root-filled soil and leaned slightly towards the fire. While the ribs were cooking, Weng and Bo 'Hok cleared a sleeping area. They also built a rack over the fire where we laid out the skewers of meat and lengths of firewood. The light was fading rapidly as I went to search for a species of wild ginger. Crushed in half a coconut shell with a smooth river rock, the ginger can be mixed with salt and chilli. We boiled rice, and when the meat had finished roasting, we cut it up and dipped each piece into the mixture. The smoky aroma and crackling succulence of the pig blended perfectly with the fiery ginger *sambol*.

Squatting on my haunches, I could feel the fat running down my forearms and dripping from my elbows. I was totally absorbed in the meal when I heard a vaguely familiar droning sound growing louder and louder. I looked up through a gap in the jungle canopy and saw, for perhaps five seconds, a commercial airliner. It was streaking its way across the evening sky. As I watched, the light from the setting sun transformed the plane into a golden comet followed by a pure white vapor trail. It was a strange sight from where I crouched by the fire surrounded by the darkening forest and night sounds. I explained to Bo 'Hok and Weng that the airplane was bigger than a longhouse, but was unable to explain what kept the plane in the air.

The plane disappeared, and we continued eating, but the significance of the incident continued to grow in my mind. The passing plane had allowed me to see clearly how much I had adapted to the jungle over the previous four months. I imagined myself sitting in the plane, looking out over the rain forest for the first time. The uninterrupted vista of treetops swept to the horizon in all directions. Far below, at the edge of a small clearing, almost hidden from sight, I could see myself seated by a campfire with two brown-skinned jungle men, speaking an unknown language. Nearby lay the steaming carcass of a wild boar. From that perspective I suddenly realized what an astonishing situation I was in: submerged in a sea of giant trees, hunting wild animals, a bloodied parang at my waist—the stuff of pure fantasy six months earlier.

✦   ✦   ✦

Apart from my feet, I was in excellent health. My stomach had flattened, and I had developed an acute sense of smell and hearing. I could distinguish small movements of animals on the jungle floor and imitate many of the natural sounds of insects and birds. More significantly, I had shed my Western concepts of time, comfort, and privacy. When I first entered the jungle and let go of my margins of safety to become vulnerable to a place I didn't understand, it was terrifying. I had slowly learned, however, to live with the fear and uncertainty. Also, I realized that the physical journey was not the great accomplishment. The value of the trip lay in everyday encounters, and the destination gradually became a by-product of the journey. Again I reminded myself that it was my ability to understand the local people and adapt to their way of life that had allowed me to get this far. I then realized, for the first time, that if I had come this far into the jungle, what could possibly stop me now from reaching the east coast of Kalimantan? Yes, I was definitely going to make it. I had spent six years thinking about this moment, but instead of the giddiness and surge of pride I would have anticipated, I felt serene and confident. Not that I wasn't thrilled. I could feel my face flush and tears come to my eyes, and I tried to hide these emotions. My daydream of crossing the Borneo rain forest was going to come true; that knowledge gave me an incredible sense of power and self-assurance.

That night the jungle was perfectly black, and a cool wind blew through the shelter. Bo 'Hok and Weng and I fell asleep joking about the condition of the tattered shoes I had attached to my feet that morning with adhesive tape. The nylon uppers were so rotten from the climate and constant damp they had completely detached from the soles. When I could, I planned to stitch the shoes back together with nylon fishing line.

We reached the Saban village of A Pau Peng the next afternoon. My toes were swollen together, and the tropical ulcers that had started as small sores now dripped lymph down my legs and ankles like clear candle wax. On each of the previous three mornings the pain had increased, and I felt so dreadful I couldn't talk during the first hour of walking. I was feverish, and each footstep made me feel nauseated. By midmorning my feet would lose all sensation, and I could begin to relax. A Pau Peng was located on the upper Bahau River, and this is where Bo 'Hok and Weng would head east for another week to reach their own land at the headwaters of the Malinau River. That night we went over our journey day by day, and I gave them shotgun shells for their wage. We went to bed early that night in an empty farm hut, and before dawn Bo 'Hok and Weng nudged me awake to say goodby. They returned to the jungle, and I never saw them again.

The next week was a blur of strangers and backwater communities. After Bo 'Hok and Weng the quality of guides plummeted. The two-hour trip downstream to Long Berini was thoroughly forgettable. I enlisted the services of a geriatric betel-nut addict and a young tough who could not walk without a crutch because of a childhood accident with a parang. As boatmen they were totally inept, constantly running aground and choosing the wrong way through the rapids. We agreed on a half-day journey so they could return upriver to A Pau Peng before nightfall, but after one hour in the longboat they pulled in at the first village and went in search of more betel nut. They then demanded lunch from the headman's wife, and the three of them conspired to convince me to give them money for the meal. This is not the custom, and when I pointed that out, they all agreed. The guides (I never learned their names) ate like gluttons, downed two giant glasses of *arak*, belched horribly, then flopped over for a sweaty afternoon siesta on a porch dotted with dog shit. An hour later they staggered to their feet and announced in a threatening manner that it was time for them to return to A Pau Peng and that they would like to get their day's wage, plus rental for the longboat. We had a nasty argument, and I paid them for half a day. They accepted my gift of tobacco then jeered at my generosity, because they knew they were trying to cheat me. This introduction to the people of Kalimantan came as a shock, and I suddenly felt very alone.

The people of Long Berini were working in the gardens, and the village was deserted until dusk. I went for a walk to find someone interesting or sympathetic, but what I encountered was village life at its worst. Mange-ridden, copulating mongrels were stuck back to back at every turn, and the naked children were filthy. The buildings were architecturally boring, which came as a surprise because the simplest rice-storage huts in Sarawak and Kalimantan can be visually stimulating. Beautiful utilitarian joinery is possible with the parang and adz if there is some attention to detail and a sense of proportion, but here in Long Berini the low level of craftsmanship was immediately evident, giving the village a cheerless, temporary appearance. The afternoon walk gave me an idea of what to expect that evening. I don't remember the meal, only the snaggle-toothed, cross-eyed, dumb-staring, *arak*-breath faces that surrounded me until I thought I might pass out from the effort of being pleasant. The people of Long Berini spent the entire evening apologizing for not having white sugar or tinned food. They were poor in the worst possible way. They had lost all sense of pride and village spirit. There was no music or dancing or any sign of weaving or basketmaking that might suggest simple pleasures in daily work. Chinese antique dealers from Tanjung Selor had made a sweep through the village the year before, and there wasn't a single rice-wine jar, headhunting knife, or other artifact to remind the people of their heritage. The little sympathy I could muster for them disappeared as soon as we began discussing guides and a dugout to take me away the next morning. We bargained for hours and finally agreed that a man would take me downriver in a dugout the next morning for two sticks of tobacco and two shotgun shells. I was glad to leave that wretched village, but the next one was no better. Similar evening scenes were repeated for the next five days as I inched my way down the Bahau River.

The communities on the upper Bahau River have few opportunities to trade because of the fickle nature of the river. The water level constantly changes, and the people are isolated in the villages. The communities are poor, and when they see an opportunity for gain, they grab it. I must have looked like a portable shopping mall with my shotgun shells, colored beads, salt, fabric, and medicine. I realized that my Indonesian had improved, because I could sit down with as many as a dozen villagers and patiently negotiate a fair deal for guides. With revolting hairless dogs lifting their legs on my pack and the prospect of yet another meal of tapioca leaves and rotten fish, I was often tempted to pay inflated prices just for the pleasure of saying goodby to my hosts. Unfortunately word travels from village to village very quickly, and once it's learned there's a newcomer willing to pay more than the going rate, the negotiations become even more prolonged and complex. Extra charges are thought up, and a price will not be settled until every possible avenue has been thoroughly covered. Until an agreement was reached I would have to stay in the village. No one was particularly concerned if I stayed or left because as long as I was in the village there was the likelihood I would part with some of my possessions — the more the better. There was no easy way out. Travel arrangements required a minimum of two or three tough bargaining sessions.

The young man who took me from the village of Long Uli to Long Peliran is memorable because he was the very worst guide I had on my entire journey. He arrived at my room in a cloud of cheap cologne late one morning dressed for the muddy slog in long, skin-tight, white pants and a T-shirt that read: "American Disco Fever." A pair of 1950s-style sunglasses straddled his black, bristled skull, and a compass hung from his neck. Dangling from his waist was a souvenir-quality parang suitable for opening letters and spreading marmalade on toast. I knew it was going to be a bad day. A homemade shotgun was slung over one

165

shoulder, and in his back pocket sat a little snub-nosed 22-caliber six-shooter. He waved the pistol in my face and exclaimed with a well-practiced sneer, "Can shoot! OK, *Tuan*?"

"Sure thing," I replied, and off we went for the three-hour journey. We walked at a totally distracting pace. Quick sprints interspersed with long stops and exclamations (his) of "*Lelah!*" (tired) . . . "*Susah!*" (difficult). Sweat beaded up on our foreheads and streamed down our faces, and we would hurry off again. For an hour we continued sprinting, stopping, sprinting, and every so often the young man in white would turn to me on the trail and brandish his gun menacingly.

"Can shoot! OK?" he repeated. On this cue I would nod perfunctorily, and we would plow on. It was madness to carry on like this, and soon I was thoroughly pissed off.

"*Tuan* can walk strong!" he finally gasped.

"Fuck you," I replied brightly.

He refused to speak Indonesian, and our conversation was limited to his ten-word English vocabulary. His repeated garbled phrases became incomprehensible, and I had to cut him off. I taught him to sing: "Zippity doo dah, zippity aye. My, oh my, what a wonderful day. Plenty of sunshine heading my way. Zippity doo dah, zippity aye."

He practiced his song for the next two hours, and I was left in peace. I provided encouragement at regular intervals to maintain his interest, and by the time we marched into Long Peliran he was sounding terrific.

Long Peliran, a Kenyah village situated on the left bank of the Bahau River near Sungai Lurah, was approximately thirty-five miles downstream from where I had left Bo 'Hok and Weng six days earlier. It was the home of the proud possessor of the Singer sewing machine. Although I had no reason to suppose that in any other way the village would be more cheering than the others I had visited in the last week, I arrived at Pa Lampung Padan's house in Long Peliran to find the people there delightful. Enshrined in the common room of Pa Lampung Padan's house was the sewing machine from Marudi. His wife was full of life and obviously delighted with her husband's great journey. I stayed for two days; then Pa Lampung sent me downriver with a long-boat full of friends. "How much for guides and the boat?" I ventured to ask. He laughed at such a ridiculous question then filled my arms with a stem of bananas and skewers of smoked deer meat.

Once I left Long Peliran, I began covering incredible distances — fifteen to twenty miles in one day. The river widened to as much as 100 feet, and the sun became a problem. After seven weeks in the shadows, my skin began to burn. Each day or two I joined a different group going downstream, and the longboats I traveled in kept getting larger, until we were using the standard 40-foot, eight-man dugout canoes. With a skilled crew these boats could get through the really big rapids that lay between the village of Pudjungan and the mouth of the Bahau River.

Fifty years before, Charles Hose, the British Resident of Sarawak, had written this about upriver travel in Borneo: *The Kenyahs are experts in handling these boats, and unlike the other tribes, seldom have accidents. It is a very moving sight to see a boat slowly gliding downriver to the head of a fall, the men standing up and leisurely dipping the ends of their paddles in the water to keep the boat's head straight, and straining their necks to find the best spot to shoot the falls. Suddenly they drop down on the thwarts and paddle for all they are worth, the boat dashing into the foaming mass of waves between huge boulders. The roar is deafening, and the water splashes in on all sides. For a moment it seems as if it would be impossible to get through, but pace tells, and by wonderful handling the boat, often full of water, slips around into a less troubled part, where the crew obtain a short breathing space in which to bale out the craft and prepare for the next rapid.*

This description is all too true. For three days we traveled in this fashion through six named sets of rapids and numerous un-named smaller ones. I must have bailed tons of water with my dinner plate. If there were any lingering resentments about the upper Bahau River communities, they were quickly erased by the excitement of the river. This was the way to travel. Giant 8-foot monitor lizards swam in the shallows, and monkeys and large herds of wild pigs wandered along the big gray river rocks and open riverbanks. The hunting was fantastic. In every shade of green, the dense jungle grew 150 to 200 feet high on both sides of the river.

I traded two sticks of chewing tobacco for a large conical sun hat and could then luxuriate in comfort under the intoxicating, languid tropical sun. It was a relief to be out of the perpetual shade and dampness of the rain forest. The sunlight made my skin tingle, and my clothes were dry. I didn't have to wear my shoes, and my feet appeared to be healing now that I wasn't walking.

At the junction of the Kayan River, we switched boats for the last time, and I climbed into *The Pioneer*, a 60-foot open-deck river trader powered by three 40-horsepower outboard motors. *The Pioneer* was on her way downstream to the trading post at Long Bia and would arrive the next day before noon. Whether or not Long Bia lived up to my expectations, my arrival there would mark the end of my first crossing of the island.

Behind me lay four months and one thousand five hundred miles of jungle travel. The last day on the river *The Pioneer*, with thirty assorted passengers on board, started off in a jungle mist before sunrise. An hour later the blue sky and sunshine broke through. Logging camps began to appear, and we arrived in Long Bia just before the heat of the day. Most of the passengers were still sleeping soundly as the bow eased into the muddy riverbank below the trading post.

I climbed up the riverbank with my woven rattan backpack. It contained a blackened cooking pot, a bamboo section of wild bee's honey, my mosquito net, and less than 50 of the original 250 shotgun shells. The rest of my goods, the tobacco and beads, had been extracted from me by the villagers on the Bahau River. I looked at my tattered clothing and realized how wild I must look, even in a small village such as Long Bia. I smoothed out my khaki shorts and straightened the knotted camouflaged shoe-laces on my ridiculous footwear and, just as I had imagined it weeks earlier, walked up to the white Colonial-style missionary bungalow that overlooked the river. How I had waited for this moment! Before I reached the second of five carefully swept front steps, I was greeted from behind the screen door with a surprisingly loud, "Well, what do you want?" spoken with a strong accent from the American South. The voice belonged to Ian, the Mission Aviation Fellowship (MAF) pilot. He wore mirrored aviator sunglasses and, without opening the door, stood with his hands on the hips of his ironed trousers waiting for my answer.

"What do I want?" I echoed weakly. "Well, I just arrived and thought you might like to have a chat." It was painfully obvious to both of us that nothing could have been further from his mind. After weeks of looking forward to this meeting, I was at a total loss as to what to say. I continued uncertainly, "If you're not too busy, that is . . . well, you know, I could always come back later on, I guess." This was followed by an uncomfortable silence as we looked at each other through the screen door. My vision of Long Bia and a friendly reunion with a fellow Westerner evaporated.

I was backing down the stairs when Ian's wife, Julie, appeared beside him and invited me in. After removing my shoes, I was immediately led to the bathroom to wash up and was confronted by a brand-new bar of Dove soap, a white porcelain washbasin, and a blue terrycloth handtowel with matching washcloth. I looked at the baby blue flush toilet and the shower with the blue plastic curtain and suddenly realized that I really didn't want to be there. I had an almost uncontrollable urge to climb out the window, to be back in the rain forest looking at walking leaves and catching Malay lorikeets with Bo 'Hok and Weng. I wanted to chase a wild pig through the jungle with hunting dogs and a spear. The last place in the world I wanted to be was in that bathroom washing my hands with a bar of Dove soap. I reconsidered and then washed my dreadful-looking feet in their sink.

As I washed my feet, I glanced in the mirror above the sink and was shocked at what I saw. I had a penetrating half-mad look to my eyes, a look of such unblinking intensity that immediately I realized why Ian hadn't been eager to invite me into his home. I stared into my own eyes for what seemed like five minutes then towelled my feet dry.

On the verandah, Ian and Julie were sitting beside a white wicker table. Their two infant children, Michael and Janie, were playing on the polished hardwood floor. I sat down and glanced at what was on the table. I stared dumbly, and perhaps too intensely for my host's comfort, at four perfectly shaped chocolate chip cookies neatly arranged in the center of a sparkling white dish. They looked like some sort of offering or monument to the memory of white rule. At first, I was merely hypnotized by this apparition, then outraged. I touched one. It was real, and still warm. I wanted to make the cookies disappear. They were intruding on my fantasy, my vision of a dank jungle world of buttressed tree roots and wild-animal sounds. The cookies also smelled delicious. They transported me back to my grandmother's kitchen and the strawberry-shaped ceramic cookie jar of my childhood. I was overwhelmed by conflicting emotions, and in the end I did the only thing possible. I took the cookies in my hands and ate them. Without a word I ate every last one. After months of living in the jungle, it would be obscene to describe what those cookies did to the inside of my mouth. The sensation of white sugar, melting chocolate morsels, and the scent of vanilla essence. Ooooh! . . . the decadence . . . the saliva . . . the shame!

Ian and Julie were perched nervously on the edge of their seats staring at me, perhaps waiting for me to disappear. I looked at the Christian paintings, calendars, and framed scriptural quotes that covered the walls. I had been in the jungle too long to make any sense of them. All these symbols seemed trite and out of place. And their puppy. That sweet-smelling, freshly shampooed, little bundle of white fluff would have been torn to pieces in thirty seconds by the village hunting dogs.

I started to explain my route from Kuching, but soon realized that Ian and Julie weren't listening. I sensed that I had interrupted something important. I was correct. After a two-month wait, they had just received a package from the United States. They were anxious to make sure everything was there. I let my voice trail off, and they gravitated back to their cardboard treasure chest. Yes, it was all there: the instant pudding, the taco and pizza mixes, the Kraft Parmesan cheese in its distinctive green container, Jell-o, some Dinty Moore Beef Stew in family-sized tins, and a jar of Orville Redenbacher's Gourmet Popping Corn. What can one say about these things?

After their excitement had died down I mentioned that I was planning on going to Data Dian, a village in the mountains where I wanted to do some trading. I asked Ian about a possible lift in the mission plane. Without a moment's hesitation he replied, "No, we can't do that!" Ian went on to say that there was a backlog of vital mission supplies that had to be airlifted to the highlands. "There's just no way we can take someone like you, there's no room."

Their lack of interest in my arrival was a shock, but I reasoned they were there to do a job and to help the village people. I couldn't expect special privileges. The people should come first. I also realized that it must have looked very self-indulgent of me to be wandering around the jungle without any specific purpose that they could see.

We were all uncomfortable, so I decided to leave. I collected my shoes at the door and walked away from the house speechless. As I left I heard the "click" of the screen door as it was locked behind me. That must have been their way of saying goodby. From a distance I could hear the sound of a child being spanked. The puppy barked.

I wandered over to the small corrugated metal mission warehouse next to the landing strip. I was curious to see what things were essential to village life in the area. I expected medicines and tools, perhaps educational material. I stood with my hands and face pressed against the wire-mesh window, peering into the dim interior. When my eyes adjusted to the dark, I could see the vital mission supplies that Ian had referred to. I listed them in my journal. There were Eveready flashlight batteries, Roma and

Ayam brand tea biscuits, Baru Baru laundry soap, Tancho lavender-scented hair pomade, souvenir-quality headhunting knives from the coast, Jackson Super Milk Toffee Sweets, Super Bubblegum, linoleum, white sugar, tins of instant chicken noodle soup, infant formulas from Switzerland, soft drinks, Bliss Peppermints ("sweetens the breath"), and wind-up plastic penguins from Hong Kong.

It was all neatly arranged in colorful cardboard boxes. Looking into that storeroom, I caught a glimpse of my own culture. The taste of chocolate lingered in my mouth, and I could feel my roots.

The owner of *The Pioneer* had given me the name of Nyonya Nam Sun, the sister-in-law of the local trader, Tokay Moumein. I couldn't think of anywhere else to stay that night, so I asked directions to her house. Word of my arrival in Long Bia traveled quickly, and by the time I found Nyonya Nam Sun's house, everything had been prepared. Nyonya Nam Sun had been expecting me. The room had been cleaned, and there were frangipani flowers on a low dressing table. The mattress, though twelve inches too short for me, was covered with a clean, flower-print sheet. Nyonya Nam Sun brought me sweet black tea, and twenty minutes later she produced a delicious lunch of fried fish and rice with a bowl of bitter-melon soup. It was good to be speaking Indonesian again and to be eating with my fingers.

"Would 1,000 rupiahs ($1.60 U.S.) be all right for the room and two meals?" Nyonya Nam Sun asked me.

"One thousand rupiahs is fine," I replied, "but 1,500 rupiahs would be better." I was so touched by her hospitality that I offered her this extra amount. Nyonya Nam Sun smiled then brought a second helping of lunch.

I left Long Bia the next morning intending to end my journey across the island at Tanjung Selor near the mouth of the Kayan River. In a dugout canoe with six paddlers, we headed into the main current. We glided past timber camps and areas of a clear-cut forest. Log rafts became more frequent, and the river was dark brown and muddy from the erosion caused by hill logging.

Almost every longboat had an outboard motor, and the people wore Western clothes. It was upsetting to see these things. Also, I worried about the police in Tanjung Selor. If they detected me, which was highly likely, I would have a hard time explaining my expired passport and nonexistent visa. The real jungle was far behind, and we were rapidly approaching the downriver commercial centers. The sores on my feet had erupted again, and I wanted to go to a hospital. The missionary family had repulsed me with their self-centered, insulated existence, so I sat in the dugout, despondent, waiting for my adventure to come to its disastrous end.

I had lost my momentum and confidence. I felt so miserable I didn't bother to paddle. I sat on the duckboards like a doughy lump, feeling sorry for myself because after so much time and effort the trip was going to end badly. Maybe the entire project had been a farce sustained by my foolish pride? I felt like a fool, but during the next couple of hours I started to recall many of the remarkable moments of my journey. Faced with my imminent arrival at one of the squalid coastal boomtowns, I became uncertain what to do. I had to make an important decision. I asked myself: could I possibly contemplate a return to the jungle? I was exhausted, depressed, and half-crippled. The jungle had just spat me out like a piece of old chewing gum. And what were my chances of making it through another eight hundred miles of jungle in my condition? I could be back in San Francisco within a week, and the temptation to go was great. Get on a plane, I tried to convince myself. Don't be a fool!

I'm not quite sure what prompted me, but early that afternoon, 137 days after entering the rain forest, I decided to turn back. I was within a day's journey of Tanjung Selor. I ignored the confused protests of my Kenyah companions, and fifty miles from the ocean we made a slow, wide arc in midstream and started back upriver. *"Orang gila!"* (crazy man), one of the men muttered.

I waited ten days at Long Bia for my feet to heal. Following Nyonya Nam Sun's suggestions, I washed them several times a day in salty water, and by keeping the weeping sores covered with bandages, the swelling gradually subsided and the ulcers began to close. I slept with my feet elevated and spent my days collecting trail information from visitors and piecing together a hand-drawn map that, with luck, would lead me back to Sarawak. One day I spent four hours stitching the patchwork remains of my shoes back together. The first crossing of the island had taught me how to travel. The return trip would test my limits. I planned to recross the island by a much more difficult and uncertain route.

⋆　　⋆　　⋆

For six days I listened to the missionary plane come and go, but on the seventh day there was silence. Rumor quickly passed through the village that neither of the two mission planes was working now and the daily flights had been cancelled. Despite the letdown of my arrival in Long Bia and the disastrous meeting with Ian and Julie, I hadn't lost my ability to recognize a transportation opportunity. I realized that Ian and I were now drawn together in a moment of common purpose and need. I decided to make him an offer.

His problem was that while both mission planes were grounded, the peppermint breath mints and marching plastic penguins were threatening to burst the walls of the small mission warehouse. My problem was that I wanted a lift to Data Dian, a Kenyah village on the edge of the highlands, to do some trading. The anticipated exchange of goods that I could buy from the trading post at Long Bia would put me in a barter position that would finance my second crossing of the island.

Ian and I made a deal. If I could help him get one of the planes in the air, he would give me a lift. I was allowed fifty pounds of merchandise, and Ian would waive the strict mission restrictions on the transport of tobacco and ammunition (the two most valuable and portable commodities in the highlands).

Both the mission planes were single-engine Cessnas. One had a broken radio, the other needed a valve job. I didn't have any experience with radios, so I suggested repairing the plane with the burned valve. I didn't share with Ian the information that my entire mechanical experience consisted of tuning up my 1964 Volkswagen and rebuilding an Italian motorcycle engine when I was sixteen years old. I do have a knack with tools and once replaced a wheel bearing using only a small hatchet, a screwdriver, a rock, and a cold chisel. Ian seemed to have a marginally more adequate tool kit, and so we began.

By noon there were a lot of airplane parts on the ground, and I kept reminding myself that if things went badly, I could always quietly disappear into the jungle. I also figured I wouldn't have to go on the test flight.

"Yes, we're doing just fine," I kept telling Ian as we ground the valves by hand, using sticks tipped with rubber suction cups. But looking at our work, I began to feel uneasy. We continued throughout that afternoon and early evening, and the next morning we were still at it. We had, by then, selected two villagers to assist in the reassembly. A crowd of about twenty people watched us wrestle with the valve-spring assembly. In their eyes we were performing magic, and they weren't too far wrong. Using feet, knees, and hands, our two assistants held the cylinder heads immobile in the dirt as Ian and I carefully levered the powerful valve springs back into place. With deft touches on our makeshift "waterpipe, tree branch, screwdriver, wooden wedge and vice grip" valve-spring compressor, we finally managed to drop the last two shims into place. Dripping with perspiration, we sat back for a rest. The most difficult part was done. By two o'clock that afternoon the engine had been reassembled. I didn't notice any extra parts lying in the grass, so I figured we were through. I congratulated Ian on the fine job, and we arranged to meet at the maintenance shed at ten the next morning for the flight to Data Dian.

I spent the afternoon carefully selecting trade items with Tokay Moumein, the third-generation Chinese merchant who ran the trading post in Long Bia. I now knew what to buy, working on a profit-per-pound ratio that Muhammad Aidid had taught me, which I had developed over the last four months. With the use of an old handheld hardwood balance beam graduated with slivers and dots of inlaid ivory, I bought exactly 35 pounds of *sugee*, colorful seed beads for the women's baby carriers, blocks of salt, batik fabric, sewing needles, and nylon fishing line. With my remaining shotgun shells I was at my 50-pound limit. I also bought all the antibiotic ointment and bandaids in stock to hand out as gifts. While I was in the trading post bargaining over prices, I heard the sound of a small aircraft overhead and guessed that everything had gone all right with the test flight.

By eleven the next morning we had the red-and-white mission plane fueled and loaded to capacity. Next to the tin of gasoline, boxes of wind-up, plastic penguins and lavender-scented hair pommade were strapped down in the back. We taxied to the end of the airstrip. Ian checked the wing flaps and instruments as I fastened my shoulder harness. The roar of the engine made conversation almost impossible.

"How did the test flight go?" I asked.

"What?" Ian yelled back, unable to hear me.

"How . . . did . . . the . . . text . . . flight . . . go?"

"What test flight?"

"Yesterday afternoon . . . the test flight . . . you know . . . I heard the plane overhead."

"Oh, that was a plane from another mission. I don't have enough flying hours left this month to waste any of them on a test flight." He went back to his preflight check.

"Oh," I finally said to no one in particular.

I gazed through the spinning propeller and down the bumpy runway, which ended with a 100-foot drop to the river. I tightened my seatbelt and waved weakly to our assistant mechanics, who were proudly standing at the edge of the airstrip waiting for the big takeoff. Julie stood nearby. Janie, the younger child, was in her arms.

I was deafened by the roar of the engine, and a terrific vibration shook the little plane as the engine strained to reach maximum power before takeoff. The needle on the RPM dial moved towards the red zone. If it's going to blow up, let it blow up now,

I thought. A successful forced landing in the jungle was out of the question.

Ian finally released the brakes, and we were committed to our repair job. The plane careered down the runway, lurching and bouncing wildly as we gathered speed. We shot off the end of the runway, banked sharply to the right to avoid the 200-foot wall of jungle trees on the opposite riverbank, then followed the winding river, gradually gaining altitude. I could see dugout canoes, women doing their wash, and children swimming in the brown river. Almost imperceptibly we climbed above the tallest trees and in fifteen minutes had left the river behind. We were cruising about 1,500 feet over uninhabited rain forest.

By the grace of God, I thought. I had slunk down in my seat and was still shaking. Ian smiled, gave me a knowing wink, and with a laugh slapped me on the knee. "We're on our way, buddy!"

I decided to give Ian special dispensation. He was forgiven for the chocolate chip cookies and the plastic penguins. We had become friends.

CHAPTER NINE · MUSIM TAKOOT, THE SEASON OF FEAR

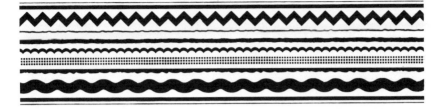

THE LAST sounds I remembered hearing before falling asleep were the rhythmic tones of the *gampang* (hardwood xylophone), the wind, and the pattering of rain on the leaf roof of the longhouse. It was uncomfortable sleeping on the plank floor, but whenever I woke up I could hear the *gampang* being played softly. By dawn the music had stopped and drops of water were falling from the eaves and nearby branches. Through my mosquito net I could see a rooster, perched on a low windowsill, crowing small puffs of steam into the crisp morning air. My feet felt cold on the smooth hardwood floorboards as I tied my sarong and wrapped a blue-and-white checked bedsheet around my shoulders. Walking down the longhouse porch, I came upon the familiar wrinkled and smiling faces of two old men, Pa Bit and Pa Ulay. From beneath a shared blanket they invited me to sit with them at their morning fire burning neatly in the bottom half of a dirt-filled tin trunk that had once been painted bright blue with red flowers. The men thumped a huddled mass of dogs with pieces of firewood in order to make room for me. Yelping and whining, the dogs disappeared into the heavy mist that billowed down the 200-foot covered porch. As we sat talking, Pa Bit's daughter appeared with a breakfast of boiled rice, smoked deer meat, and black tea. Tiny shafts of sunlight gradually began to appear, slanting down weakly through gaps in the roof as the fog lifted and the morning air began to warm.

Here in the village of Long Sungai Anai I was above the impassable Ambun Rapids of the Kayan River. *Ambun* is an Indonesian word meaning mercy. From Long Belun Alim, on the Bahau River, I had walked for two days, thirty miles, with a group of rattan cutters through the jungle to avoid that boulder-filled gorge of waterfalls and perpetually rising mist. The Ambun Rapids were the last major obstacle blocking my way to the Apo Kayan — the highland plateau of central Borneo. From the highlands six major rivers flow down to the Celebes, Java, and South China seas. The Apo Kayan is part of the large white patch on my map bordered by comments such as "Unsurveyed," and "Limits of Reliable Relief Information." Few Westerners had come this far. Over the next two months I would discover and map a network of trails that spread throughout the rain forest — linking rivers, garden plots, and villages.

I wanted to leave for the village of Long Nawang in the morning. It was a nine-hour walk through the jungle, and I was told that I needed a guide because the trail was difficult to follow. I asked Pa Bit and Pa Ulay if they could come with me, but they were busy splitting lengths of rattan with their long-handled knives. I continued down the longhouse porch looking for a guide, but after spending half the morning searching in vain, I decided to go by myself. I had survived my travels through the interior for more than four months, and since it was only "one more day's walk" to the main Kenyah villages at the headwaters of the Kayan River, I felt comfortable trying to find the way alone. Pa Bit helped me sketch a crude map of the rivers and mountains, but suggested that it would be foolish to go without a companion. Other people in the village were much more adamant. They went to great lengths to warn me of the confusing trails, the long distance, and the dangers of walking alone in that particular part of the jungle. The hand-drawn map looked simple enough, so I couldn't understand their attitude. There was an urgency to their voices that seemed exaggerated, an apprehensive tone that I couldn't quite identify. For a moment I thought I could detect a note of fear. Still unfamiliar with how the Kenyah expressed themselves, I assumed they were simply being overly cautious. I left the village late that morning, keeping in mind that I could return if the trail was too difficult to follow.

Within an hour I was beyond the last shimmering green fields of hill rice and had entered the deep jungle. Enormous hardwood trees blocked out the sun and created a diffuse light that filtered down through the tangle of vegetation into the depths of the rain forest. There was cool shade along the narrow dirt footpath, but the humidity and the weight of my woven rattan backpack soon had me streaming with perspiration. I had just replaced the plaited carrying straps, and they were still stiff and uncomfortable. They soon began cutting into my skin, so I removed my shirt and used it as a shoulder pad. The occasional breeze that blew across my bare midriff helped to keep me cool. I followed a good trail through stands of giant bamboo, some of it eight inches wide and ninety feet tall. I encountered a now-familiar landscape pattern of knee-deep exposed tree roots, hanging-moss forests, and single-log bridges that provided slippery passage over mud-and-vine choked waterways. The walking was slow, but I was in no hurry.

At times the jungle closed in, and I had to follow tunnels cut through the interwoven mass of barbed vines, aerial roots, fallen branches, and dense shrubbery. These tunnels were cut for the local people, so I was forced constantly to duck. Sometimes I crawled on my stomach. Massive dead tree trunks covered in blue-green moss that appeared to have been caught in midfall by the tangle of vines and branches leaned at fantastic angles. Glittering armies of black ants filed across the trail, disappeared into a mat of twigs and rotting leaves, and reappeared a few yards farther on as they marched over a fallen tree and out of sight. Enormous heart-shaped leaves, three feet across, curtained either side of the trail, and I felt as if I were a small bug crawling through some fantastic garden. The staccato bursts of insect sounds, rasping and vibrating, filled the thick, moist air until I couldn't hear my footsteps. I recognized the lilting call of the bulbul and the distinctive leathery wingflap of the hornbill. I called to the birds, and sometimes I could get one to follow me. They would stay with me for a mile or so, keeping just out of sight. When one bird lost interest, I would try to attract another.

I found myself imitating nearly every sound that I heard. I was trying to talk with the jungle.

Gibbon monkeys, with their "whoop-whoop" cries, swung hand over hand through the canopy. I stood behind a buttressed tree root watching two wild pigs dig up a creekbed with their powerful snouts. A slight gust of wind brought clusters of fragrant white flowers down from the treetops. The five-petaled flowers spun like little propellers, slowly descending to the jungle floor. I stopped walking and filled my lungs with the thick perfume that hung in the air.

The light, the temperature, the sounds, and the smells of the rain forest were in a perpetual state of change. Walking through patches of warm aromatic air, I would suddenly encounter the stench of putrefying flesh or feces. Everywhere I looked there were signs of decay and regrowth. Sprays of purple orchids sprouted from dead branches, and wherever one of the giant trees had crashed to earth, ripping a hole in the roof of the jungle, young saplings had sprung up, competing for the narrow patch of sunlight.

I crossed many rivers that day, but the water was never more than waist deep. Clear and cool, it ran slowly enough to be crossed safely. With my parang I would cut a six-foot sapling for balance, heave my pack high onto my shoulder, and slowly make my way to the opposite bank. I kept my shoes on to protect my recently healed feet from the painful river rocks, and the cold water felt wonderful rushing past my bare legs. On the far bank the trail would sometimes invisibly follow the river for a few hundred feet before reentering the thick foliage. To pick up the trail again I walked up and down the edge of the forest, looking carefully for footsteps or the telltale sign of where a parang had slashed the undergrowth. When the trail narrowed and disappeared, I knew I had gone the wrong way. I would retrace my steps to the last trail junction and continue on. I carefully marked each fork in the trail with a blaze in case I became lost and had to return to Long Sungai Anai. By midafternoon I was beyond the point of being able to return, but I still felt confident I was making good time and that I would be able to reach Long Na-wang before dark. Pa Bit's map and directions were excellent.

I sat in the sun at the edge of a clearing in the jungle to enjoy the sight of sun on the long grass and unfolded my banana-leaf lunch packet of boiled rice, dried meat, steamed vegetables, and chillies. Grasshoppers made short energetic flights across the shoulder-high buffalo grass; swarms of brightly colored butter-flies clustered on the jungle floor. It was a perfect day for walk-ing: dry, few leeches, a reasonable trail, and no sense of urgency. I hadn't seen a soul all day and had completely forgotten about the warnings from the people in Long Sungai Anai. I wiped my fingers on the banana leaf and let it drop at my feet where it would soon be reclaimed by the jungle. Pushing my way through the buffalo grass, I reentered the green darkness of the rain for-est. Within minutes I realized the grass must have had sharp serrated edges because my face, hands, and legs were covered with a crisscross of shallow, stinging cuts.

An hour later, at the crest of a densely forested mountain trail, I was looking up at a towering wall of vines and branches when I noticed a flurry of movement at the base of the trees. Obscured by shadows, I could see women and children fleeing towards the undergrowth. Within moments the jungle had swallowed them up, leaving a small group of men standing at the edge of the clearing. One of them instinctively reached for his parang. The men were apprehensive, but I had no idea why. To reassure them, I approached as nonchalantly as possible, smiled, and slowly re-moved my pack and parang. In spite of the awkwardness of the situation, I let them see I was unarmed. We exchanged greetings mechanically. The men, dressed in ragged shorts or loincloths, were carrying blowpipes and spears. Their earlobes had been distended, and intricate blue tattoos covered their throats, chests, and arms. The men had been squatting on the ground, leaning against their heavy cargo packs. Woven out of shiny golden brown rattan, the packs contained rice and sections of green bamboo filled with wild bee honey. One of the loads was a dead boar trussed securely on a stake. Long strips of fibrous bark had been passed through slits in the hide and fashioned into shoulder straps. It was easy to spot the man who had carried the pig: his buttocks and legs were smeared with blood and covered with flies.

I spoke with the group in Indonesian for about five minutes. I told them where I had come from, what I was doing in the jungle, and why I was by myself. These people were Kenyah and were fluent only in their own language, so I got the feeling that they didn't understand much of what I said. I wanted to let them know there was no reason to be afraid. They seemed to relax slightly, but no real conversation developed. We never sat down. The uncertainty of the situation made it too awkward to linger, so we all put on our packs and said goodbye. I felt confused about their reaction to me, and as we quietly walked off in opposite directions, I glanced back and saw the last two men standing at the edge of the forest holding their blowpipes. The looks of suspicion and terror on their faces made me catch my breath. I managed a friendly wave before we lost sight of each other. The women and children never reappeared.

Minutes later I stopped at the end of a narrow ridge. Peering through a gap in the vines and branches, I caught a glimpse of the Kayan River valley. Below me the expanse of distant treetops stretched far away into a blue-gray haze. I could see faint wisps of smoke filtering through the branches into the afternoon sky. Beneath that immense green canopy were eight major Kenyah villages. The only knowledge I had about the people in the villages came from obscure museum journals, a World War II account by Tom Harrisson, and stories from missionaries who had made infrequent visits over the years. Although a token form of Christianity was practiced here, I knew this tribal area had retained strong ties with animistic traditions. It was still a world of supernaturalism, omens, and black magic.

As I stood there, I remembered the group of Kenyahs I had just met. The startled expressions on their faces haunted me. I couldn't understand why the women and children had fled at the first sight of me. The incident made me reflect on the rumors and

184

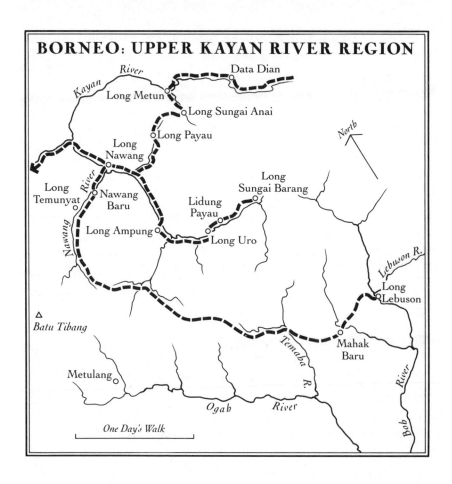

BORNEO: UPPER KAYAN RIVER REGION

Kayan River

Data Dian

Long Metun

Long Sungai Anai

Long Payau

Long Nawang

North

Long Temunyat

Nawang River

Nawang Baru

Lidung Payau

Long Sungai Barang

Long Ampung

Long Uro

Lebuson R.

Batu Tibang

Long Lebuson

Temaha R.

Mahak Baru

Bob River

Metulang

Ogah River

One Day's Walk

warnings I had heard about the Apo Kayan. I recalled a night three weeks earlier in the mission station of Long Bia when Nyonya Nam Sun had cautioned me not to walk by myself in the farm clearings or to go out at night. "People are afraid," she had warned. She had also mentioned the words *bali saleng*. Back in my room at the trading station I found the definition in my dictionary: *bali saleng* meant the black ghost. Still standing on the trail, fragments of overheard conversations drifted back to me: ". . . jungle spirits . . . blood sacrifice . . . spring-powered shoes for jumping over trees . . . pregnant women abducted . . . selling blood to oil companies."

Superstition, I reassured myself, folk history, part of their oral traditions. I started walking again, but my mind was no longer focused on the trail. I began searching my memory for more recollections.

There is an established Kenyah tradition of making blood offerings before starting any new longhouse construction. On previous occasions I had seen the blood of a rooster or pig poured into a posthole before the first post was placed; prior to Colonial times a proper sacrifice would have been a young girl, a slave, or a captive. With this offering the power of *bali tanah*, the spirit of the earth, would have been invoked to bless the project and protect the men during construction.

On the east and south coasts of Borneo, near the towns of Samarinda, Tanjung Selor, and Balikpapan, as well as to the north in Sarawak, huge construction projects are underway: bridges, high-rise buildings, roads and hydroelectric schemes. Each project is associated with a different spirit. There is *bali minyak*, the spirit of oil; *bali jambatan*, the spirit of the vehicle bridge; and *bali rumah tinggi*, the spirit of the high-rise. All of these spirits require blood offerings, and shamans known as *dayungs* are hired to perform the ceremonies. No construction project could be started without first calling in a *dayung* to appease the appropriate spirits; otherwise the local labor force would refuse to begin work for fear of spirit retribution. There are many well-documented cases of major projects that experienced endless difficulties until the proper ceremonies were observed. Com-

186

pany reports tell of equipment failures, unseasonably bad weather, widespread illness, and absenteeism. Vehicles have been known to disappear into muddy roads overnight. Even PERTAMINA, the national oil company of Indonesia, hires a *∂ayung* to help launch a project. The company has learned from experience.

Officially, animal blood has been substituted for human blood, but few, if any, inland people believe in this. From the central highlands all coastal development plans are viewed with suspicion and fear. The villagers reason that if one longhouse pole traditionally required the blood of one human being, then how much blood from how many people is needed to construct a 30-story concrete office building? I had heard people from the highlands refer to construction projects in terms of their cost in human blood. By village estimates there are "200-person" hydroelectric schemes and "100-person" bridges. Development projects are rarely seen as employment opportunities.

The role of a *bali ∂aleng* is to collect the blood. He is half-man, half-spirit; he lives in the forest; he is believed to be employed by large companies. I had heard that the standard price for five pints of blood was one million rupiahs ($1,500 U.S.). For a big project many *bali ∂aleng∂* are employed. As I continued walking, I realized that among the inland people I might be mistaken for a *bali ∂aleng*, but feeling confident in my ability to speak Indonesian, I assumed I would have no trouble explaining who I was.

What I did not know was that the description of *bali ∂aleng* changed regularly, and that he came only at a very specific time of the year. At the time I happened to be traveling through the Apo Kayan, the description was "a tall, white-skinned man with brownish hair who walks by himself in the jungle. He will come over the mountains from Sarawak during the season of grass cutting."

My long day's walk came to an abrupt and welcome end when I arrived in Long Nawang just before dark. People were in the fields cutting grass, and because of the omen, they had been expecting me for the last two months. I received a noticeably cool reception. Usually when I entered a village in Sarawak or Kalimantan, the children would get very excited, following me closely. As they jumped up and down, their delighted voices would rise above the usual din of barking dogs and crowing roosters. The first evening many people would come to the headman's room to greet me. We would drink rice wine, laugh, tell stories, and, if people were in the mood, dance to the music of the three-stringed *sapeh* until late at night. After being in the jungle for even a short time, it was a thrill to be included in the clamor and excitement of the longhouse.

That first night in Long Nawang was different. I sat alone with the headman, Pa Biah Leng, and his wife. There were no visitors, and the longhouse was unusually silent. After dinner Pa Biah rolled himself a large conical cheroot with a scrap of used notebook paper and some of the tobacco I had given him. He was dressed comfortably in a checked sarong and white singlet. His jet black hair was still glistening from his evening bath in the river. He was a well-preserved 63-year-old. As the match flared, I could see the carefully penciled school lessons illuminated along the length of his cheroot.

Without looking at me Pa Biah asked, "*Tuan*, why have you come to the Apo Kayan?"

"I wanted to come here because few white men have traveled through these jungles. I have shotgun shells I want to trade for gold and for *gaharu* (the aromatic hardwood)."

He seemed skeptical that anyone would come from so far away for the reasons I gave. That evening, after I spoke to Pa Biah about my encounter in the jungle, he told me the story of *musim takoot*, the season of fear. He explained that every year during October and November people are isolated in their fields, weeding the ricefields and constructing small farm huts in preparation for the harvest. This period of the year used to be one of the traditional headhunting seasons because it was relatively easy to ambush individuals who were working far from the villages. Headhunting no longer occurs, but the seasonal fear has been sustained by the belief in *bali saleng*.

"The people are afraid," Pa Biah warned me. "Don't travel by yourself; it is not safe. The people know you have come to the valley. They may hurt you if they see you alone in the jungle."

The red glow from Pa Biah's cheroot gradually faded, and as he coaxed the fire back to life with his foot, we sipped hot bitter tea from chipped enamel mugs. Ibu Iting, his wife, sat nearby. She was making thread by pulling strands of cotton from the edge of an old piece of fabric. While holding the ends of two strands in her left hand, she twisted them together by rubbing them between her right hand and thigh. She threaded her needle and continued to listen to our conversation as she patched a well-worn pair of trousers.

"Last year," Pa Biah continued, "*bali saleng* was described as a brown-skinned man with long black hair and pointed teeth. He wore a powder blue, short-sleeved, military-type shirt with matching shorts. He had a special set of spring-powered shoes that enabled him to jump four meters in the air and ten meters away in a single bound. He could spring through the air to cover long distances quickly and capture people by surprise. After tying up his victim with strips of rattan, he would take the blood from the wrist or the foot with a small knife and a rubber pump. The corpse would then be hoisted with vines up into the jungle canopy so that searchers could not find it."

Listening attentively, I tried to imagine a police department's composite sketch of such an individual. The image of *bali saleng* was still too farfetched for me to take seriously.

"A *bali saleng* cannot be killed by man," Pa Biah continued. "Bullets bounce off him, spears cannot pierce his body, and when he gets old he will take on a young man without family and train him."

Pa Biah went on to tell me that the year before a pregnant woman was reported to have been killed by a *bali saleng* near the village of Long Ampung. Pregnant women are considered prime targets because they contain the blood of two people.

That night the people of Long Nawang locked themselves into their family quarters and did not open their doors until daybreak.

I listened to Pa Biah's stories with interest, but I failed to recognize my own imminent danger. I was placing too much confidence in my knowledge of the language and too little importance on the power of fear. Instead of accepting the people's beliefs as something real and adjusting my behavior accordingly, I was relying on a false sense of security. With nearly eighteen hundred jungle miles behind me, I had become careless.

The next morning I got up and left at dawn — alone. I didn't get far. Four hours up the valley, as I followed the Kayan River southeast from Long Nawang, I was attacked in the village of Long Uro. The first thing I heard was the frantic pounding of children's feet along hardwood planks of the longhouse porch. There were a few startled cries from the women then the sound of men's voices. It all happened very quickly. It took me a moment to realize that I was the cause of the commotion.

A group of about two dozen men, some armed with spears, came down to the trail where I was standing. After some excited questioning and gesturing (not all of which I understood), I felt their hands on me. I was stripped of my pack and forced to the ground. I didn't resist. I sat in the dirt with my back to a drainage ditch as the men formed a tight semicircle in front of me. For the next two hours they fired accusations at me in Indonesian. I was repeatedly questioned and cross-examined. My mind became alert, and I was careful not to show any fear. They wanted to know why I was by myself, why I didn't have a cooking pot, what I was doing in the Kayan River valley, and how I had come over the mountains from Sarawak. My answers didn't sound very convincing, and I soon realized how vulnerable I was. The experience of facing so many frightened people was intimidating. My belongings were ransacked; shotgun shells, diaries, salt, clothing, and half-finished letters to friends littered the ground. I was repeatedly asked about the contents of my pack. After two men had gone through everything, I realized that they had been looking for spring-powered shoes, the small blood knife, and the rubber pump.

Over and over they repeated two questions: "Why do you walk by yourself?" and "Why aren't you afraid of *bali ʃaleng*?"

The fact is that no one in Borneo walks by himself in the jungle. It is too easy to fall down or to get lost or sick. Every year people disappear in the rain forest without a trace. Solo travel isn't done except by the spirits. It was difficult to explain to these villagers why I had no fear. By now hours had passed, and I felt my energy fading. These frightened, angry people, with their excited sing-song manner of speaking, were exhausting me. Here in a village of practicing animists was a middle-class Westerner arguing about evil spirits in their jungle. By consistently basing my answers on logic and reasoning, I was only making the situation worse. It would have merely increased their suspicions if I had claimed not to believe in spirits. How could I possibly be convincing? I asked myself. It became irrelevant and unimportant to me whether they understood who I really was. By this time I wanted only one thing: to be able to leave the village safely. I realized that I had to accept their fear and deal with it on their terms. It was absurd for me to try to convince them that one of their greatest fears was unfounded. A solution came to me unexpectedly.

The Kenyah, as do all the inland people, have a tradition of amulets, charms, and spell-breakers. The collective term for these items is *jeemat*. A *jeemat* can be made from a wide assortment of materials; the most common are seedpods, bones, wood shavings, crushed insects, beeswax, cowrie shells, and odd-shaped black pebbles known as hook stones. A *jeemat* can be made by man or found, but the most powerful ones (the hook stones) are given by a spirit or ghost. Directions for their use are revealed during a dream. It is very bad luck to lose or give away a charm that has come from the spirits. *Jeemats* are usually worn around the neck or wrist and are an important part of one's personal adornment. They are visible proof of one's faith in the power of the spirit world.

With this in mind, I remembered I was wearing a small, stuffed fabric banana pin that a friend had given me before I started my trip. The pin was about three inches long and had a bright yellow, polka-dot peel. The banana was removable. It could be dangled at the end of a short safety string. Until that moment in Long Uro, I had used the pin only to amuse people.

"This," I said, gesturing to the pin, "is my *jeemat*. It protects me from *bali saleng*." It caught them off guard; it also aroused their interest. One of the men came forward to touch the banana, but I cautioned him not to. He stopped three feet away from me.

"It has very strong *obat*," I said. *Obat* has many definitions: magic, power, or medicine. "Be careful, this charm was made especially for me by a spirit. That is why I'm not afraid to walk alone in the jungle." The mood of the interrogation changed as interest shifted to my banana pin.

"Where did it come from?" "What is it made of?" "Do you have more?" "How much would one cost?" they wanted to know.

I did not concoct my banana-pin story because I thought my tormentors were simple-minded or childish. Quite the opposite. The Kenyah have a highly developed relationship with the spirit world. I couldn't think of any other story they might believe. From generations of experience, they know how to coexist with both good and bad spirits. Firmly rooted in the twentieth century, I certainly didn't have anything to teach them. I was the outsider, the ignorant one. I had great respect for all the inland people. With their unique forms of architecture, social organization, and sophisticated farming techniques, they have established themselves in an incredibly difficult environment. The decision to present the banana pin as a powerful charm not only helped save me in this situation, but also forced me to reconsider how I was responding to the people. I stopped being the observer and began to accept their supernatural world, and my journey was never the same. In that single moment I grew much closer to my experiences.

The tension eased after I had revealed the power of the banana-pin charm. A few obstinate older men insisted on going over the fine points of my story, but the rest seemed to think I was probably harmless. I was flushed with relief. The blood and adrenaline pounded through my body and made my fingertips and toes ache. I felt light-headed and blessed to have survived this incident unharmed.

I was free to go, but it was too late to continue up the valley to my original destination — Long Sungai Barang. I had to spend the night in Long Uro. Dozens of eyes stared at me through knotholes and cracks in the rough wooden walls as I ate a miserable and lonely dinner. I was served half-rotten fish pounded in a mortar, bones and all. Having finished my meal, I strung my mosquito net in a filthy corner, unrolled my mat, and escaped into an exhausted sleep.

During the night there must have been more discussion because in the morning, just after I left the village, I came upon a young man standing at the side of the pathway. He was barefoot, well muscled, and dressed in blue shorts. He wore white gloves and held a large unsheathed parang at his side. He didn't respond to my greeting as I approached, but as I passed he fell into step a few feet behind me. I continued on for a short while then decided it would be better to confront him. I turned to speak, but he had vanished into the undergrowth. I knew that he could be no more than fifty feet from where I stood, but I couldn't see him. For months this jungle had seemed so benign and giving. How quickly it had become frightening. It was clear to me that at any moment I might be ambushed and killed.

Farther up the valley I passed abandoned farm huts and stopped briefly in the village of Lidung Payau to ask directions to the village of Long Sungai Barang. On the far side of Lidung Payau, I saw what I soon realized was a cage fashioned out of logs six inches in diameter. The structure was raised off the ground and had a slat floor that let excrement out and the flies in. The cage measured six feet by five feet by four feet and had a shingled roof. It was "home" not to an animal, but to a man. There were no doors or windows. I later learned that the inhabitant, barely visible between the gaps in the horizontal logs, had lived in the cage for more than two years. I don't know what his crime was. The cloud of furiously buzzing blackflies must have driven him mad. I looked upon this wretched man as a fellow sufferer, but when I tried to speak with him, he moved to the far side of his cage, and I could sense his fear of my presence.

I no longer had my sense of security and self-confidence. I lost track of time. As my anxiety mounted, a few hundred yards began to seem like miles. My thinking became erratic and unsound. There was no turning back, and for the first time since leaving Long Sungai Anai three days earlier, I began to panic. I sensed that I was being watched. Soaked in perspiration, I paused frequently to look over my shoulder and listen for the sound of human voices or of jungle knives slashing through the undergrowth. I scanned the surrounding walls of impenetrable green and brown foliage, but I could detect nothing. There were only the normal sounds of the jungle: the wind, the flutter of leaves, dripping water, and rubbing branches. I could see black hornbills perched nearby, so I called to them. I wanted to hear something friendly and reassuring, but their calls came back to me sounding like strangled pleas.

I hurried on to Long Sungai Barang, hoping that word of the incident in Long Uro hadn't preceded me. I wanted a fresh start. I now realized the full extent of my naiveté, my incredible stupidity. I was completely alone and vulnerable. I didn't know what else to do except to keep walking and to try to relax. I stopped frequently, considered going back, couldn't decide, then continued on. Whenever I sat down to rest and clear my mind, a new wave of anxiety would engulf me.

I knew that Long Sungai Barang was the last village in the upper Kayan River valley. If the people there weren't friendly, I would be trapped. Four hundred miles of primary rain forest separated me from the most accessible coast.

It was late afternoon by the time I entered the longhouse at Sungai Barang. I was disoriented and confused, and my legs were bleeding freely from the leeches and barbed vines. I was led to the headman's room. While he was being summoned, I was surrounded by about a dozen Kenyah men. I could feel the deep, painful grooves that the straps of the rattan pack had cut into my shoulders. My shirt was pasted to my back from the heat of the day. The men seemed relaxed and curious, but I felt they looked right through me and sensed my uncertainty.

We talked about the approaching rice harvest for perhaps ten minutes; then to my left I heard the familiar creak and slam of a sapling-powered hardwood door. In midsentence I looked up, expecting to see the headman, but there before me stood a young, white-skinned woman with golden hair. She was dressed in a flowered sarong and a blouse. She was barefoot, pretty, and smiling. I was completely unnerved. It just wasn't possible for her to be there. I became incredulous and even more confused. Finally I just smiled back and felt my pent-up fears and anxieties begin to dissolve.

The first thing I noticed as she stood there was the fragrance of her skin. It wasn't the scent of soap or perfume; it was the scent of another culture, another world, a fresh, wonderful smell that made me question my attraction to smoky jungle campfires and eating wild animals. We spoke Indonesian. There was no urgency to our voices. In Kenyah fashion we began with trivial matters in order to mask the real intent of our conversation, and gradually we led up to the important questions. More people came into the room. They sat quietly, watched, and listened. Eventually the temptation to speak our own language was overwhelming. The woman smiled again and in perfect English said, "I'm Cynthia. I live next door. The headman won't be back until late tonight. Would you like to come over to my place for a visit?"

CHAPTER TEN · MEETING A FOREST ECOLOGIST

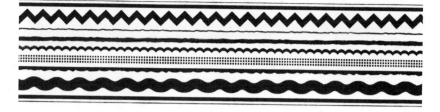

YNTHIA closed the door, and we removed our shoes. The longhouse sounds of rice pounding and roosters faded. I put my pack on the rough wooden floor then glanced around the large room. A row of newly installed windows illuminated the quiet interior. The window shutters were hinged at the top and propped open with sticks. The room was an unlikely but charming combination of herbarium, kitchen, and bedroom. Plant presses bursting with specimens were stacked in orderly fashion on high shelves, and dozens of live orchids grew on the walls. The jumble of familiar objects made me feel at home immediately: a bathing suit was draped over a chair, and at the foot of the bed lay a rumpled copy of the English newspaper *The Guardian*. I half-expected to see the remains of a croissant and a dish of raspberry jam on a white breakfast tray. Mixed in with the tabletop clutter of reference books, notepads, and typewriter, were a magnifying glass and a pair of binoculars. Perched on its shiny metal stand a green mosquito coil sent a thin ribbon of smoke into the thatched roof. Beneath the table I noticed another familiar object, a case of Scotch; the bottles appeared to be unopened.

Cynthia showed me the slat-floor lavatory alcove then boiled water for tea on her indoor fireplace. I ladled water into a plastic tub and washed. First I removed the powdery white lines of sweat from my face, then the dried blood from my legs and feet where the leeches had been. I towelled myself dry and joined Cynthia by the fire. I was beginning to feel much better.

We were both nervous after our surprise meeting, but it seemed likely that we could become friends.

"All right, what are you doing here?" I asked with a laugh.

"No, that's my line," Cynthia responded. "Where on earth have you come from?"

"That's becoming a very popular question," I replied. I gave her a brief account of the *bali saleng* legend and went on to describe what had happened to me during the previous several days.

"Well, you should be safe here," Cynthia spoke without hesitation. "I've never heard of *bali saleng*, but you can stay with me. I'll say you're a relative. The people in this village trust me."

The water boiled, and we had tea; then we talked for an hour without interruption while Cynthia told me the story of how she had arrived in the Apo Kayan. Four months earlier she had been flown from the coast to Long Sungai Barang in one of the mission planes. The pilot helped unload her 12-month supply of research equipment and personal belongings then took off, leaving her standing at the edge of the tiny grass airstrip. Cynthia was twenty-seven years old. In her bags she had an English/Indonesian phrase book and a dictionary.

Cynthia was taking part in UNESCO's Man and the Biosphere Program. One aspect of the project is the study of interactions between people and tropical forests in East Kalimantan. For a year she would conduct research into the long-range effects of shifting cultivation on the secondary forest surrounding Long Sungai Barang, an area that had been selected by fellow researcher Timothy Jessup and Herwasono Soedjito of the Herbarium Bogoriense, Java. The people of Long Sungai Barang have an extensive knowledge of the plants they use for medicine (40 species), food (150 different species, including 67 wild species), and crafts (43 species). The people are keen gardeners and have introduced to their land many exotic crop species, such as papayas, scallions, cloves, guavas, tomatoes, coco, and others. In addition to their gardening interests, the people of Long Sungai Barang are intelligent, hardworking, and generous with their knowledge. It was an idyllic place for Cynthia to conduct her research.

That afternoon, as people were returning from their garden plots, we swam in the river, and a dozen naked boys and girls came to join us. I pretended to be an alligator, swimming underwater and grabbing their legs, causing the children to scream in mock fright. Little girls brought bouquets of jungle flowers, and suddenly I realized what a wonderful village I had walked into.

We were called to the headman's room that evening for dinner. I brought gifts of tobacco and shotgun shells and was introduced to some of the important older men and women. Both Cynthia and I spoke Indonesian during the evening, and as we ate I told the story of my overland journey from Sarawak. The headman wanted to know which way I had come and what villages I had visited. "How much is an Indonesian hunting dog worth in Sarawak?" one man wanted to know. Remembering my Muhammad Aidid lessons, I told the man exactly, in terms of Malay dollars, shotgun shells, water buffalo, and Japanese diesel engines. Everyone laughed at my detailed response to the man's casual question. The mood at dinner was relaxed, and there was no mention of the incident in Long Uro the day before. Cynthia explained to everyone that I was her *saudara* (relative) and would stay in her room. That arrangement was slightly scandalous but acceptable, and after dinner we wandered up and down the creaking floorboards of the longhouse porch meeting people. Bottles of *arak* appeared, and back in Cynthia's room the first bottle of Scotch was opened. We drank it warm, straight up, in glass tumblers. I don't recall how much alcohol we consumed or how many people came to visit, but I made a point of collecting as many allies as possible before the *bali saleng* story caught up with me. We all got very drunk, and I ended up sleeping on the table. Skylights had been installed in her roof, and in the middle of the night I woke up to find shafts of pale moonlight penetrating the darkness of the room. I remember lying on my back on the

199

table with my hands held behind my head thinking how good it felt to be in a safe place. I fell asleep with a palpable sense of relief.

♠   ♠   ♠

The mornings in Long Sungai Barang were chilly, and Cynthia and I got into the habit of sitting side by side in front of the little fireplace warming our bare feet and drinking cups of thick black coffee. Sliced bananas sizzled in the wok as we talked about her work.

Development planners in the Indonesian government believe that traditional hill farming is ruining the fertility of the rain forest by depleting the soil. In the process of clearing the land to make the farms, significant amounts of valuable export timber are being burned. These were two of the main issues that Cynthia was looking into. She explained that development planners in East Kalimantan were also operating under the assumption that the rural people randomly destroyed the forests in order to create farmland that would be abandoned after a few years when the soil was ruined.

In the highlands, at least, those assumptions were not true. For more than a hundred years the people have practiced a long-fallow form of shifting cultivation that is based on forest maintenance. Cynthia believed that the principal threat to the forests of Kalimantan was the two dozen major timber companies, not the peasant farmers who grow rice to feed their families. Cynthia pointed out that in the past swidden agriculture, commonly known as slash and burn, was responsible for the clearing of primary forest, but the villagers were no longer cutting down primary forest. Village populations had stabilized or were in decline, and there was less need for land.

The rural people make their farms in what are called "old fields," which are previously farmed areas that have remained fallow long enough for the forest to regenerate. Cynthia introduced me to *Prunus arborea* (a kind of cherry tree). The tree grows in old fields and appears as a little seedling by the fourth year. When this tree is in its twelfth to fifteenth year, the farmers know that the soil can once again support crops. There are perhaps half a dozen other plants that are indicators of good soil. The people would never go to the tremendous effort of cutting the forest unless they knew the soil was ready. While they wait, medicinal plants (not usually found in primary forest), rattan, *gaharu*, tree resins, and other useful products are harvested from the secondary forest.

"The people here have a very keen sense of forest management. We are learning a lot from them. Obviously there have been problems," Cynthia went on. "If fields are too large, Imperata grass, known locally as *alang-alang* can take over. Once it is established, the trees will possibly never grow again. The development planners complain about land use by shifting cultivators, but the worst damage being done to the forest, apart from logging, is on the government-subsidized resettlement areas near the coast, where a Wild West frontier mentality prevails. Chain saws and gasoline are easily obtained for clearing the forest, and with a nearby market for rice, the villagers make their fields as large as possible. Farming practices on those resettlement schemes, where no one has a long-term interest in maintaining the forest, are going to have to be reconsidered."

But why, I was curious to know, if the soil in the highlands was still fertile, were so many communities migrating to the coastal areas?

"The main reason people are leaving the Apo Kayan," Cynthia told me, "is that it is so difficult to obtain basic commodities like salt, gasoline, fabric, tobacco, and especially steel tools and cooking pots. The river and overland trade routes, as you well know, are very difficult. A round-trip journey by longboat can take two to three months. There is very limited access to wage labor, and there is a lack of adequate health care and schooling. People's expectations have been raised, and they want to be a part of the coastal cash economy. They can't participate here because they are totally isolated."

One morning when Cynthia went out to check some of her sample sites, she left me with a stack of research material. It was slow reading because of the technical aspects of her work, and then I came upon her plant list. I found the Kenyah translations and Cynthia's personal comments most amusing. The list revealed as much about life in Long Sungai Barang as it did about Cynthia's astute observations and sense of humor.

Here are a few samples from more than two hundred species of successional vegetation from secondary forest. The Kenyah names are in parentheses.

SABAICEAE FAMILY, *Meliosma nervosa (Bulit yap)*: the chicken-soup tree, a food source and an indicator of good soil.

EUPHORBIACEAE FAMILY, *Glochidion breynoides (Lundu demah)*: the afternoon nap tree. And in the same family, *Macaranga wincklerii (Daun lukok)*: the cigarette-paper tree.

ASCLEPIADACEAE FAMILY, *Tylophora cissoides (Aka bulu mah Bungan)*: the rice goddess's (Bungan) crotch-hair vine.

MORACEAE FAMILY, *Ficus (Aka pinut)*: figs, the afternoon-snack vine.

ASTERACEAE FAMILY, *Blumea balsamifera (Embung pasapun)*: the ass-wipe weed, listed as a medicinal plant.

MUSACEAE FAMILY, *Musa (Sawan demanei)*: the bachelor's wild banana (a primitive erect fruit).

All of this information was tremendously interesting, but after a few days a new dimension was added to our talks. During these weighty conversations I frequently found myself looking at Cynthia's hair or the line of her neck. I occasionally lost track of what we were talking about. Then one afternoon, between discussions of sustained yield management of forest products and the importance of women to agroforestry in central Borneo, I realized I was becoming attracted to Cynthia at precisely the same rate I was losing my interest in forest ecology.

I wasn't sure what Cynthia was thinking, but I began to consider the consequences of our becoming lovers. I knew that in a village situation it was impossible to keep such a secret; then there was the question of our being related. More important, I realized there was a possibility I might have jeopardized Cynthia's safety because of my *bali saleng* status. The question of jungle spirits may sound silly to Westerners, but in the central highlands of Borneo I had to think my way through a very delicate situation.

There was also the question of human endurance. I hadn't been to bed with a woman for more than five months, and after three nights on the dinner table I was finding it difficult to sleep. In the village setting my natural instincts seemed inappropriate, and the situation was made worse by the fact that I couldn't bring myself to explain to Cynthia what I was feeling. So the sexual tension increased along with the evening Scotch consumption.

At about this time the *bali saleng* rumors spread through Long Sungai Barang, and Cynthia passed on the warnings, "Don't go anywhere by yourself. And don't do anything suspicious. The people feel comfortable with you because you're staying with me, but some of them are asking questions."

One man had raised the issue of what I was doing in the jungle. "He walks alone," the man had pointed out. "If he is not a *bali saleng*, he might be working for one." When I heard this story, I knew that regardless of how pleasant it was staying in Long Sungai Barang with Cynthia I would have to go. Had I already endangered her? I had no way of knowing. The people of Long Sungai Barang continued to be friendly, but I couldn't know what they were thinking.

By way of excuse, I explained to Cynthia that I would have to return to Long Nawang in a few days to start making preparations to recross the mountains to the northwest. It was true that I needed to find a way back to Sarawak, but there was no hurry, and I would have preferred to stay. I had grown very fond of Cynthia. She was articulate, kind, attractive, and had also been wonderfully hospitable. The week in Long Sungai Barang gave me the needed rest and confidence to complete the second crossing of the highlands. The nurturing and attention I didn't receive in Long Bia had been provided by the people in Long Sungai Barang. Looking back, I often wonder what would have happened to me if I hadn't pressed on to Long Sungai Barang the day I was so terrified and disoriented in the jungle.

I realized I was still vulnerable to people's fears, but during my stay in Long Sungai Barang, I willed myself into believing everything was all right. I did this quite consciously because I believed if I could carry on for another month I could make it back to Sarawak. I simply assured myself I was safe and in control of the situation, even though that was not the case. My shaky emotional state was revealed by my decision to return to Long Nawang alone. I based my decision on the unsound assumption that if I had already made the journey between Long Nawang and Long Sungai Barang once, the second time would somehow be easier. It wasn't.

☀   ☀   ☀

On my last day in Long Sungai Barang, Cynthia and I stayed in the village and spent a comfortable morning and afternoon on the longhouse porch telling stories. When other people sat down to visit or listen, we would switch from English to Indonesian.

One of Cynthia's stories settled my confusion about where people go for casual sex. Apart from lovemaking and defecating, every human activity is on public display in the longhouse. In the close communal environment there are unique opportunities for all sorts of social interaction, but as any first-time visitor will tell you, there is no privacy. The only opportunity for couples to give over completely to their lovemaking is on rainy, wind-blown nights, when all sounds are muffled as the storm pounds away at the jungle outside. These nights are unpredictable, so people resort to using the farm huts. Because of their remoteness, the huts provide the perfect place for unabashed lovemaking. They are used by newlyweds, adulterers, unmarried couples, and even good old mom and dad, who can't seem to manage in the longhouse because the extended family sleeps in the same room.

Cynthia finished her story; then it was my turn. A small group of young women had joined us, so I talked about the special diets of the pregnant women in Sarawak.

The Chinese and Iban in Sarawak prize the yellow-crowned bulbul as a food for their pregnant wives, believing that if the women eat this bird, which sings its enchanting warbling song each morning along the riverbanks, their child will have a beautiful voice and be clever with words. These qualities will help the child attract many friends. There were other important animals for the women to be aware of during pregnancy. I read the list from my journal:

FROGS They are good to eat. They help the child develop strong legs.

TORTOISE Bad to eat because it will cause a difficult delivery. Like the tortoise's head, the baby's head will go in and out, in and out during birth.

SNAKES They are good. They make the baby's skin smooth.

EAGLE If an eagle is eaten, the child will be aggressive and will use its fingernails like claws when fighting.

OWL Should be avoided; otherwise the baby's eyes will be too large (like a Westerner's).

I asked the women if there were similar diets in the Apo Kayan, and they said no, but one woman mentioned the use of an aromatic root called *lung*. During pregnancy, when the women are feeling vulnerable or uneasy, they keep a piece of this root with them to help them feel safe from ghosts. Cynthia later identified the plant as *Homalomena sagittifolia* from the family Araceae.

I then asked about contraception.

"The Kenyah don't use contraceptives," Cynthia laughed, "only fertility medicines, as children are gold. Illegitimacy is not frowned upon nearly as much as barrenness."

The women wandered off to finish their afternoon work, and Cynthia and I took one last swim in the river before dusk. I had dinner in the headman's room, but didn't mention I was leaving the next day. I was hoping to reach Long Nawang in one day, and I didn't want anyone waiting for me on the trail. As usual, Cynthia and I stayed up late drinking Scotch, and, as usual, I spent the night on the dinner table.

In the morning I said goodby to the headman and gave him five more shotgun shells. Cynthia was going to check a number of old fields that morning, so most people would have assumed I was just going out for the day. Only minutes before I left did I pick up my pack. Three Kenyah field assistants joined us, and we walked out of the village. In silence we walked to the trail junction that led to Long Nawang. I felt terribly self-conscious as we followed the winding jungle path. I wanted to tell Cynthia why I was leaving, but I couldn't utter a word.

We stopped walking where the trail branched in two directions. Cynthia offered her hand as if to shake mine, and I took it. She smiled and then without warning pulled me close and in one motion slipped her other hand behind my neck and kissed me square on the mouth. The effect was instantaneous and I returned the kiss. We remained standing very close after we separated, and for a moment we both hesitated. Public kissing is not part of Kenyah custom, and Cynthia's helpers watched us with great interest. What now? I thought. Does this mean "goodby" or "please stay"? I still don't know, but instead of making any revealing comments, we mechanically recited our farewell lines. I mumbled the classic banal phrases of thanks, and Cynthia provided the appropriate trivial replies. Both of us chose to ignore any deeper feelings.

I turned, walked a few steps into the forest, then reconsidered. You fool, what are you doing? Go back. It's not too late. Tell her how you feel! But it *was* too late. We had lost sight of each other, and I walked on. In a lifetime an opportunity such as that would never come again. Such an unlikely encounter — the friendship and, of course, the desire. It was the stuff of romance, and I chose to ignore it. I continued walking, overwhelmed by appalling feelings of regret. Was I doing the right thing? Probably not. One thing was certain, however. I had a good idea of what to expect from the people of Long Uro later that day. I was four hundred miles from the coast as I walked down the jungle trail to face my tormentors alone.

Five months after leaving the village of Long Sungai Barang, I received the following letter.

May 27, 1983

Dear Eric,

The rains are incredible now. Low parts of the trail are up to my waist in water sometimes. The wild pigs are coming back, hornbills too. My roof leaks all over the dining room table . . . tough on visitors. The photos you sent in your second letter made the people in my longhouse very happy.

Sorry to be such a lousy correspondent, but I thought you should know the following piece of information. The people in Long Uro and Lidung Payau were very suspicious of you and thought you were the bali saleng. *You were right about the people being afraid! The fear of you remained, but it did not extend to me because I traveled with their neighbors from Long Sungai Barang. You invoked fear because no one travels alone, and it was suggested that you had killed your guides. You should think twice about coming back here.*

When I traveled through Lidung Payau several months ago, I spoke with an elder about strangers. He mentioned you (tall European) and said that a man in Long Uro was standing behind you ready to stick you with a poison dart if you had made a false move while arguing in the village. I don't know what else to say other than I'm glad you made it back to Sarawak safely.

Sorry to make this so short again. I will try to get a good recording of the night sounds for you.

Love,

Cynthia

CHAPTER ELEVEN · ASANG JALONG — SAFE IN NAWANG BARU

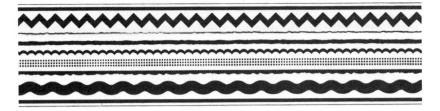

THE PLAN, as I walked from Long Sungai Barang to Long Nawang, was to continue through the villages of Lidung Payau, Long Uro, and Long Ampung as quickly as possible, hoping that no one would stop me. If someone did, I knew there would be trouble. I wanted to avoid those villages, but there was only one trail, and I had no alternative route. I considered making a jungle detour around each village, but decided against it. If I had been caught sneaking through the forest near a longhouse, I have little doubt I would have been attacked. I would have to take my chances on the main trail, which I knew well from my original walk from Long Nawang to Long Sungai Barang. Most of the people along the way would be in the fields at midday, leaving the longhouses nearly empty.

Arriving at the clearing before Lidung Payau, I quickened my pace, and within minutes I was through the village and back into the shade of the jungle. I saw a few people, but no one had shown any particular interest in me. That's one village, I thought to myself; two more to go. Walking . . . walking . . . walking; eight hours of it, and the day was hot. Sections of the trail passed through open farmland, and no clouds protected me from the sun. I frequently stopped to drink from the river and wash my face and arms, but I felt much too anxious to swim. Several hours down the trail, I emerged from the jungle once again and could see the beginning of the garden plots that led to the longhouse at Long Uro. I walked through the fields in full view of the village, imagining that dozens of pairs of eyes were watching me. Strangely enough there was no sound of human activity as I passed close to the longhouse. I expected a voice to call out, but there was only silence and the sound of my own heavy breathing. I stepped onto the steel-cable suspension bridge that spanned the Kayan River, wobbled along the undulating 12-inch-wide wooden plankway, and disappeared down the trail on the far side of the river. I found it disquieting that I hadn't seen anyone, and I had no explanation for it. I moved on quickly, wanting to put as much distance as possible between myself and the village. I hoped to reach the safety of Long Nawang that night.

I made good time that day. There were no confrontations, and I began to relax. The few people in the fields who noticed me did not respond with the fear that I had anticipated. Maybe everything was all right now that they knew who I was. Had I misjudged the *bali saleng* incident and overreacted to people's suspicions? Without further evidence of the people's fear of me, I began to relax. By late afternoon I was confident that there was little to worry about. The *bali saleng* incident had blown over.

The last village before Long Nawang was Long Ampung, and as I approached that village I had to make a decision. It was obvious that I wouldn't reach Long Nawang that night, and I was undecided whether to stay in Long Ampung, where I didn't know anyone, or to try to reach a farm hut one and a half hours downriver where I knew Pa Ubang, an acquaintance from Long Nawang, would be staying with his family. I had met Pa Ubang the afternoon of my arrival in Long Nawang ten days earlier, and he was one of the few people who had been relaxed in my presence. With less than two hours of light remaining, I decided to try for the farm hut. I breezed by Long Ampung without incident and recrossed the Kayan River just below the village. I then hurried along the trail, which at that point closely follows the open riverbanks. I came around a bend in the river and without warning found myself in full view of about twenty people bathing and washing clothes on the other side of the river. My reaction, after a slight panic, was to wave cheerfully and smile. No greeting was returned. Their blank, open-mouthed expressions of horror sent shudders of fear through my body. Washing dripped from their hands, and I could feel my heart beginning to pound. It was obvious that they were paralyzed with fright at the sight of me. Oh shit! I thought as I realized what must be going through their minds: Stranger in the forest . . . solitary man walking into the jungle at nightfall.

Only *bali salengs* sleep in the jungle. There was no way these people could have known my plans, and I hadn't had the presence of mind to say something reassuring such as, "Is there time to reach Pa Ubang's farm hut before dark? He's expecting me."

I felt helpless in this situation and didn't utter a word. Instead, I waved mechanically, and once out of sight I started to run down the trail. The pack bounced on my back and exhausted me, so I slowed to a brisk walk. Minutes before I had felt safe, and now I was in a panic. Why had I relaxed? Why didn't I explain to the people where I was going? I had been caught off guard, and I had reacted in the worst possible way. The people at the river probably continued to wash their clothes, but for more than an hour I imagined I could hear the sounds of paddles against the side of the longboat that was racing downriver to cut me off.

Frequently, as I continued at a fast pace, I thought I could hear the sound of distant voices through the trees. Then I saw two abandoned packs at the side of the trail — as if the owners had recently dropped them and bolted for the jungle. I had only a moment to contemplate this strange sight before three hunting dogs flew at me from the nearby undergrowth. I had never seen dogs in Borneo act aggressively towards people, but their snarls and raised hackles clearly conveyed their intentions. I'm dog meat, I thought. The dogs stopped their charge two yards from me. Growling and barking, they made tentative lunges at my legs from three sides. I pulled out my parang and kept walking. They pursued me in the same threatening manner for one hundred yards. Each time they came close I turned and growled at them loudly, and they stood back. The dogs frightened me, but I hadn't slowed down because the thought of having my leg savaged by a dog paled in comparison to the possible scene of an armed group of frightened villagers running me down at this late hour of the day. They certainly wouldn't have allowed me to continue, and I would have been taken back to Long Ampung for a session of threats and insults like the one I had endured in Long Uro. These people were searching for an incident to lend credibility to their terror, and I had no interest in providing them with one.

In the fading light I fell down many times on the slippery trail, cutting myself on the rocks and barbed vines; I had to reach the farm hut before dark. Wading across a waist-deep tributary stream in the twilight, I could smell the smoke from Pa Ubang's dinner fire. I stepped from the water and decided to call out when I was within hearing distance of the hut to alert Pa Ubang's family of my arrival. Before I could do so, I ran into Pa Ubang's wife on the trail as she made her way to the river for water. She spotted me first, a tall silhouette on the darkened trail. She let out a horrible scream less than thirty feet in front of me. I composed myself enough to identify who I was, but she had fled. Before I could reach the farm hut Pa Ubang rushed down the trail with a spear and a flashlight. I called out, "It's Eric . . . don't be afraid . . . don't be afraid!"

"What are you doing here, *Tuan*?" Pa Ubang asked, only slightly relieved at the sight of me. "It is very foolish of you to walk at night!"

We returned to the hut, and I explained the long walk from Long Sungai Barang. I told Pa Ubang that the reason for my late arrival was that I had misjudged the distance to his farm. I also apologized for scaring his wife. Pa Ubang told me that if I had come a day later the hut would have been abandoned as they were planning to return to Long Nawang the next day. We settled down to an uneasy dinner. Three of their children were present, and we were all unnerved by my awkward arrival. Pa Ubang locked us into the farm hut that night, and it wasn't clear to me whether it was for my protection or theirs. No one arrived later that night, and I was relieved that I hadn't been followed.

There wasn't enough room for me in the longboat, so I continued on foot the next morning and arrived in Long Nawang without incident after a three-hour walk. Pa Ubang and his family arrived by longboat late in the day because they had capsized in the rapids. The outboard motor wasn't working, and they had lost their cooking pots in the river. The motor could be fixed, but the loss of the cooking pots was serious because the nearest place to buy new ones was on the coast. They managed to borrow an extra set, but that meant they would have to return the favor by acquiring new pots at a later date.

Pa Ubang brought me the outboard motor that night and asked me if I could fix it. Water had seeped into the carburetor, and the spark plugs were fouled. We cleaned them, checked to make sure the plugs were sparking, then primed the carburetor. The first pull on the rope starter produced a backfire. I adjusted the choke, and on the second attempt the engine came to life. The entire process hadn't taken more than an hour, and Pa Ubang was speechless with delight. Word of my success with the outboard soon spread, and the next day I was asked to adjust the Japanese-made rice-husking machine so that it would process a brittle type of hill rice without breaking the grains. The Japanese/English instructions gave me some difficulty. The air-flow valve, for example, was indicated by the word *wind*. I adjusted the "wind," and eventually a steady stream of unbroken rice grains began to pour from the machine. These basic mechanical skills, I quickly realized, generated a lot of positive interest in me, so I set to work fixing things: tape players, wind-up alarm clocks, and more outboard motors.

One man produced a Royal typewriter and asked me if I knew how to operate the machine. I estimated it was at least sixty years old. The typewriter had two beveled-glass inspection windows on each side and keys for all of the fractions in one-eighth increments. The man called his typewriter *mesin tik-tik*. Mesin means machine in Indonesian; *tik-tik* is the sound produced by striking the keys.

I pulled a piece of paper out of my journal and set the typewriter on the floor in front of my crossed legs. I explained touch typing then gave a demonstration by writing a letter to a friend. The ribbon appeared to be only slightly newer than the machine.

I hadn't properly tested the functions of the *mesin tik-tik* so at the end of the first line, the carriage hung precariously from the typewriter. I adjusted the right-hand margin and again began to type. The people were amazed that I could remember the location of so many keys without watching my fingers. I typed:

Dear Heidi,

I'm not quite sure what a typewriter is doing in a place like this. It has come as a real shock to walk out of the jungle after two frightening weeks of being suspected as a collector of sacrificial blood to be confronted by this relic of Dutch Colonial days. There are about a dozen men watching me write this letter. I'm not feeling very comfortable with these people, but I'm showing them how to touch type. I'm trying to gain their confidence with my typing skills. While I'm at it, I think I'll attempt a feat that may be without precedent. I will mail this letter to you despite lack of postal service, stamps, or regular transport to the coast . . . it's two months by dugout canoe. There is one more mountain range to cross before I'm back in Sarawak, but there are no guides, and so I'm stranded. Again I'm not sure what to do. At time like this my mind wanders to thoughts of homemade chocolate truffles, toasted sesame bagels from the Polk Street/Broadway bagel shop in San Francisco, pecan pie, and the view from Hawkins Peak on a clear day on a pair of cross-country skis.

With love and a smile,

Eric

I never expected the letter to arrive, so I addressed the envelope: *Heidi, Partington Ridge, Big Sur, California.* The return address was: *Eric, East Kalimantan, Borneo.*

I gave the letter to a man who was heading to the east coast and asked if he would post it for me. The last time I saw the letter the man was rolling it up and placing it in the safest possible place: inside his bamboo poison-dart quiver. I forgot the letter, and it wasn't until six months later that I heard it had arrived in perfect condition.

On 6 November Pilot Ian and Eric Michaels arrived in Long Nawang by missionary plane as part of their monthly church visits to the remote villages of the interior. I was pleased to see the plane was still working. When Eric finished with his service, he brought me up-to-date on *bali saleng* news in Long Bia. Two weeks earlier, in the middle of the night, a father woke to see an arm coming through a gap in the wall towards his sleeping child. The man quietly reached for his spear-tipped blowpipe and stabbed the intruder three times, twice in the face and once in the arm. Blood was found near the house, but the police were never informed. The next morning the village organized night patrols consisting of two shifts of ten men each from 8:00 P.M. until 5 A.M.

"The people are very frightened," Eric Michaels told me. "My wife and I don't go out at night."

☘   ☘   ☘

After a week with Pa Ubang in Long Nawang, I once again felt comfortable with the people, but I knew there was still an underlying suspicion towards me that was unlikely to change. Then an unexpected death occurred that was to alter completely people's attitudes towards me. A young wife died in the nearby village of Nawang Baru, and for two days and nights the mourners filed in from neighboring villages to pay their respects and to deliver the traditional gifts of rice, salt, *sugee*, money, cooking oil, sugar, pigs, chickens, and clothing.

People contributed labor, cooking meals for the three hundred mourners. At the funeral I sat with a group of people from Long Nawang. On the first day, when it came time to make the offerings, I asked what would be appropriate. This gesture didn't go unnoticed, and the family of the dead woman was pleased to receive my gift of tens sticks of *sugee*, four thousand rupiahs, and two shotgun shells. The donations were written in a ledger.

On the main footpath below the longhouse, construction of the log coffin was in progress. A dozen carpenters and wood carvers were embellishing the coffin lid with delicate openwork and stylized hornbill beaks. These were later painted in black, white, yellow, and red—the favorite colors of the Apo Kayan. Family members filed into the longhouse during the first day to take their turns mourning the dead woman.

Dressed in a traditional brown-black-and-white Javanese sarong, white blouse, and fringed cap, the corpse lay on a cot in the middle of the longhouse porch. A string of tiger teeth had been placed on her breast and her lips were lightly colored with lipstick. A crowd of several hundred people sat around the cot sobbing and wailing, often caressing her hand, foot, or hair. People had come equipped with crying towels. A headdress of hornbill feathers was hanging from the gallery wall above the body. Later in the day the body was placed in the log coffin, and the decorative lid was set to one side. By nightfall the mourners had reached a state of exhaustion, and the wailing began to subside.

Earlier in the day I had noticed a cassette player near the coffin and had been puzzled by its presence. Later that night the tape player was brought out, and a young man slipped in a tape. I was expecting a "Holy Ghost" tape or some inappropriate Western music, but out of the speakers came the highlights of the day's mourning. This allowed the people a break from their sobbing, without offending the departing spirit.

A short, smiling man with twinkling eyes came to sit next to me. He tilted his head to one side and introduced himself as Pa Lenchau. He asked about my journey from Sarawak and wanted to know if I had really traveled all the way from America without companions. I told him of my guides in the jungle, and he smiled and nodded to himself as if I had solved some puzzle for him. Pa Lenchau then told me the story of Asang Jalong, a traditional Kenyah hero. Asang Jalong had taken a journey similar to my own. From Sungai Malinau ("from the east, but not as far as America") he had followed Sungai Bahau to Pudjungan, traversed the Sungai Iwan watershed, and traveled up the Sungai Kayan to Long Nawang.

"Asang Jalong traveled by himself over great distances. He was very brave," said Pa Lenchau.

"Did he take heads?" I asked.

"Oh, how many thousands! *Potong*! *Potong*!" (cut, cut), exclaimed Pa Lanchau, as he motioned with an imaginary parang.

Jalong Laing, the *kepala adat* of Nawang Baru, and Pa Ibo Usat, the *kepala kampong*, sat nearby listening, and soon they joined Pa Lenchau in a discussion concerning my name. Eric was too short for a man's name, and they believed a fixer of motors should have a proper Kenyah name. They decided on Asang Jalong. This was a tremendous compliment, but more than that, the name revealed their changing attitude towards me. Whereas the people of Long Uro had taken my habit of solo travel as the sign of a malevolent spirit, the three most important men of Nawang Baru interpreted it as an indication of bravery and courage.

This unexpected gesture of friendliness and human kindness had an extraordinary effect on me. Was it possible they were accepting me? Until Pa Lanchau came to sit with me, I had felt so isolated that I didn't dare hope my situation might improve. It seemed the people were again finally warming to me.

We sat around the dead woman for a second day and night without leaving the porch. At the end of the second day, a faint smell of decomposing flesh had started, and the coffin lid was put in place and sealed with tree resin. That night the crying towels were put away, and people were smiling again. General news was discussed, and children tentatively resumed their play. A thunderstorm with brilliant flashes of lightning and deep-throated rolls of thunder shook the forest and longhouse. Rain poured down from the night sky, and that evening we slept. Women provided me with a blanket and a black-and-tan Penan sleeping mat. Pressure kerosene lamps remained lit near the coffin, and the tape-recorded mourning continued to play.

Everyone stretched out side by side with their feet towards the coffin, and the dogs vied for warm positions in the sunken fire pits, which were evenly placed along the verandah floor. I woke in the night, and the tape had stopped. The storm had passed, and water dripped from the eaves. I noticed a hand raise up from the pile of hundreds of prostrate bodies. The hand was poised like a cobra ready to strike; then it moved slowly in a downwards arc to press the rewind button on the tape player. Soon the now-familiar sounds of mourning recommenced and I drifted back to sleep.

Next morning preparations were made to carry the coffin to the graveyard. We had an elaborate breakfast of fish, pork, fried tapioca, and rice. People had bathed in the river early that morning, and no one looked as if he or she had been sitting in the same spot for three days. Conversations were loud and animated. The formal mourning was over, and everyone was waiting for the procession to begin. During the three-hour wait for the journey to the graveyard, Pa Lenchau leaned towards me and asked, "Do you know the story of Tom Harrisson caught in the big tree by his parachute during World War II?"

I told him I had read an account of it in Harrisson's book, *World Within*. Following is Harrisson's story: *After some emasculating efforts to manipulate the suspension cords and sail into the wind, I flopped and descended crabwise. There was not anything I could do about it. I came right across the valley and over a ridge, where up-eddies and air currents played with me as if I was some sort of tubular glider out of control. They presently deposited me, with a smash, sideways on to the forest canopy at about 4,000 feet, upon a very steep hillside. . . . Then I began to slide. Looking down, it was difficult to doubt I was about to break my neck on the face of the ravine, 200 feet below. But when I got about a quarter of the way down (entangled head first in my harness, my feet wrapped up in the lines) I came to a shuddering stop. . . . A single broken branch in the tree top had pierced the parachute silk and held it. . . . I presently managed to get my feet below my head (and look something more like an old Harrovian and a gentleman should when in trouble). But I was so suspended that I could not do anything more. I was too far from my own tree or the next to swing in either direction without starting something serious up on my single securing point over-*

head. I had not the strength to climb up the lines, even if I could have cleared the harness without falling out. . . . Before long I must have passed out . . . I woke up to find myself swaying alarmingly . . . I could no longer feel my body below the waist, where the harness and the pressure of suspension held me in a vice of pure misery. The wind had got up. I must soon be unhooked from above, to crash down below. . . . I managed to assemble enough strength to look up and watch dissolution. Instead, the extraordinary sight of a small yellow man, wearing only a loincloth and a cap of hornbill feather, perched in my tree top on the theory — as I subsequently learnt — that if he unhooked the 'chute it would open again before it hit the ground. He was trying to free me and it. I summoned all the invective in all the Borneo dialects I had ever heard swear in. This caused him to reconsider: his position and mine. . . . By and by, he got other people to build an enormous ladder and improvised a pulley, between my tree and the next. Down this device some twenty little agile, excited laughing Borneans lowered me with great gentleness to the ground. They carried me over the ridge, into and across the blissful grass.

The small yellow man in the loincloth of Harrisson's story was young Pa Lenchau. He was delighted when I informed him that thousands of people had read about the incident. I told him that I was equally delighted to have made his acquaintance. Pa Lenchau and I continued talking, and his quick wit and humor soon became apparent. Our discussion became very silly, and this caused others to move closer to join the conversation.

A man produced a smallish lump of magnetic ore, which he called *batu besi berani*, the magnet rock. He asked for a needle from one of the women. The crowd knew his trick and moved closer, eager to watch my response. He held the *batu besi berani* over the needle, which was in the palm of his hand. Suddenly the needle leapt up and stuck to the rock.

"Ohhhhh," the people murmured.

"Very clever," I agreed.

I felt in a competitive mood and asked for the stone and needle. Also, I located the fishhooks in my bag. Everyone watched as I stroked the needle with the rock. I stroked it and stroked it until

I had everyone's attention. Then I placed the rock to one side and spread the fishhooks on the floor. I held the needle over the first hook.

"Ahhhhhh!" came the response from the crowd as one by one I picked up the fishhooks with the magnetized needle.

The owner of the rock looked a bit miffed, so I complimented him for having found such a marvelous rock. Of course, everyone wanted to try the trick, but soon we had moved on to discussions about even more spectacular "tricks." We talked about the American space program. One woman had listened to a crackling radio report on the Apollo moon mission, and she wanted me to clarify a few points. This did not surprise me because for weeks the villagers in the Apo Kayan had been asking me about the moon. Many of them refused to accept the story that the Americans had landed there. The final day of the funeral I once again did my best to answer the by-now-familiar questions: How many days did it take to get to the moon, and where did the astronauts sleep at night? How many *moks* of rice did they bring, and how did they cook it? What did they hunt on the moon? Finally, the women wanted to know why, if the Americans needed a big, powerful rocket ship to get there, how they could get back in a small one?

The big rocket ship question was difficult, but this is how I described the force of gravity: "Inside the center of the earth is a very large *batu besi berani*. It is so big that it not only pulls metal objects towards it, but also people, coconuts, tree branches, and water. I demonstrated by dropping my plastic pen to the floor. People don't fall off the other side of the earth because the *batu besi berani* pulls them to the ground. Inside the moon there is only a very small piece of *batu besi berani*. It is weak and therefore pulls things more slowly. I showed them how slowly my pen would fall on the moon. To leave the earth you need a rocket ship with big engines and a lot of gasoline to escape the powerful magnetic rock. Leaving the moon you need only a small engine and much less gasoline. Traveling away from the earth is similar to traveling upriver through rapids. Leaving the moon is the same as traveling downriver." I was pleased with this analogy, and my simplistic explanation.

I glanced around the longhouse porch, but there was still no sign that the funeral procession was about to begin, so we continued our conversations.

"Do you know where gold came from?" I was asked by two Christian gold miners from the nearby village of Mahak Baru.

"I have no idea," I replied.

"After Noah built the Ark and all the animals were aboard, the flood came. All the bad people and all the extra animals in the world were drowned," the two men explained. "When the flood waters receded, the bodies rotted, and in time the bones decayed into little flakes. These flakes turned into gold and are now found along the tributaries of the upper Mahakam River."

Early in the afternoon carrying poles were lashed to the sides of the coffin, and people began to move off the longhouse porch. We formed two long lines leading to the river. The coffin passed between the two lines, and during this part of the journey, the husband rode on the coffin with his arms hugging it tightly. The coffin was ferried across the river in a longboat then carried to the Christian graveyard. The burial was over in a matter of minutes, and the large crowd that had been together for the previous three days immediately dispersed.

I walked back to Long Nawang with Pa Ubang, feeling tired but much more confident about my position in the community. During the funeral I had taken the opportunity to ask the headman about guides to take me to Sarawak. I knew it would be days before I could expect a reply, so I settled down to making friends in Long Nawang.

Pa Ubang's father, Pa Deng Chok, was the next person to take an interest in me. He was seventy years old, and, like Pa Lenchau, he had such smiling eyes that I had to look closely to see if they were open. Pa Deng Chok, I later learned, had been watching how I acted in Kenyah company. Once he felt friendly towards me, our conversations took on a new depth. We began discussing supernaturalism. He slowly revealed his trust in me by describing the important omen birds and the basics of using fresh pig livers for divination. When divining the future the Kenyah are very practical. If the liver conveys bad omens, the men will sometimes blame the ignorant pig then try a new liver. I once watched as four consecutive pigs were cut open, until the proper omens were found.

I asked Pa Deng about dream interpretation, and one day he took me to the village *dayung* (shaman). When we entered the *dayung*'s room the man was seated on the floor with his eyes closed mumbling unrecognizable phrases. Facing him was a young girl of about twelve. Her parents and five or six other people sat nearby. On the floor was a brass tray with a trussed-up chicken and an old headhunting sword. On the flat side of the sword a chicken egg was somehow balanced on its end. We sat down, and Pa Deng explained that the *dayung* was in a trance, interpreting the girl's dream by speaking to the benevolent white goddess, Bungan Malan.

Pa Deng spoke quietly, "As long as the egg remains balanced, the interpretation can continue. When the egg falls over, contact with the spirit world is broken and the dream story stops."

I couldn't understand the Kenyah words, so I watched the egg. It refused to topple over. Several minutes passed, and the tension in the room increased. How long could the egg remain upright? The dogs moved about the room, the floorboards creaked, but the egg remained perfectly motionless. After another minute the egg seemed to relax. It rolled over onto its side, and the *dayung*'s droning stopped. I examined the sword and the egg later and could find no rational explanation for why the egg had remained upright.

Pa Deng and I spoke with the *dayung* about dream stones. He told me that sometimes when people awaken after a dream they discover a smooth brown stone the size of a thimble in their hands. This stone can give the person magical power or strength or can be used to tell the future. The person with the dream stone will go to the *dayung* and tell him the content of the dream. In a trance the *dayung* will hold the dream stone and give an interpretation.

Over the following days Pa Deng showed me some of his magic charms that he kept in a small fabric pouch. He laid them out on the floor and unwrapped each one. There was a deformed mouse-deer's horn, similar to a unicorn's, that he had found growing from the middle of the animal's head; a three-inch rattan segment that appeared to have grown in two directions at once; an irregular pig's tusk; and two curved black stones known as hook stones. The hook stones were set to one side, and the other items were rewrapped and returned to the pouch.

Pa Deng described where the first stone came from. In 1941 he had gone to the jungle to collect bamboo. He began splitting a length of it when his parang became jammed. He discovered the blade had lodged against a claw-shaped, black stone inside one of the bamboo segments.

Later, in a dream, a spirit spoke to Pa Deng, "There will be a rain of bullets (*hujan peluru*), but you will be untouched and will administer medicine, provided you keep the stone with you."

Pa Deng had been confused by this dream, until months later when the Japanese Imperial Army marched into Long Nawang by surprise and massacred all the Europeans who had sought refuge in this remote outpost at the beginning of the war.

The second hook stone had been passed down to him from his grandfather. In a dream a spirit had spoken with Pa Deng's grandfather and had told him he would be receiving a gift. Grandfather awoke perplexed and wondered about the meaning of the dream. He felt troubled, and so he took his dogs and went to the forest to hunt. The dogs pursued an animal, and when their drawn-out cries told him the quarry was at bay, he closed in. To his confusion he found his dogs in a circle, barking furiously, but there was no animal. Grandfather wondered about this strange behavior until he noticed a thin vine of rattan from which hung a hook-shaped black stone the size of his thumb. As soon as he touched the rock, the barking ceased and his dogs milled around his feet whining. He placed the rock in his dart quiver and returned home to tell his wife of the strange incident. Her first reaction was to ask where the meat was and where he had been for so many hours.

Later a spirit entered the body of a *dayung* and told Grandfather the meaning of the stone. "The hook shape means the charm will bring you luck. You are to save the stone and pass it down through your family. If you sell it or give it away, you will die."

♣   ♣   ♣

The significance of my participation in the funeral continued to be revealed by people's behavior. A man walked for two days to invite me to his village, and one evening two fathers presented their eligible daughters.

"Five months without a wife is too long," I was told.

I complimented these men on their beautiful daughters, but expressed concern that they were only about twelve or thirteen years old.

"Oh, don't worry about that," they reassured me, "they will grow up very soon." I got the distinct feeling these men were interested in having a motor mechanic in the family.

A group of older men at Nawang Baru reinforced my feelings of acceptance by including me in their private evening talks. They spoke Indonesian rather than Kenyah so I could participate. For the first time in many years I felt stimulated by the exclusive company of men. I listened to stories about a lost Hindu shrine. In the jungle there was a statue of Ganesh, whom they described as a seated fat man with an elephant's head. Then the subject of *palangs* (penis pins) came up. We touched on the matter lightly, and I was given directions to the hut of Pa PK, the local expert in these matters.

Pa PK was the *tukang palang* of Nawang Baru, the penis-pin craftsman of his village. Throughout the island people have been manufacturing and using a curious assortment of charms, potions, and other sex aids that can be traced back at least five hundred years. Most villages have one or more specialist at performing various operations and making some of the more sophisticated items of pleasure. Materials as varied as goat eyelashes, antique trade beads, feathers, knotted fishing line, and chicken bones are utilized to achieve maximum sexual pleasure.

I was invited to share a breakfast of rice and fish with Pa PK, and as we sat together I recalled an incident that had occurred a year earlier in the main reading room of the San Francisco Public Library. I had come across the following passage by Tom Harrisson in the *Sarawak Museum Journal* dated 1964: ". . . a cross piece driven through the male penis . . . the basic operation simply consists of driving a hole through the distal end of the penis: sometimes, for the determined, two (or more) holes at right angles. In this hole a small tube of bone, bamboo, or other material can be kept, so that the hole does not grow over and close. It is of no inconvenience once the initial pain of the operation — always done by experts from the lowlands — has been overcome.

"When this device is put into use, the owner adds whatever he prefers to elaborate and accentuate its intention. A lively range of objects can be so employed — from pig's bristles and bamboo shavings to pieces of metal, seeds, beads, and broken glass. The effect, of course, is to enlarge the diameter of the male organ inside the female, and so to produce accentuated points of friction, quite evidently giving a peculiar sort of sexual satisfaction to the female recipient."

I was astonished at what I read. What sort of community could encourage that practice, and why did they do it? Taking clues from footnotes and a brief bibliography, I decided to pursue the subject. As I read on, I wondered if they did it for the pain or it if was just another "proof of manhood" ritual? I was surprised to learn that the main reason the men used the *palang* was that the women insisted on it. Until as recently as the 1960s, a young man would not be considered as prime marriage material without one.

My reading indicated that some of the erotic devices were in common use well before the Portuguese began trading in Southeast Asia in the sixteenth century. In 1521 Pigafetta, who accompanied Magellan, noted, "The males large and small have pierced their member near the head from one side to the other with a device of gold or of tin as large as a goose quill. . . . They say that their women want it this way and that if they did otherwise would not copulate with them. These people use this because they are of a weak nature."

Further reading uncovered more facts. Miguel de Lorca in 1582 wrote, "They have a very abominable custom . . . they have the genital member pierced, and through the hole they put a dowell of tin on which they put a ring-like spur. They use 20 kinds. To discuss them would be immodest."

To sum up the European attitudes at the time, I refer to the famed *Boxer Codex* of 1590, translated by Carlos Quirino and Mauto Garcia (Philippines *Journal of Science*), ". . . and finally in the sin of the flesh, they are used to a thing which is the newest and never hitherto seen nor heard—which seems to be the guide to vice and bestiality that they have in this particular region. The men commonly place on their genital member a wheel or ring with round spurs. . . . Some wheels or rings are very large, there being more than 30 kinds, each with a different name, and in general a name sacred to their language . . . a custom invented by the Devil so that men may offend more with this vice our Lord God."

These accounts came from the southern Philippine islands — the area where these practices seem to have originated. Despite the claims of immodesty, weak moral fiber, and crimes against God, the use of these devices continued to spread . . . and for good reason. The women obviously enjoyed them greatly.

As far as sexual mutilations go, those practiced in Borneo seem pretty mild. They are for giving pleasure rather than preventing it. With the millions of genitally mutilated women now living in Africa and the Middle East (as the result of clitoridectomy and infibulation), it seems all the more remarkable that in Borneo it is the men who willingly undergo painful operations for the sole apparent purpose of pleasing women.

The earliest Borneo reference comes in 1847. Robert Burns,

a grandson of the famous Scottish poet and pioneer of European travel in many of the island areas, gives a very accurate account of the penis pin: "On males arriving at the age of puberty or more commonly before marriage, the Utang (palang) is adopted and without this marrige does not take place. It consists of a round ring (frequently two or three of wood, bone, brass or gold about an eighth of an inch in diameter) passed horizontally through the gland of the generative organ, and projects about a quarter of an inch on each side: when more than one is used they are placed transversely."

🌲　🌲　🌲

After breakfast Pa PK and I got up from our patch of sunshine and went to his room. I offered him rolling tobacco, which he placed in a brass tin. Continuing his work on a bamboo fish trap, he began to speak. "Before performing the *palang* operation, it is necessary for the man to stand in the river until his penis is shriveled up like a little boy's. Then the bamboo penis compressor (*katiputin*), with the two guide holes, is put in place. I then quickly push the sharpened iron rod through the flesh."

Upon hearing this I flinched slightly. "How many of these operations have you performed?" I asked.

"*Banyak!*" (many), he replied with pride.

In payment for such operations, Pa PK may receive a small gift of soap, fish, or tobacco. In many cases there was no charge. He considered his work a special sort of public service.

"One method of determining the length of a man's *palang*," Pa PK continued, "is to measure the length of the second joint of his thumb. The *palang* should be about half an inch longer."

I cast furtive glances around the room, casually comparing thumbs. Then Pa PK proudly stated that he had not one, but two, *palangs*, placed at right angles. "Just like the four-bladed propeller on the monthly missionary plane," he explained as he held his hands together in prayer. I wondered if this could be a new development on the standard missionary position.

I commissioned Pa PK to make a set of *palangs* for me, and he gladly accepted the task. Every time he saw me during the week it took to complete the *palangs*, he inquired as to when I would be having the operation performed.

"Perhaps tomorrow," I would reply, "when the water in the river is colder."

On my way across the island I had collected similar stories, and I delighted Pa Lenchau and Pa Ibo Usat with descriptions of sex aids I had learned about in different communities in Borneo. These stories were much more amusing to them than the *palang* stories with which they were so familiar. I think some of them may even be true.

The Bahau River villagers are given credit for initiating the practice of creating raised scars on the uppermost surface of the head of the penis. The technique is not widespread, but was traditionally performed by the individual on his own penis. A series of longitudinal incisions were made with a sharp knife. The cuts were then rubbed with ash to create as much scar tissue as possible. It is more common now to visit a government dispensary so that the incisions (usually three to five) can be made by a doctor using an anesthetic. The hospital method involves suturing up the incisions in such a way as to create the raised parallel ridges.

Months earlier Muhammad Aidid had revealed to me the secrets of *mata kambing*, as well as *minyak lintah* — the leech oil. The second procedure is very involved and doesn't attract many users for reasons that will soon become obvious. Take two or three large buffalo leeches and drop them into a small amount of coconut oil; seal in a vial and place in the sun for approximately two to three months, or until the leeches are completely dissolved. Some impatient individuals try to hasten the process by frying the leeches in oil; however, that is not the recommended method if one wants to obtain the maximum effect. When the oil is ready, take some stalks of the sharp-edged buffalo grass and lightly score the penis along its entire length until it is reddened and bleeds a little. This is to allow the oil to penetrate. Then smear the penis with the leech oil and cover with a section of bamboo of the desired length and diameter. Fasten the bamboo around the waist with a string and keep in place for about a week.

The penis will permanently swell to fill the inside of the bamboo. One must remember to pierce the bamboo at the end to allow free urination. The theory is that the tissues of the leech will pass on to the tissues of the penis the ability to grow many times their original size.

Mata kambing, literally the eye of the goat, is mainly used by the coastal Malays and Iban. From a freshly killed goat you carefully cut out the eyelash and surrounding connective tissue. When detached, it forms a natural ring with the upper and lower bristly eyelashes radiating outwards. You stretch this over a stick about the same circumference as your penis. Then let it dry. Directions for use: First soak the *mata kambing* in warm water until soft and pliable. Then slip it over the head of the penis. It should fit snugly without cutting off circulation. This goat eyelash tickler is also available commercially and comes wrapped in a white packet with blue printing: Love's Magic Ring — Potent to Man, Joy to Woman. It can be purchased in the coastal bazaars in three convenient sizes: small, medium, and large. It lasts about one year with normal use.

Despite the ingenuity that leads to the creation of fishing-line ticklers embellished with wooden beads and exotic bird feathers, the village people appeared sexually conventional in most other ways. There seemed to be little if any interest in masturbation or prostitution. Homosexuality does not seem to be practiced. Abortion and contraception are not problems — everyone apparently wants children. It is not uncommon for a woman to have six to eight children, and breastfeeding is likely the only form of contraception. The occurrence of venereal disease is infrequent, and rape is a crime that these people barely know about.

♠   ♠   ♠

These evening talks with the men provided me with a sense of relief, a sense of being in a place where people were concerned about me. During the daytime I would walk through the village and visit with the women and the children as they worked. With my new name and new friends, I realized, at last, that I was safe in Nawang Baru and that my days of fear in the rain forest had come to an end.

INTERLUDE · THE PENANCE OF LONG LEBUSON, A ROYAL WELCOME

I STAYED in Long Nawang and Nawang Baru for several weeks trying to arrange guides to take me over the mountains to Sarawak, but there were innumerable delays that prevented me from leaving. While I waited for new travel opportunities to present themselves, I decided to make a two-week journey through the headwaters of the Mahakam River to search for *gaharu* and the alluvial gold found in the small streams that flow south into Sungai Ogah. I wasn't willing to risk a third visit to the villages on the upper Kayan River, so I flew over those villages in the mission plane from Long Nawang to Mahak Baru. From Mahak Baru I proceeded overland. First to Long Lebuson, then west, returning to Nawang Baru by way of Sungai Temaha, Sungai Metulang, and Sungai Nawang. This journey was made remarkable by an incident that I witnessed on a tributary of the upper Boh River.

Word had spread through the forest: The plane was coming back. Days before the droning sound of the red-and-white, single-engine missionary plane could be heard over the jungle canopy, the people of Long Lebuson were on their hands and knees carefully manicuring the 500-foot-long grass runway with curved, 3-inch-long grass-cutting knives. They were performing penance by transforming the overgrown clearing into a perfect stretch of suburban lawn suitable for croquet and cement garden gnomes. The people worked with the devotion of cargo cultists, pausing only occasionally to look up through the opening in the rain forest, hoping the plane would come soon. Heat waves rippled the ground as sweat rolled off brown-skinned Protestant and Roman Catholic noses. With my eyes closed, the barely audible ripping sounds from dozens of grass knives reminded me of cattle grazing. The air was filled with the smell of hot, freshly cut grass.

Two months earlier a young boy had thrown a grass bomb at the regular mission plane as it was taking off. The harmless clod of soil and grass missed by a wide margin, but the pilot had noticed the childish gesture, and it was decided at the coastal head office to teach the people of Long Lebuson a Christian lesson. Air service to the village was immediately suspended. When I arrived in the village by dugout canoe, the people had run out of salt, fuel, and medicine; they had not received mail for eight weeks.

It is a six-week, one-way journey to the coastal markets from Long Lebuson, and there was talk about organizing a major expedition to provision the village if the flights weren't resumed. In the past people had organized their trade journeys in accordance with the uncertainties and time involved in going to the coast and returning by longboat. In recent years, however, the villagers had become reliant on the grace of Mission Aviation Fellowship (MAF). They were now learning a painful lesson: The MAF giveth, and the MAF taketh away. Deprived of vital supplies, as well as accustomed luxuries such as sugar, candy, cigarettes, infant formulas, and soda crackers, the villagers were suffering. The prolonged punishment was excessive and completely contrary to their customary laws, which would have resolved the issue within a few hours. Who were these white people who treated the Kenyah like children? There was a lot of unspoken resentment; revenge was inevitable.

Shortly after my arrival, word reached us from Mahak Baru that the plane was coming in two days. The village would be officially pardoned, so final preparations were made to receive the honored guests. The plane arrived late one morning. Pilot Ian had brought his wife, Julie, their child Janie, and Ian's seventy-year-old parents, who were visiting from Fort Worth, Texas. Michael had stayed behind in Long Bia.

The royal welcome began on the grass runway, where the entire village had gathered. The heat was ferocious. First, a bamboo flute, drum, and homemade guitar ensemble honored the guests with a few tunes. Then the handshaking commenced. Several hundred people lined up between the river and the longhouse, and the visitors were obliged to shake everyone's hand — not once, but several times, because those at the head of the line re-formed at the rear.

The white-skinned entourage lurched into the longhouse an hour later, after shaking more than a thousand hands. Lunch was served, but rather than a communal meal, the guests were invited to enjoy their meal as hundreds of villagers jammed into the room and settled down to the elaborate Asian pastime of staring at Westerners and commenting upon every nuance of gesture. This gawking behavior, so utterly contrary to my experience of local hospitality, confirmed my suspicions that something was afoot.

I accepted an invitation to join the meal and noticed that during lunch there was no dialogue between the guests and the Kenyah. I knew how little it would take to make everyone relax, but I didn't feel it proper to intervene. This was a matter between Mission Aviation Fellowship and Long Lebuson, so I left them to it. I felt sorry for Ian for having to bear the burden of an arbitrary administrative decision. After lunch I excused myself and took an afternoon nap.

Six hours later I returned to see how things were progressing. The family was backed against a wall by a growing crowd of spectators. I knew that Ian and Julie spoke some Indonesian, but apparently there had been little conversation. I checked in again at 10:00 P.M. and saw that Ian's father had finally taken positive action: he was fast asleep on the floor. His poor wife had managed to remain in an upright position, but continually nodded off. I couldn't bear to watch any more, so I said good night and went to bed. I was told later that the guests of honor had been put through their paces by performing solo dances and songs for the entire village until 2:00 A.M. The MAF administrators on the coast were responsible for this fiasco. They created this situation weeks earlier with their insensitive handling of the grass-bomb incident. I sympathized with Ian and his family, but there was little I could do to make things easier for them.

Back in Long Bia, when we were dismantling the airplane engine, Ian had told me his story. He had been a U.S. Navy pilot in Vietnam and had survived two hundred bombing runs over North Vietnam. Not until his return to the United States did he fully realize what he had done to the people in the jungle villages. Ian became a Christian; then he discovered MAF. His work in East Kalimantan was, I suspect, an attempt to make up for all those bombs. Considering our backgrounds, I found it a strange irony that Ian and I should meet in central Borneo. Both of us were set in motion by the war in Southeast Asia. Ian enlisted. I left the country several weeks before an FBI agent arrived at my parents' front door.

☙ ☙ ☙

The following afternoon the festivities continued. The two rival churches (Protestant and Roman Catholic) decided to have a longboat race on the muddy Sungai Lebuson. Sensibly dressed in stitched-leaf, wide-brimmed sun hats, the village people formed small friendly groups along the river bank or beneath the shade of the river trees. The guests were seated comfortably on a log with a good vantage point.

Two brightly painted, 18-man longboats were haphazardly drifting downstream when, without warning, the paddles churned the water and the longboats streaked downriver. There was yelling, cheering, splashing, and a terrific thumping of paddles against the wooden hulls as the Protestant boat scored a narrow victory. After a short rest the boats were turned around and raced upstream. Again the men furiously churned the warm, brown water to a froth as the two boats dashed for the non-existent finish line. Surging through the water, the men were bursting with vitality and pride, but just as the Roman Catholic longboat was about to take the lead, the alert Protestant congregation prematurely declared victory for themselves by breaking into wild applause. Competition longboat racing (an introduced sport) is relatively new, and the rules haven't been firmly established. General shouting marks the start, and resounding applause signals the finish. Common consent determines the winner, but, of course, the spectators are seldom in agreement with each other.

The regatta continued. Pa Bit, a member of the Roman Catholic longboat crew, put forth the suggestion that although the Protestant boat was obviously faster, the real issue of church supremacy should be determined by the strength of the men. Representatives of the rival congregations agreed and decided that the contestants should switch longboats. They did so, and the matter was quickly resolved with a third win by the Protestants. The third win marked the end of the older men's competition, and I must say at this point that there was a noticeable amount of ill feeling towards the Protestant paddlers.

The older men were soon replaced by swaggering younger fellows with special broad-bladed racing paddles slung over their shoulders. Taunting each other, they waded out to the longboats to show the young women and God what they could do. What they lacked in finesse, they more than compensated for in power. Paddles were lost in a blur of arms and frothing water, and the Roman Catholic crew scored a stunning victory. But they had cheated. There had been an extra paddler in the longboat. The offending paddler removed himself. The boats raced again, and the Roman Catholics lost.

For one congretation to have scored so many wins was clearly unacceptable to the crowd. The riverbanks emptied as men, women, and children splashed through the shallows grabbing boats, paddles, arms, and legs in the attempt to establish their own church's superiority. For the next hour the races continued sporadically until every possible combination of crew had scored such a confusing assortment of wins and losses in each other's boats that the real winner was unknown. Eventually the crowd lost interest. The important goal had been achieved: everyone felt victorious.

In the afternoon Ian accepted a formal apology for the grass bomb. The guilty boy apologized, and everyone wore a solemn face for the occasion. The villagers desperately wanted the plane service resumed. Ian agreed to resume flights, and soon the plane was ready for the return flight. The little red-and-white Cessna flew away loaded with wild fruit, necklaces, ceremonial swords, sugarcane, and trussed chickens. Such was the generosity of the people that a large pile of food and gifts had to be left behind because of weight limitations for takeoff. The people were satisfied: they had subtly extracted their revenge, and the plane would come back. Moments after takeoff the mission plane buzzed the village, dipped its wings, and disappeared over the jungle to the east. The sound of the plane grew indistinct. Only then did it occur to me that although the people of Long Lebuson had been pardoned, they still didn't have any salt, fuel, medicine, or mail. The plane had arrived empty.

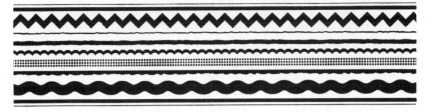

Y OUR PATH is like a river," said Ibu Iting, holding my hand by the light of a kerosene lamp and caressing the lines on my palm with her fingertips. It was nice to be touched like that by a 60-year-old woman, and my mind flitted from the meaning of her words to the sensation of having my hand stroked so nicely.

"*Tuan*," she continued, "do you see this second line below your fingers? It travels the entire width of your palm, through many areas of confusing smaller lines. This line is your life path. The smaller lines are your obstacles. Like the rapids in a river, they cause turbulence, but your path extends through the difficulties, and you attain your goals. The line also extends around to the back of your hand. This means you will have a long life journey. You have trouble making up your mind, but once you see your goal there is nothing that can stop you. In your hand I see the sign of blind determination and courage. You take risks. You like to cause mischief."

Ibu Iting went on to read my thumb and toes. "The back of your thumb has four deep lines. These are your children. You will have four sons. And here (taking my right foot in her hand), your first and second toes on both feet are grown together as far as the first joint. This means your mother will die before your father." I wasn't sure about those last two comments, but her observations about determination and mischief were to stick in my mind.

Later that night Pa Ubang, Ibu Iting's son, returned to the longhouse with bad news. On his face was a look of total resignation. He ate his meal of fish and rice then came over to where I was seated by the fire.

"Mr. Eric," he said with a sad face, "we have a problem. I think the big longboat has been taken by men from another village. If this is so, we cannot go to Sarawak to find work, and you cannot go back to your home. I promised you, and now I am very ashamed."

"Which village is trying to get the boat?" I asked.

"You will be angry, Mr. Eric."

"Which village?" I asked again.

"Long Uro," came the reply.

"Long Uro?" I exclaimed in amazement. I couldn't believe what I had heard. The words tumbled around in my head like two bricks in a cement mixer. I felt defeated. Would I ever be able to extricate myself from the clutches of that village which lay half a day's walk from the village of Long Nawang where I now was. Suddenly I felt light-headed. I got to my feet and walked to the end of the longhouse room. The floorboards creaked and bounced on the hardwood joists as I paced up and down the darkened room trying to sort out the implications of what Pa Ubang had said. He was right about one thing: I was angry. In fact, I was totally pissed off.

Looking back, I can see my anger in this situation was unfair. I was still reacting to the *bali saleng* incident that had frightened me so badly and destroyed my sense of safety. It took years for me to settle my mind about what happened that day in Long Uro. Eventually I was able to understand that the men who had thrown me to the ground and pulled my pack apart were victims of their own fears and fantasies. They weren't intentionally malicious towards me, but at the time the attack occurred it was quite impossible for me to step back and look at the situation rationally. When I heard they were claiming the longboat, my own fear and resentment made me respond with anger.

There was also a practical problem created by this competition for the longboat. Very few locals travel to Sarawak from the Apo Kayan, and if I missed this opportunity I might be stranded in the highlands for months. I was anxious to complete my second crossing of the island, and perhaps this made me respond in an overly aggressive manner. And then on the everyday, childish level, I just wanted to get even with those bastards. I would have to act quickly, though. I would have to force myself to do something I have never been good at — taking positive and immediate direct action.

I might have been overreacting, but I suspected the men in Long Uro were partially motivated by a desire to put me in my place — a little farewell gesture to humiliate me in public.

Pa Ubang and his parents had not seen me like this. I had rarely felt so angry in my entire life, but there I was, hyperventilating and muttering to myself in English and Indonesian, gesturing with my hands as I spoke. Pa Ubang seemed willing to accept the situation, and in Kenyah fashion masked his deeper feelings. I could not follow his example; then I remembered the lines on my hand and Ibu Iting's comments: You are determined; . . . nothing can stop you once you make up your mind; you like to create mischief.

Mischief? Right! A devious plan began to form in my brain. By the time I sat down on the floor next to a bemused Pa Ubang, I could see my goal. We would get the boat and travel over the mountains to Sarawak. I visualized the scenario then worked out the practical details with Pa Ubang.

He quickly described what had happened earlier that day. Eleven men from Long Uro wanted to go to Sarawak to work and had claimed rights to the big cargo boat we wanted because some of them had originally brought the boat from Sarawak two years earlier. Actual ownership, I noted, was credited to people in Long Sungai Barang, Cynthia's village. Long Uro had asked to use the boat, and that request had been tentatively accepted by the owners. At this point the people of Long Sungai Barang were unaware of our interest in their longboat.

"What can we do to get the boat?" I asked Pa Ubang.

"We would have to make a better offer to Long Sungai Barang for the longboat, and we would have to pay the Kommandan

Polici and the Camat (District Officer) for permits and a Letter of Clearance for each man. There is a quota system for the number of workers that can go to Sarawak. Only one group can go at a time. First you need a boat; then you can get a permit. We don't have a boat or enough money for the necessary bribes, so it impossible for us to go before the men from Long Uro."

"How much money do we need to get the permits and the boat?" I asked.

My alternatives were to fly down to the east coast of Kalimantan on a mission plane and face the immigration officials, or somehow find another group of Penan to walk me over the mountains to Sarawak. That trip could take months, and I wanted to avoid the experience of walking back to the coast. I knew the villagers' intended journey by longboat was my best chance; I didn't feel like being patient.

"How much?" I repeated to Pa Ubang.

"The Kommandan Polici will ask ten thousand rupiahs for each man's Letter of Clearance, and the Camat would need at least five to ten thousand rupiahs for the permit. Then we would have to give something valuable to the headman in Long Sungai Barang. Something very valuable and unobtainable."

Visions of shotgun shells danced in my head. Compared to some of my other Indonesian experiences, this situation did not seem hopeless. Money was the problem, and I felt there was a likelihood the boat would go to the highest bidder. I was willing to exchange whatever I had for the pleasure of paddling down the Kayan River waving goodby to the men from Long Uro. I relished the possibility of seeing the incredulity on their faces.

"Pa Ubang," I suggested, "this is what I think we should do. Tomorrow send someone secretly to Long Sungai Barang to find out what Long Uro has offered for the longboat. Have him tell the headman that we want the boat and that I am willing to pay twenty shotgun shells and two jerry cans of gasoline. Also, give me the names of the men from Long Nawang and Nawang Baru who want to go to Sarawak. I will talk to the Kommandan Polici and the Camat tomorrow."

"Yes, *Tuan*, but who will pay?"

"I will pay for the permit and the letters. Do you think this is a good plan?"

"Oh, I think that would be a wonderful idea." Pa Ubang was excited now. "Would you really do that?"

"It would be my pleasure," I assured him, "but if we are successful with this plan, no one must know how we got the boat until after we leave."

Pa Ubang was positively beaming with delight at the thought of putting one over on the people from Long Uro. There was a small chance, of course, that I had been set up by Pa Ubang, but it didn't matter. I was locked into a game of wits with these master schemers, and that was motivation enough to sustain me. It was a strange thing that I was in their yard, playing their game with their rules; and yet from the start I had a very strong suspicion we would get the longboat.

To a casual observer the next few days would have seemed uneventful. The people in Long Nawang and Long Sungai Barang went about their usual tasks. The women pounded rice with five-foot-long hardwood poles, and the men cut timber and collected rattan in the jungle. Behind the scenes, however, quiet talks were being conducted up and down the Kayan River. Four days later the arrangements had been made. Fifty thousand rupiahs ($77 U.S.), forty rounds of shotgun shells, ten gallons of gasoline, and three hundred sticks of chewing tobacco secretly changed hands, and we obtained our permits. A day later our runner returned from Long Sungai Barang with news: the longboat was ours. While we were making plans for our departure, the men from Long Uro arrived in Long Nawang. They were greeted hospitably, and no antagonism was shown by any of us. With an air of barely concealed confidence and arrogance, they examined the longboat then leisurely set about planning their imminent departure.

At first they were dumbfounded by not being able to get permits. The Kommandan Polici was unable to offer suggestions or to clarify the situation, and the Camat had unexpectedly gone hunting for a few days. No one else was talking, which immediately aroused their suspicions. Their confusion changed to outrage when with apparent innocence we began work on the boat. A protest was lodged with the *kepala aɔat*, and we stopped work, but only briefly. The dispute was soon settled with the arrival of five men from Long Sungai Barang. They confirmed our arrangements for the longboat, and there was nothing the men from Long Uro could do. This maneuver might set them back two to three weeks, until another boat could be arranged. It was bad enough that they had lost the rights to the longboat, but what really bothered them, I suspect, was the fact that they knew I was somehow involved.

One of the rumors that circulated was that I had paid the headman of Long Sungai Barang forty thousand rupiahs for the boat. Another story suggested that the people from Long Uro were not good Christians and were being punished by Jesus. The church members from Long Uro periodically went on tour up and down the Kayan river, performing religious skits for the other villages. They considered themselves to be better Christians, but the *bali ɔaleng* incident had revealed their lack of true faith. Many people felt they deserved to lose the boat. The village skeptics were amused. I feigned total ignorance.

I knew the true story would come out eventually, but by then we would be in Sarawak, paddling down flower-scented waterways with the smell of barbecued pork on our fingers. Meanwhile, I was safe in Long Nawang. The Kommandan Polici had heard of the *bali ɔaleng* incident and knew what might happen to me if the men of Long Uro caught me alone in the jungle. He therefore agreed to give us a week's head start before issuing the travel permits to the men from Long Uro. Because they eventually made arrangements to travel in two lightweight longboats, there was a slim chance they might overtake us, but I put that thought out of my mind and concentrated on preparing for what would be my last journey through the rain forest.

As soon as the dispute was settled, we set about repairing the longboat for the journey over the mountains. A longboat over the mountains? Wait a minute. My map showed a low pass at 4,500 feet, but surely we weren't going to haul a one-ton boat and 1,500 pounds of equipment over those slippery, densely forested slopes. Or were we?

I had by now been introduced to the eight men and three young women who would make the trip with me. I was having a terrible time remembering names. There were the following:

Pa Ubang Deng and his daughter Ros Ubang
Pa Bia Den and his wife, Isteri Lang
Pa Ulay Arang
Pa Awang Arang
Pa Jugeh Taseh
Pa Angin Arang and his wife, Isteri Iting
Pa Bit Ibau
Pa Gong Jalong, a student

In Indonesia it is a sign of respect to refer to a man as *Pa* (Father) and a woman as *Ibu* (Mother), so I called all the men *Pa* until I could associate their names with their personalities. Like Pa Lampung Padan, they were making the journey to Sarawak to find work and purchase goods that are unobtainable in the highlands.

For more than a year the 40-foot longboat had been stored out of the weather in a shed just above the highwater mark on the riverbank. The longboat was heavy with damp, and it was with some difficulty that the eight locals and I dragged it down to the gravel riverbed and turned it upside down to dry in the sun. The four-foot-wide hull had been made from a single trunk of *meranti merah* (*Dipterocarpeae ʃhorea*), the best timber for boat building. Each side of the boat was built up with two overlapping hand-hewn planks that ran its entire length and were clinched to the hull with long steel nails. There were no seats, but duckboards covered the middle two-thirds of the longboat.

Our first job was to pound strips of cloth and cardboard into the cracks in the hull. Two-inch-wide strips of thin metal sheeting were placed over the cracks and nailed along each edge to form a durable patch. Then the inside seams between the planks were caulked with a sticky, fibrous tree bark. The men prepared a combination of tree resin and motor oil. This mixture was boiled down to a puttylike consistency, and when it was cool, but still quite sticky, we pressed it over the caulking to make the seams waterproof. New ribs were added, with sectional braces to stiffen the boat for the long overland journey.

Next the hull was turned right side up and set upon a bed of dry banana leaves. I was alarmed when Pa Awang set fire to the leaves with his lighter and the boat disappeared in a tremendous wall of smoke and flames. Had they lost their senses? I watched as my fifty thousand rupiahs went up in flames. Finally the smoke cleared, and there was the longboat: black as a cinder, but otherwise undamaged. We then planed the hull with our parangs to remove all the burrs and splinters. This burning/scraping procedure made the hull smooth, so the boat would move through the water more easily. The burning also helped to get rid of excess moisture, thereby reducing the weight of the longboat.

Pa Ulay and Pa Awang were in charge of the repairs. They were meticulous in organizing the work, a fact that was brought home to me when I observed their thoughtful planning in the precise placement of the longboat on the wide riverbed. When we began work in the early mornings it was light and cool on the gravel, but just as the heat of the day began, the shade of the river trees reached out to protect us from the sun. We worked only until eleven o'clock, when a picnic lunch of steamed rice and vegetables was brought down from the longhouse. Different families took turns preparing the midday meal. After lunch everyone drifted off, to do other work or to take naps, as was the usual custom. I would swim in the Kayan river or visit my friend Pa Lenchau in the nearby village of Nawang Baru.

As we finished lunch one day, Pa Ubang helped me make a list of things to bring on the trip. I had never traveled overland with so many people and didn't know what to expect. In addition to the gratuities to the Kommandan Polici, the Camat, and the headman of Long Sungai Barang, I wanted to contribute to the general expenses.

Counting on his fingers, Pa Ubang dictated the essentials as I wrote them down in the back of my journal. I would need a ten-day supply of salt for twelve people, about eight blocks or ten pounds; two hundred sticks of *sugee* (Lombok brand chewing tobacco); a 12-foot-by-7-foot stitched-leaf raincover for the sleeping shelter; farewell photographs of each man and his family; fourteen fishhooks; my share of rice: forty-five *moks*, or three *gantangs*, which equal twenty-three pounds; two bottles of *arak* for the farewell; four bottles of *arak* for the arrival in Long Busong, the first village in Sarawak; five bamboo sections of pig fat for cooking; four bars of Sunlight laundry soap; seven packages of clove cigarettes; and my remaining ten shotgun shells.

"Fine," I said, scribbling down the last items, "but, Pa Ubang, if we aren't taking a shotgun to Sarawak, what are the shotgun shells for?"

"The shotgun shells?" he smiled. "They're your gift to me."

I agreed to this "tip," knowing that some of the permit money had already found its way into Pa Ubang's hands. But what was I to do? Was I expecting a firm handshake and a formal thank-you for the permits and the letters? In the United States a similar situation might have made me angry, but here in rural Indonesia I simply accepted the most obvious facts and didn't fall into the futile game of trying to find out what was really going on. We had the boat and the permits; that's all I cared about. Pa Ubang's need for my goods was certainly no greater than my need for his expertise. We each understood that.

Work on the longboat was finished the evening of the fourth day, and by that time the men from Long Uro were sullenly working on two derelict longboats. I avoided all contact with them and was grateful for our five-day head start.

We left Long Nawang the morning of 22 November 1982. The longboat, built for eight men, was dangerously overloaded as it sat in the shallows tied to a tree. There were twelve adults traveling, plus two hunting dogs. For the eleven Kenyah villagers this day marked the beginning of their *peselai*, the long journey.

These people might be gone for years, and I would probably never return. There were tearful farewells at every landing stage. First we headed upriver. Flowers, food, and other bon voyage presents were exchanged, and at Nawang Baru Pa Lenchau was waiting for me. He looked peaceful and composed at the edge of the river. He tied two antique trade beads from his family cradle board to my wrist so that I would come back to the Apo Kayan. He was a sweet, smiling old man who looked at me with dancing eyes and grinned. He knew and I knew that he was largely responsible for saving me weeks earlier, but we didn't talk about it, and he didn't attempt to express his feelings with words. Before I got back into the boat he simply said, "Goodby, *Tuan*, safe journey." I knew that I would never see him again, and that made me sad.

One of the difficulties of my trip was this continual saying goodby to friends. I was never in one place long enough to enjoy a sustained friendship, and I found that frustrating. I would meet someone I liked, and within a day we could be great friends. The next day I might be gone. But there were some obvious advantages to this situation. The knowledge that I would soon be leaving intensified the quality of the relationships. I wouldn't waste my time with people who didn't interest me or who were a drain on my energy. It was a valuable lesson. How quickly I fell back into bad habits when the trip was over.

Rice wine and *arak* were offered to us at every landing stage in Nawang Baru, and as we came downriver for the last time before our departure, we stopped for a second goodby where friends had gathered at the riverside in Long Nawang. By now the children were wailing and the wives and older relatives began to cry. The dogs howled, and in their excitement furious fights erupted. Roosters began to crow, and the final departure from Long Nawang collapsed into total pandemonium. In the end even the men from Long Uro couldn't resist seeing us off. It was a grand spectacle as we drunkenly passed beneath the great 200-foot steel-cable suspension bridge that spanned the river. We were all overbalancing, and the impossibly large jumble of cargo piled amidships threatened to overturn the longboat. We reached midstream and began to pick up speed. People on shore laughed and ran along the riverbank waving and calling their last farewells. The longboat slipped around the first bend in the river, and suddenly, apart from the rush of water against the hull, there was silence. We had left, but it took me perhaps a quarter of an hour to comprehend fully that I was in motion again. My journey seemed so effortless at times like this. I was always quick to forget the exhausting slog, the uncertainties, and the preparations that led to these moments. I surveyed the muddy river and felt as if I were flying.

Everyone settled into place, and the baggage was tied into the boat with thin strips of rattan in case of a capsize. Pa Jugeh selected his paddle and moved to the stern to steer. The young men provided the muscle power at the bow while the more-seasoned boatmen took their places between Pa Jugeh and the baggage. A light afternoon rain shower cooled us as we drifted and paddled down the greenish-brown Kayan River. The sun was soon out again, and when it became uncomfortably hot in midstream, we kept to the shade of the big river trees.

The dogs stood on top of the pile of supplies, eagerly sniffing the air for the first scent of wild game. The thick aroma of clove cigarettes mixed with the sweet fragrance of jungle flowers. After an hour we arrived at Sungai Pernasi and began to pole the boat up that tributary. Branches met overhead and created a cool, green shade. The air was noticeably fresher and the water perfectly clear. Birds were occasionally heard, but the general mood was one of peace. We all were lost in our own thoughts as we moved upstream through the overhanging forest. The only sounds came from the boat poles bumping the hull and the gentle rush of water. Late in the afternoon the longboat was eased into the gravel bank, and without discussion we set about making camp and cooking rice. Two of the men went off with the *jalla* to catch fish. Within forty-five minutes we were sitting down to our evening meal. This was to be our routine for the next ten days.

Most of us were coughing and sniffling from chest and head colds, and that night we talked about *uap* (steam) and disease. The dry season was just ending, and with the arrival of regular nightly rains, the floor of the forest was blanketed in rising steam. It is believed that the *uap* carries illness from the ground and that until the ground has been thoroughly cleansed (once the rainy season is well established) people will continue to get sick.

Each day the river became narrower and more shallow, and soon we were only knee-deep in the rapids, hauling the longboat upstream over the slippery rocks and fallen logs. By this time I had developed a bad cold, my hands were blistered from the poling, and the soles of my feet were bruised from the effort of dragging the boat mile after mile over sharp river rocks. Quite literally I wasn't pulling my own weight, so I decided to make things easier for the men by walking along the river bank, but there was nowhere to walk. The banks came down to the river at a steep angle, and if I had ventured into the jungle, I would have become lost. After an hour of stumbling along in the shallows, I rejoined my companions and the longboat. There at least I had something to hold onto.

In the middle of one particularly difficult section, where the river was choked with boulders, Pa Ulay called out to the others to stop for a moment. It appeared that there was something wrong with his foot. Everyone paused as the wild torrent thundered beneath the boat and around our bare legs. Pa Ulay calmly reached into the water while still maintaining his hold on the boat and grabbed a 12-inch fish that he had inadvertently trapped between the rocks with his foot. He flipped it into the longboat as if this were his usual way of catching fish. I'm certain everyone was astounded, but no one reacted to the remarkable incident.

We continued to haul the boat, and as we worked our way upstream, the dogs combed either side of the river trying to detect the scent of game. The men whistled and called to the dogs to keep them within hearing distance, and occasionally we stopped to listen to the tone of the dog barks. The dogs will let out a distinctive bay when they have located an animal, and the men respond with a whoop to let the dogs know they are on the way. With the exception of large boars, two good hunting dogs can pull down any animal or chase it back towards the waiting men.

Pa Ubang and I were washing our clothes in the river one afternoon when the long drawn-out howl of a hunting dog reached us. "Jep," said Pa Ubang, immediately recognizing his dog's voice. The other men were fishing upstream beyond hearing distance, and in a moment Pa Ubang put a spear in my hands, and we were dashing through the forest towards Jep's now-frantic barking. I had never been able to keep up the chase before. Either I would run the wrong way or fall down long before the game was cornered. This time Pa Ubang crashed through the undergrowth calling to his dog and with me right behind him. Leaves slapped my face, and thorns raked my legs, but I stayed on my feet.

We were quickly gaining on the unseen animal when suddenly through the trees there was a flash of movement, and Pa Ubang accelerated ahead of me, leaving me temporarily alone. Pa Ubang's second dog had arrived moments before, and as I stumbled onto the scene, Jep took the giant deer by the throat and brought it to the ground. The deer had a full set of antlers and was immediately on its feet again. Ignoring the dogs, the deer went for Pa Ubang, who was ready with his spear, sinking it into the deer's shoulder, but a flurry of vicious thrashing kicks knocked him flat. The dogs sank their teeth into the deer's haunches, and in the ensuing scuffle of legs, teeth, antlers, and flailing hooves I realized I was standing there like a dumb spectator while Pa Ubang was in trouble. Still I hesitated; then everything shifted into slow motion.

I felt as detached from the scene as if I were watching a movie. Pa Ubang's hands went up to protect himself, and my own hands tightened on the spear shaft. Dogs, man, and wounded deer blended into one. In a dream I saw myself step forward and ram the spear tip into the deer's side. It slid in easily, and I pressed the shaft home. Hooves flashed by, and the life went out of the animal. It was so simple. The dogs backed off, and Pa Ubang sat up. I looked at him and the dogs and realized we were all panting heavily. I had never killed an animal with a spear, and at that moment it felt like a very sophisticated weapon.

I held the bloodied spear and remembered the childhood games in my parents' yard: the imaginary animals and my fantasy jungle. What I had felt as I stalked the camellia bushes with my bamboo spear was the natural instinct to hunt. That sensation had been repressed at an early age, and not until I stood with Pa Ubang panting beside the deer carcass did I fully recall that feeling: the urge to hunt. At that moment the physical sensation of being a hunter hit me with its full force. Only then did I understand why these people preferred to hunt with spears and dogs rather than with guns. Guns are impersonal. Anyone can pull a trigger. By hunting with a spear the hunter is giving the animal a chance. It may be a small chance, but the accompanying element of doubt created for me, at least, the most exquisite sensation of being drawn back into man's past.

"*Tuan*, you have killed the *payau*. I thought you would never move. You waited for the last moment," Pa Ubang's voice broke into my thoughts.

I glanced at his legs and was shocked. They looked as though someone had taken a cricket bat to his shins. The skin was broken in many places, and massive swelling had already started. His legs would soon be an ugly mass of black-and-blue lumps. I apologized for my hesitation and said that I hadn't known what to do.

"*Tidak apa* (it's all right), Mr. Eric," said Pa Ubang. "The bones are not broken, and I can walk."

We dragged the carcass to a nearby stream and butchered it. When Pa Ubang disemboweled the carcass, he removed the penis and set it aside. I had never seen that done before, and was surprised that it was more than a foot long. Pa Ubang told me that it would be sold to a Chinese pharmacist downriver.

"What for?"

"For deer-penis whiskey," he replied nonchalantly. "The Chinese and Malays believe that by strengthening the kidneys a man increases his sexual appetite. Deer-penis whiskey is for strengthening the kidneys."

It wasn't until months later that I confirmed this story in a shop in San Francisco's Chinatown. The man behind the glass-topped counter filled with dishes of unrecognizable medicines gave me a recipe for deer-penis whiskey. "Take one dried deer penis (nine to twelve inches long) and slice thinly. Soak the slices in whiskey or brandy for forty to sixty days. Strain. Drink one shot-glassful per day until vitality is restored."

⚵   ⚵   ⚵

After five days' travel, the stream became so small we could no longer travel along it. We had come to the end of Sungai Pernasi. We unloaded the boat, and for the first time I heard to name of our next destination — Sawak Iran Pass. I felt grave misgivings about this stage of our journey. Moving through the rain forest is tremendously difficult with just a small backpack; now we were faced with the challenge of hauling a 40-foot longboat weighing nearly a ton over a mountain pass to the first stream in Sarawak. The boat was cumbersome, slippery, full of splinters, and with ease could crush toes and fingers against rocks and logs.

We shoved the longboat out of the riverbed and began hauling it through the jungle. A pathway was cut, and log skids were placed along the jungle floor. We made good progress for more than a mile on the slight incline. The hours passed, and we slowed down as the slope gradually became steeper. Soon it was impossible to slip the hull along for forty to fifty yards at a time. We would heave it forward two or three yards and then stop. By midday we were covered with mud and sweat, and I was dazed from the effort. I had expected a low pass over a hill, but it was becoming increasingly obvious that for the first time my map was correct. We were working our way up the base of a very tall mountain. We stopped for lunch and then walked ahead, clearing a path with our parangs. Arriving at the end of a narrow valley, we were confronted by a 30-degree slope. The men took no notice of the steep hillside and continued up the slope, positioning logs and hacking at saplings and rattan vines. We brought the boat to the base of the incline and lined it up with the new path. Then we took a rest. My companions had come this way before and knew what to expect next.

Physical labor in Kalimantan is often rated in terms of how many pieces of *sugee* are required to complete a specific job. For everyday tasks men place a pinchful of the stuff behind their upper lips. Like coca leaves in South America, *sugee* makes the work easier. With this in mind I was alarmed when I noticed the men filling their mouths with entire sticks of *sugee*. They chewed for a short while; then we started to move the big boat up the hillside. The *sugee* must have taken effect because five minutes and one hundred yards later we were still inching the monster up the mountain. Emotions were running high as we grunted and farted our way up through the dense forest. But the slope was too steep. We began to falter, and soon the longboat was stuck fast. No sooner had we stopped than Pa Jugeh cried out in a clear voice the beginning of a Kenyah work chant.

"*Dua Telu!*" (two, three), he sang to the others.

"*Ta-pat!*" (four), the chorus of six men immediately yelled back.

We heaved on the boat, but it wouldn't budge.

"*Kua Kua!*" (all together now), screamed Pa Jugeh.

"*Men-at!*" (move it), the chorus grunted, and miraculously the longboat moved. Not much, but enough to create some momentum.

Everyone strained, and the longboat continued to inch forward.

"*Dee Da Duh-Niee!*" (straight to the top), Pa Jugeh gasped.

"*Pen-at!*" (let's go), the others yelled, and on we struggled.

It was a great battle. We continued for about forty yards, until Pa Jugeh announced a rest. He grabbed a short block of wood out of the longboat and jammed it behind the stern to keep the boat from sliding back down the mountain.

The old wads of *sugee* were spat out; then, like artillery shells being rammed into the breach, fresh sticks of *sugee* were stuffed into the gasping mouths. The only time I tried *sugee* I got sick, so I chewed on a piece of sugarcane.

The trail was crawling with leeches, and our legs were covered with the slippery, brown creatures. Now that our hands were free we plucked off dozens of them. I ground my leeches to a bloody pulp between two rocks while the others chopped them up with their parangs. While this was going on, Pa Ubang tied the skinned and severed deer skull, with the antlers and eyes still intact, to the bow of the longboat.

This grisly figurehead led the way, and we continued at a deadly pace throughout the afternoon. The chants became more desperate, and although I couldn't understand the Kenyah words, the rhyming shouts blended wonderfully with the powerful rhythm of work, and I felt a surge of extra strength. I desperately wanted to be a part of this mad effort, but I was losing strength rapidly. I struggled on mechanically until I broke out in a cold sweat. "Just a bit farther," I tried to reassure myself. I staggered drunkenly for another fifty feet, until the jungle began to spin and I collapsed exhausted by the side of the boat. A rest stop was called, and Pa Ubang, whose legs were so hideously battered, came over to where I sat in the mud. In a quiet voice he said, "*Tuan*, you must rest. We are used to this work, and we will take the boat to the pass. Sit here awhile. Then meet us at the top. It is not far. Are you all right?"

I said I was fine and then threw up in the bushes. How could they continue? Maybe it was the *sugee*, or perhaps it was part of the male ritual to hide their exhaustion. I was mystified by their endurance.

The men took their positions on either side of the longboat and dug their powerful toes into the muddy trail. Pa Jugeh took a breath, and the men braced themselves.

"*Ilun Ahan masak paku!*" cried Pa Jugeh. The boat lurched forward and disappeared from sight. There was the sound of scrambling bare feet, a few grunts, then silence.

"*Ilun Ahan masak paku?*" I repeated to myself as I sat in the cold mud. Literally this phrase meant Ahan (a woman) cooks ferns. Hardly the sort of expression one would expect to inspire such a display of brute strength. When I felt better, I followed the skid marks made by the boat. The trail got steeper, and soon I could hear muffled yells from somewhere high above me on the mountain. When I caught up with the boat twenty minutes later, there was little doubt the men had reached the pass. The international border runs along the narrow crest of the mountains, and there the longboat sat, tottering between two countries, its bow in Sarawak and its stern in Kalimantan. *Sugee* littered the ground, and the men were totally spent. They were also delighted with their ascent of Sawak Iran Pass. The longboat looked absurdly out of place on top of the mountain in the middle of the forest. I thought of the Ark on the summit of Mount Ararat. We were a day's walk from the nearest river and four days from the nearest village.

Everyone rested, and I asked Pa Ubang about Ahan and the ferns. Kenyah folklore, he told me, is full of stories about Ahan, a legendary cook—unmarried, beautiful, graceful, strong, and very much desired. The term *ilun* indicates that her mother has already died. Ahan embodies the qualities of the ideal Kenyah woman and stirs up the deepest passions in men. She is so clever that her pot of rice is cooked before the smoke from the fire has risen twelve feet, and ten grains of rice in her pot are enough for ten men. Strong stuff by Kenyah standards.

We left the boat where it was and walked three or four miles back through the jungle to camp. The women had prepared a delicious meal of deer meat and hill rice. Early the next day we returned to Sawak Iran Pass, and to the longboat.

The ascent had been a magnificent effort, but how were we going to get the boat down from its precarious resting place? I watched as 100-foot lengths of rattan were attached to the longboat in four places. They would control the speed of descent. The loose ends were wrapped around tree trunks like boat winches then slowly let out as men maneuvered the unwieldy boat down the mud-and-rock cliffs. The slopes were so steep on this side of the mountain that it was difficult to stand up without holding onto the longboat or the trees. If the longboat had broken loose, it would have shot down the mountain like a runaway freight train and smashed against the big trees far below.

Yet the skill of these people was such that within only two hours we were off the pass and had moved the boat into a perilous ravine choked with thorny vines and slippery rocks, one of the headwaters of the mighty Rajang River. Four hundred fifty miles downstream, where it flowed into the South China Sea, the river was 3½ miles wide, but here it was a humble trickle, perhaps 2 inches wide and half an inch deep. From this spot it was another day's journey before we would reach a section of river deep enough to float the longboat. We walked back to the Kalimantan camp and began shuttling our belongings over the pass in stages. We were to cross the 4 steep miles of the Sawak Iran Pass six times that day, carrying a wide assortment of goods: sleeping mats, axes, a chain saw, hundreds of pounds of rice, spears and blowpipes, fishing nets, cooking pots, plus clothing and other personal belongings to last a year or more in the timber camps of Sarawak where my companions hoped to find work.

An entire day was spent moving the baggage and longboat to Sungai Sihet, where we set up camp at a place called Long Iran. The sleeping shelter was built; then half the men went fishing, and the other half went off with the dogs to hunt. The women started a smoky fire to keep away the clouds of sand flies, chopped a tremendous pile of firewood, and sorted the baggage. Before I fell into a brief sleep, Pa Ubang's daughter Ros brought me a cup of lemonade. I was delighted, but where had the lemons come from? This lovely gesture was typical of their thoughtfulness throughout the journey. Ros had carried the lemons from Long Nawang.

The afternoon was spent repairing and strengthening the longboat. Extra planks were cut to add eight inches to the sides for the rapids downstream. Larger ribs were added, and cross-braces were lashed in place with rattan. The hull was set on fire once again, and with this task completed we were ready for a dawn departure the next day. If the men from Long Uro were going to catch up with us, this would be the spot. Once we started downstream we would easily outdistance them. They, too, would have to haul their boats over the mountain and stop at this camp to make repairs.

Work continued into the evening. Hundreds of fish were split open, salted, and placed on drying racks over a series of long fire pits. A pig and another deer were cut up and smoked. This huge stock of food was to last until work could be found in Sarawak. Hunting downriver near populated areas would be difficult, and the logging operations had ruined the fishing and chased away much of the wild game.

When dinner was finished, the men came one by one to my sleeping mat to use my razor and hand mirror. They shaved the downy whiskers from their cheeks in preparation for our arrival in the village of Long Busong the next day. Everyone then lay back in the 50-foot-long sleeping shelter for quiet conversations and storytelling. Individual men began to sing, and in the darkness, above the insect chorus and the crackling fire, I recognized the sound of Pa Jugeh's voice, with its beautiful, resonating quality that lulled the rest of us into silence. His song consisted of drawn-out phrases interspersed with brief pauses to mark the end of each verse. I didn't understand the words, but it was obviously a very sentimental song, and we all lay still listening quietly. When the song came to an end, no one spoke for a few minutes.

"What was that song?" I asked Pa Awang, who was lying on his bed mat next to mine.

"That is a special song for *peselai*," he replied. "It is for the wife who is left behind. We Kenyah believe that on quiet evenings like tonight the wife can hear her husband's voice. It comes to comfort her over the months or years that he may be gone."

The other purpose of the song, I assumed, was to let everyone know that you are thinking of your wife and missing her. Such a sweet, simple gesture was totally unexpected after the three days of heroic struggle on the mountain.

At dawn we repacked the longboat and dragged it along the shallow riverbed for the first hour. Then we all climbed in, stood up, and poled our way down quiet stretches of river; the sensation of floating was utter luxury. In contrast to the last three days, the jungle now slipped by with little effort on our part. I fastened my sun hat beneath my chin and joined the rhythm of the boat poles. I was soon overwhelmed with excitement.

We were back in Sarawak, and in a few more days I would be out of the jungle. Now I could relax and feel assured that I had made the right decision to turn back from the east coast two months earlier. I had survived, but the second crossing had nearly destroyed my confidence in my ability to recognize danger signs and to function under stress. My life had been seriously threatened, and I had become careless in a situation where the warning signs had been clear enough. I told myself I would never make that mistake again. The vulnerability that confidence breeds — I would remember that one. The tension and anxiety of the past weeks began to ease, and in their place grew a sense of well-being. I felt immensely relieved.

This was how I had wanted to end the journey: in a state of euphoria, floating down a quiet jungle stream, chest pounding, feeling strong about having been able to test my limits of endurance. It was not so much the physical aspects, but the incredible mental gymnastics that go along with such a journey: the loneliness and the constant doubting of my ability to be changed by a strange environment. Learning to feel comfortable with being vulnerable and to laugh at all the problems I made for myself: these were the real lessons. I continued to pole the longboat in unison with my companions, and my good feelings continued to grow. There is no other way to describe the giddy physical sensation that I experienced than to say I tingled all over. That's what was happening, and I could not stop smiling.

Pa Jugeh Taseh had become my favorite person on this trip. All these people were tireless and friendly, but what made him special was his ability to sense everyone's mood. He knew just when to quicken the tempo of the poling by vibrating the boat with quick jolts of his feet while perched on the stern post. The shudder would run the length of the boat and excite everyone to pole with renewed spirit. Pa Jugeh would respond with a delighted laugh as we glided through the magic forest.

The thick, sweet fragrance of the flowering *aran* trees was heavy in the air. Huge branches stretched over the water and deposited pinkish white flowers into the river and longboat. I watched the flowers come down in the morning breeze and noticed how they gathered in each quiet bend of the river. I began to daydream about the special moments of the journey; a kaleidoscope of events from the previous seven months blinked on and off in front of me. Suddenly I was jolted out of my reverie. The dogs shot off the longboat and into the river like a couple of deck torpedoes from a PT boat. A pig had been sighted at the edge of the river, and the boat was poled into the mud bank at full speed. The men disappeared into the undergrowth, and I sat in the longboat with the women, enjoying the sounds of the river. I sat sideways in the boat and took a quick nap. The next thing I knew there were startled expressions from the women. Four men were carrying Pa Ulay towards us. His knee was slashed open, and he was bleeding heavily. The men explained what had happened. The dogs had run down and cornered a monstrous wild boar, and in the final moment six men surrounded the animal, with the dogs nipping at its heels. Pa Ulay leapt forward with his parang and slipped. He fell right in front of the maddened boar. In an instant the pig grabbed his knee, and despite the instantaneous rain of blows and spear thrusts, Pa Ulay's knee was ripped open to the bone. Boar tusks have a cutting edge that is sharp enough to shave your fingernail.

Pa Ulay was fully conscious, but his breathing was heavy and irregular. His face paled and turned a gray-white as we washed the frightful wound. We pressed the flesh together and covered the gash with a pile of gauze pads bound tightly with strips of cloth, and the bleeding stopped. Pa Jugeh and Pa Ubang arrived minutes later with the four legs and the pig's head. These were thrown into the boat. The dogs leapt aboard, and we hurried downriver towards Long Busong, where Pa Ulay could have his knee properly cleaned and stitched by the government dresser. The river deepened, and we put down the poles and began paddling. We paddled nonstop, and during that time we left the beauty of the deep jungle. I hardly noticed the transition, but within three hours I could see the first old rice fields covered in secondary jungle. Pa Ulay was resting comfortably when Long Busong, the first village we had seen in more than ten days, came into sight. It was situated on a low hill where the meandering Busong River joined the Balui (upper Rajang). The people of Long Busong were Kenyah who had migrated from Kalimantan ten to twenty years earlier; we could expect a warm reception.

Some children were playing on the log landing platform, and as we pulled up they paused to watch our approach. Not until we were tied up and I staggered slowly to my feet, easing out leg cramps, did the children notice I was not Kenyah. They literally jumped when they saw how tall I was. Then we all began to laugh. It was a great joke to them that they hadn't spotted me earlier. Looking at photographs of myself from that time, with my Kenyah sun hat, parang, and brown skin, I think I must have looked like the genuine Kenyah article.

We carried Pa Ulay to the government dresser and strolled to the longhouse to announce our arrival. I removed my tattered shoes and, gripping the slippery notched pole ladder with my toes, climbed up to the longhouse porch without using my hands. I placed my pack in the headman's room, and then we sat down for tea.

Many of the people in Long Busong had relatives in Long Nawang, so there was a great deal of news sharing. I liked the way people told stories. There was never any urgency or competition to blurt out the gossip before someone else did. The storytelling had a gentle pace. It always unfolded slowly, building up a momentum of its own. The best stories came last, when the listeners and the storytellers had warmed up. That afternoon we began with an account of recent births and important funerals and marriages, followed by our departure from Long Nawang and where we had camped each night. Each detail of our maneuvering the longboat over the mountain was described. When Pa Jugeh or one of the other men got a good response to a particular aspect of the narrative, he would backtrack and try the same story from a slightly different perspective. This habit, I assumed, was to help them get the feeling right in their own minds. They were masters at telling each other's stories. When one man grew tired of talking, another would effortlessly pick up the thread. Nothing was written down. Their laws, histories, and folklore were interwoven and preserved through singing and storytelling. I was always impressed by how people could remember the most minute details of a journey. I once commented on this ability to people in Bario, and they laughed at my ignorance. "This is nothing compared to the old stories," they told me. "A good singer or storyteller could continue for three days. Only a few old people still know these things. Everyone else has forgotten."

Later that afternoon I looked for my shoes. They were utterly worn out, but I had kept them as a memento of my journey. I wasn't planning to have them bronzed, but I had patched them dozens of times, and each patch represented a different story or place. The history of my walk back and forth across Borneo was stitched into those shoes, and now I couldn't find them. I searched for an hour before I discovered the remains beneath the longhouse. Nearby stood the culprit: a hairless mongrel.

In its revolting mouth was one last small fragment of my dear shoes. The dog hadn't been playing with the shoes; he had eaten them both. All that was left were two black rubber soles covered with dog saliva and bite marks. I was heartbroken. Thousands of leeches had dined in those shoes, and now they were gone. The shoes, in an absurd way, had provided a sense of continuity to my trip. They were made by Nike, and during the trip I had often thought of sending the manufacturer "before" and "after" photos, with the caption: "Nike jogging shoes are not just for jogging." Accompanying the photos would be a brief story of how the shoes survived the 2,400-mile journey through the rain forest. It would have been a great advertisement.

I found a pair of rubber thongs in my pack and tried to forget the shoes. I failed.

⍏ ⍏ ⍏

The evening rice was boiled in a black cast-iron pot large enough to feed twenty people. Sweet black tea was served immediately after dinner. Then, to my surprise, all my companions climbed beneath their bedsheets and went to sleep. The trip has finally caught up with them, I thought, although it seemed a little odd to leap from dinner straight into bed.

I did a quick circuit up and down the longhouse porch, pausing briefly in the shadows at the far end to pee over the railing before returning to our room. I strung up my mosquito net and climbed under my smoky bedsheet. Lying back with my hands behind my head, I realized that everything in my pack smelled of smoke. My bedding and the still air inside my mosquito net reminded me of the interior of my brother-in-law's Weber barbecue. I would have to do some washing soon. I closed my eyes and could hear people milling about on the porch. Soon the gentle melodic sound of the *sapeh* drifted through the longhouse. Children whispered outside our door, and I thought I could detect the sound of bare feet padding on the giant hardwood floorboards. I listened more carefully and caught the sound of someone pumping up a pressure kerosene lamp. Something special was going on — people were definitely gathering on the verandah. One *sapeh* was joined by another; then came the unmistakable sound of a male dancer stamping the loose floorboards with his bare foot. This was followed by a low cry. The *sapeh* continued. The commotion grew in stages before I realized what was happening.

Glancing around the room, which was lit only by two kerosene wicks, I suspected everyone was pretending to be asleep. We remained "asleep" and ignored the clamor that was by this time shaking the longhouse like an earthquake. Our hosts then quietly filed into the darkened room to shake feet and tug on arms until we "woke up." Everyone from our boat had anticipated this move and had been lying in bed fully dressed in their best clothes — wash-and-wear shirts and polyester slacks, with cheap sunglasses and wristwatches as accessories. Every hair had been meticulously plastered into place with generous amounts of lavender-scented pomade. Even their powerful jungle feet had somehow been stuffed into shiny, plastic, imitation-leather shoes that made them limp with pain. We ventured onto the verandah in single file and took our seats along the raised section of the longhouse porch next to the outside railing. I wondered where the men had hidden their bizarre outfits during our journey over the mountain. The women had prepared themselves for the big party by dusting their lovely olive-toned cheeks with thick white powder that had the appearance of corn flour. In their silky black hair were Woolworth-quality hair clips decorated with plastic flowers and bows.

Everyone was ready for the big welcome party, and an hour and a half was devoted to drinking *arak* and "waiting for the mood to be right." I produced our four bottles of imported *arak* to speed things up, and before long the mood of the people seated nearby was well on its way to "right."

An older man stood up and was helped into the dancer's costume by two young girls. Over his head they placed a bearskin vest trimmed with rows of black-and-white hornbill feathers and seashells. A flap of stiff animal skin large enough to cover his rear end was fastened around his waist with a thin cord. That was the *tabit*, a portable seat originally designed for sitting on damp ground when loincloths were still in fashion. A woven rattan cap with long, Argus pheasant feathers was placed on his head. Finally, a magnificent headhunting sword with an intricately carved antler handle was fastened at his side. The *sapeh* began to play, and the man looked up at the ceiling then down at the floor, his hands hanging loosely at his side and a dreamy look to his face. Gracefully he extended his arms and began a series of circular steps — first to the right, then to the left. He stamped the floor and let out a scream. He smiled and seemed pleased with himself. Such a fine warrior. Still circling in a crouch, he glanced over his shoulder, looking for his imaginary foe. Once sighted, he exchanged menacing gestures and silent taunts before drawing his parang and leaping into battle. He screamed again, and the tempo of the dance quickly speeded up. He slashed the air with his blade, thrusting and fending blows until the imaginary foe lay headless at his feet. The man had fought a terrific battle and everyone applauded wildly. The dancer removed his costume and climbed into a black-and-yellow Adidas track suit.

Younger men, full of *arak*, took turns dancing, hoping to impress the women. In the space of thirty minutes the skilled dancers had taken the floor, and a score of imaginary heads littered the dance area.

Comic relief was next on the evening's agenda. I lifted a cup of *arak* to my lips and realized that all eyes were watching as the nubile maidens of Long Busong descended on me. It is considered good manners to exhibit a certain degree of modesty in these situations, so the first thing I did was bolt for the back railing. Three hundred Kenyah villagers laughed and jeered as I was reluctantly dragged into the light of the kerosene lamp and coaxed into the warrior's dance costume by three young women whose beautiful faces were grotesquely contorted by their efforts not to laugh. They arranged the vestments, and the *arak*-inspired crowd made rude comments. I squirmed as the bearskin vest settled onto my bare shoulders. It was saturated with cold sweat from the first six warriors and really did smell like a dead bear. There was a problem with the headdress. My sweet attendants were quite incapable of reaching my head, and with mock disdain I refused to stoop over. They jumped, they tugged on my arms, and they took turns trying to lift one another. They pleaded with their eyes, but I was unmoved. Finally a man from the front row got down on all fours at my feet to make a human stepladder. Children rolled on the floor, holding their sides. I gazed into space with a look of disinterest. One of the young women then climbed onto the man's back and placed the feathered headdress onto my head. It took both her hands to tie the thing securely under my chin, and while she did so she pressed her body against me for balance. The damn bearskin vest was stiff with age and didn't convey the slightest sensation of her small breasts. She had an intoxicating fragrance of nutmeg to her skin, and she breathed lightly on my face. This is very nice, I thought to myself.

The attendants withdrew, and I was left alone at center stage. Some of the people were already laughing at the mere sight of me standing so tall with the hopelessly small feathered cap perched on my head. This was great entertainment! The people in the upriver communities are not malicious, but, for whatever reason, there is no better pastime than watching a white stranger lose his dignity in front of the entire village.

I placed my hands together and bowed respectfully to the elders. They nodded back, and as the *sapeh* music started up, I struck my pose. It was that of the green sea turtle from Arnhem Land, which aboriginal dancer Nandjiwarra Amagula had taught me beside a pool table on Groote Eylandt in the Northern Territory of Australia in 1973. I faced the audience crouched like an upright frog, flippers held at shoulder height, head turned to reveal a flattering feathered turtle profile. I paddled briefly, looked from side to side stretching and withdrawing my neck. I let out a scream and paddled some more. The audience was confused.

"Penyu" (turtle), I said, and the crowd fell about screaming with laughter. I stood up and did my very best to perform traditional *ngajat*. The *sapeh* continued its mesmerizing tempo. I moved in a tight circle, arms extended, my hands carving what would have to do for sinuous shapes through the night air. I crouched, then rose up moving slowly across the floorboards, always turning, looking, circling — searching for a worthy opponent and shouting my challenges. I must have done well because when my imaginary foe came into sight, I blanched. With a look of terror on my upturned face, I indicated that I had summoned up the Kenyah equivalent of Goliath. I looked him up and down then headed for the headman's door. I pretended the door was jammed. I turned to face the audience, and the sight of Pa Jugeh with tears of laughter in his eyes spurred me on. Another scream to give me courage and out came my parang. We circled one another, and in order to look menacing I grimaced. There were snickers from the audience. Parangs slashed through the air like helicopter blades. I ducked, feigned, jumped, held my hands over my head, and did everything I could to stay out

of the way of my imaginary opponent's murderous blade. Soon I was in full retreat, clearly outclassed by this marvelous warrior. In desperation I held up my hand and called a halt to the combat. This was something new, and everyone went quiet.

Addressing Goliath, I said, *"Tunggu sebentar, apa itu?"* (Wait a moment, what's that?) I pointed over his well-muscled shoulder glistening with beads of sweat. He was a brilliant swordsman, but lacked basic street sense. As he turned to look, I gripped my parang like a baseball bat and put his head into the left centerfield bleachers. A shove with two fingers, and over went the body. The concept of fair play was never embraced by headhunters, and the audience exploded with laughter. They understood my ploy and loved it. I was winded from the effort and laid the dancer's outfit on the floor by the musicians. Immediately a glass of *arak* appeared from somewhere, and strong hands held my neck as the burning liquor was poured down my throat and bare chest.

The dancing continued, but the tobacco smoke and *arak* were making me dizzy. I felt I had to get some fresh air. I walked down the notched pole ladder in the darkness and continued through damp, knee-deep grass towards a small bamboo suspension bridge that crossed the Busong River. As the swaying structure bobbed beneath my bare feet, I carefully stepped to midspan and leaned against the handrail to rest. A warm wind blew across the fields, carrying with it the smell of the jungle. I could hear music and laughter and dancing feet. From where I stood the longhouse looked like a cruise ship alive and jumping with happy people. Beyond the black river the jungle mountains stood tall and foreboding beneath the star-filled sky. I stood on the undulating bridge greeting my favorite constellations. I hadn't seen some of them in months. Little Kite, my name for the Pleiades; Delphinus, the dolphin; and the great horse Pegasus, galloping across the night sky. There was my own constellation, Pisces. I relished the wildness of this remote scene and the rare luxury of being alone. Months before, I had felt desperately in need of solitude and privacy. How I had changed. Now I felt an overwhelming urge to return to the party. I walked back to the longhouse and joined my drunken friends until dawn.

CHAPTER THIRTEEN · TO THE MOUTH OF THE RIVER

I ARRIVED in Belaga bazaar by mid-December in a 40-foot longboat carved out of a single tree trunk. The months of jungle living had come to an abrupt end with the unexpectedly quick descent of the Balui River. Belaga was the same sleepy, stuccoed-brick, soft-drink-consuming, rooster-fighting, chain-saw-advertising outpost I remembered from five months earlier. As before, the outwardly indifferent Chinese merchants, dressed in baggy, striped pajama pants, seemed to take scant interest in commerce, preferring to devote their time to sitting at the backs of their darkened, musty shops full of jumbled merchandise watching Kung Fu videos, or sleeping on lurid Formica-topped tables trimmed with chrome, towels draped over their faces to keep away the flies. These wealthy men controlled the upriver trade of jungle products, and their children studied business administration and law at universities in Britain, Canada, and the United States.

The evening I arrived in Belaga I went to sit in a coffee shop in order to be by myself. An ancient ceiling fan squeaked and wobbled unevenly as the wooden blades batted giant cicadas against the walls, occasionally cutting one of the insects in half. From the cool concrete floor one of the cicada heads, with wings and thorax intact, buzzed to life and flew out the door of the coffee shop, leaving its abdomen behind. Ten minutes later, seemingly unperturbed by its accident and once again attracted by the light, the head and wings flew back into the shop only to be swatted against the wall by the same overhead fan. Blind persistence — I could relate to that.

The realization that I would be in Kuching within a few days worried me. I was feeling uncertain and found myself drifting from the past to the future with a regularity that I found disconcerting. I couldn't concentrate, and my spirits, which were still bolstered by the momentum of activity, which had culminated in the ascent of Sawak Iran Pass, were on the wane. I sensed that the impending emotional letdown of coming to the end of my journey was going to be horrific.

Jungle travel had become timeless and exhilarating. In contrast, my arrival in Belaga was like going over the handlebars of a bicycle and slamming into the concrete. Belaga represented the big city for my Kenyah companions, but for me this upriver outpost was merely the first taste of the familiar way of living that awaited me in the cities beyond the mouth of the river.

I knew there was no welcoming committee waiting for me at the coast—no breasting the tape, no snipping the ribbon. No one, in fact, had any idea what I had just put myself through. This realization gave me a feeling of satisfaction. I was beginning to enjoy feeling insignificant. I relished the idea that the journey had been such a private affair. No sponsorship pressures, no deadlines or obligations to anyone but myself. I had been free to take my time, and that had been one of the greatest luxuries of the trip.

In Belaga I decided to stay in one of the nondescript, second-story hotels above the single row of shops that faced the river. I was planning to enjoy the privacy and comfort of a shower stall and a room to myself. The room looked neat in a 1950s kitsch sort of way, and there was a sturdy lock on the door. I placed my pack at the foot of the Formica-clad bed and changed into my sarong. With a new bar of sandalwood soap, I was soon showering beneath a tepid dribble in an airless, concrete cubicle encrusted with green slime and smelling of stale urine. Thus refreshed, I went in search of a restaurant.

I labored through a meal of cold rice, pet-food-quality tinned sardines, and an omelette that had been fried in rancid coconut oil over a smudgy kerosene flame. The kerosene fumes had permeated the food, so after dinner I tried a cup of lukewarm instant coffee to remove the taste of sardines and kerosene, a hard candy to get rid of the synthetic coffee flavoring, and a beer to erase the memory of the meal. Then I set out to find my traveling companions to see how Belaga was treating them.

Ever practical and resourceful, my Kenyah friends had found free accommodations in a riverside warehouse. They had bathed in the river, and when I found them, they were just finishing an evening meal of hill rice, smoked river fish, and wild boar. Our differing responses to arriving in Belaga illustrated what a creature of habit I am. How quickly I reverted to my conditioned concepts of comfort and privacy.

We sat crouched in the low-ceilinged section of the warehouse that smelled of damp hessian sacks. In the dark it was impossible to make out people's faces, but the faint red glow of cigarette ashes and the distinctive voice patterns indicated the position of each individual. Earlier I had asked the hotel manager about possible jobs for these men and had been told of a timber concession on the Tubau River, a day's journey from Belaga, where the Chinese contractor was hiring Indonesian laborers. In the darkened warehouse I was beginning to explain this news when I was interrupted by the arrival of three ominous silhouettes framed in the only doorway. I stopped talking. A powerful yellow flashlight beam pierced the darkness and came to rest on my face. This threatening and irritating gesture was accompanied by two unnerving questions in English, "What are you doing here, and where have you come from?"

These words were spoken by the police inspector, who was flanked by two subordinates. I asked the man with the flashlight to please take the light off my face. The blinding beam was lowered to the rough wooden floor. Then the questions were repeated. I was seated with twelve illegal aliens, and with an expired passport in my pocket I anticipated serious problems. Fortunately, I had prepared for this situation by explaining my "official story" that afternoon to Pa Ubang and the others.

"These are my good friends from Indonesia," I said. "They

helped me get a ride downriver from Long Busong, where I was stranded for three weeks. I'm thanking them for their help and saying goodby."

The officers were very polite and begged my pardon. In English they explained that they were there to do their job and must ask the Indonesians a few questions. Pa Ubang identified himself as the spokesman, and his face was soon illuminated by the flashlight. I listened as he sweated through his own careful answers concerning where the group had come from and what they were doing in Belaga without passports.

"We have papers from the Kommandan Polici and our Camat in Long Nawang. We have come to look for work in Sarawak." Pa Ubang handed over the sheet of paper we had worked so hard to obtain.

The interrogation continued, and one of the police assistants turned to me and commented on how lucky I was to have received permission to go upriver as far as Long Busong. "Usually visitors are not allowed to go farther than Bakun Rapids."

"Yes, I was extremely fortunate," I lied and waited for his obvious next question, Where is your upriver permit? To my surprise, he never asked for the nonexistent document, but he did ask Pa Ubang and Pa Jugeh to go with him to the police station. I spoke up and asked the inspector if there was any problem or if I could help, but he motioned with his head in such a way that indicated I should not become involved. The three policemen shook my hand courteously then escorted Pa Ubang and Pa Jugeh to the concrete footpath that led to the bazaar.

Illuminated by a single streetlight, both these men looked ashen as they were led away. I feared they might be sent back to Kalimantan or fined. Even if they were allowed to stay, the Kenyah realized they would be cheated by their employers. The five men, three police, and my two friends, walked down the footpath and disappeared into the night. I don't know what happened to them, and I never saw them again. I didn't even have a chance to thank them for the journey. This was upsetting to me, but I was now at risk and could not afford to await the outcome of the discussion at the police station. I would have to hide until the express boat left for Kapit the next day at dawn.

A few minutes after the departure of the police, I said goodby to the rest of my traveling companions. This was done in nearly total darkness. I moved from one cigarette glow to the next shaking hands as we wished each other good luck. Leaving the warehouse, I decided not to stay at the hotel. As the only Westerner in Belaga everyone knew where I had taken a room. I collected my pack and walked into the shadows that led to the river. I thought it highly unlikely the police would have any further interest in me, but just in case someone decided to ask for my passport or upriver permit, I wanted to make certain they would not find me.

No moon was showing through the cloud cover as I made my way down the treacherously steep and muddy riverbank. I removed my thongs and dug into the mud with my fingers and toes. I felt my way along the water's edge until I found what I was looking for: the submerged, narrow, 30-foot plank that led to the floating fuel dock. Moored to the far side of the dock was the barely discernible shape of the big riverboat. I placed my left foot on the plank, and it rolled to one side. I centered my pack on my back and tried again. Like a tightrope walker, I stepped onto the unstable plank and held my hands out while steadying myself with my back foot. I reminded myself to keep breathing and moved forward. Balance . . . pause . . . step . . . balance . . . pause . . . step. The night was very dark, and the river current swirled warmly around my calves. It was impossible to turn around, and only when the water level on my legs began to drop did I realize I was approaching the floating dock. I stepped across the fuel dock and slid back one of the cabin shutters and climbed into the 60-foot riverboat. A single kerosene wick sent up a sooty wisp of smoke and illuminated the interior of the boat. There was a family of six stretched out on one of the two parallel benches that ran the length of the boat and faced each other. I found a clear section of hardwood bench, rolled out my sleeping mat, strung my mosquito net from the ceiling and was soon fast asleep. During the night I awoke to hear the soothing patter of raindrops drumming on the cabin roof.

Just before dawn more passengers clambered aboard, and at first light the engines started up. A bone-jarring vibration ran the length of the boat and coaxed the sleepers into upright, if not altogether wide-awake, positions. A few blasts on the air horn ten minutes before departure; then we were away from the greasy, brown, mud banks. The air freshened, and soon the jungle-lined shore was speeding past at a terrific rate. We lurched and rolled our way through the boiling Pelagus Rapids a few hours later; then the river widened and became more placid. Log-loading stations reappeared, and there were barges piled high with hardwood logs. I glanced about the stifling, cigarette-smoke-filled cabin and realized that months earlier I had been on the same boat, but traveling in the opposite direction. At that time the passengers with their jungle knives, body tattoos, and brass ear weights had seemed exotic beyond belief. Now as I sat half-deafened by the roar of the engines, these identical-looking people were poking at my belongings and speaking to me in their own language. They wanted to know where I had found the excellent jungle knife, woven rattan pack, and intricately stitched Kenyah sun hat. When I told them I had just come from the Kayan River via Long Nawang, their excited questioning gave me the first hint of what I had actually accomplished. Few, if any, of these people could claim to have made such a journey. They were interested and delighted by my stories of their ancestral homelands, and I knew I was no longer a stranger.

The express arrived in Kapit at 11:30 A.M., and thirty minutes later I was on the last downriver boat headed for Sibu that day. By this time I was literally shaking in anticipation of seeing the South China Sea. I was also beginning to suffer from the cultural bends. I was surfacing too quickly, but there was little I could do to slow down the inevitable return to the city streets filled with unknown people.

The afternoon was punctuated by a medley of events that became a blur in the confusion of heat, noise, diesel fumes, and the dreamy state of mind I had fallen into. Only one event stands out from that boat trip. From a muddy riverbank a woman was carried aboard on a plastic sheet. She was in the middle of labor, and something had gone wrong. Blood plastered her thighs, and she was moaning weakly. The central aisle of the boat was by now filled with rice sacks and some recently loaded and still-steaming deer and wild pig carcasses. Those items were stacked out of the way. A space was cleared, and a sheet was strung up in a modest attempt at providing some privacy. Once the woman was settled, the helmsman didn't wait for instructions. He reversed from the riverbank and jammed the throttle full ahead. Seven hundred horsepower of Detroit Diesel roared to life, and people staggered for balance as the sleek riverboat accelerated down the Rajang River in a nonstop dash to Sibu Hospital, two hours downriver. There was a general concern that the woman or the child might die before we reached Sibu, and older women made their way to the back of the boat to offer assistance.

The air horns never ceased their racket as they blasted all river craft out of the way. The woman was still conscious when the helmsman rammed the express launch into a cluster of similar craft at Sibu wharf. Boat owners on all sides yelled abuse, the woman was carried to a taxi, the engines shuddered to a stop, and the rest of the passengers sat motionless, stunned into silence by the hours of engine noise and pounding waves. The smiling helmsman was exhilarated by his heroic charge down the river. I staggered to a hotel and slept.

Arriving in Kuching by riverboat the next day, I climbed to the top of the concrete steps that led from the muddy river. The distinctive scent of creosote and rotten fish filled my lungs as I stood on the splintered wharf and surveyed the street scene before me. The main bazaar of Kuching is small and well ordered by Asian standards, but I felt as if I were watching the rush-hour mayhem of bodies and vehicles struggling through downtown Manhattan. Standing alone at the edge of this tide of people flowing through the markets, I realized I would have to relearn some skills: how to hail a taxi, cable my bank for money, and buy some clothes. People were looking at me, and I felt self-conscious holding my Kenyah sun hat. I attached it to my pack, but my woven rattan pack also looked out of place — I noticed young Malay women were giggling at the sight of me. I placed the pack in the trunk of a cab and gave the driver directions in Malay. He was Chinese and didn't understand. We tried broken English, and five minutes later I was back in the frangipani-scented room overlooking the familiar expanse of terra-cotta rooftops dotted with sleeping cats. For the next few days I didn't speak to anyone. I was indexing five hundred pages of journal entries. I wanted to complete that task before the memory of my journey was broken by the avalanche of distractions and mad activity that I felt approaching, and perhaps I also needed to order my thoughts and impressions of the trip while ordering my pieces of paper. And it was a way of delaying acknowledging that the end of the trip had now come.

On the morning of day three in Kuching, I woke up in a heavy sweat with my heart pounding. I was having a nightmare that I had been captured in Long Uro. I took the dream seriously and was convinced that a spell had been cast on me or that a *dayung* had sent an invisible needle or knife through the air and that I would soon fall ill.

I showered and left my room before sunrise, wandered through the Chinese section of town for a couple of hours, then went in search of my friend Grace. At the very end of Carpenter Street, I found her in the front courtyard of the See Ang Kong Chinese temple, working in her mother's fruit stall. We had talked about supernaturalism during my earlier visits to Kuching, and after listening to my dream, Grace insisted that I have the spell broken by a *bomoh*, a Dayak spirit worker.

Grace explained what I would have to do. "The fee is two red candles, one small package of incense, two eggs, twenty cents' worth of biscuits, and a bottle of beer. If the exorcism is successful, you can offer a gift as you like. This is our custom." The 60-year-old Dayak woman lived out of town, and we would have to take the bus. Over the following days we made two attempts to organize a visit to see her, neither of which was successful. Inexplicably I felt pressed for time, so I left Kuching on the night flight to Kuala Lumpur, still in a state of anxiety because of my dream.

The flight arrived at midnight, and I selected a sleepy immigration officer at the Kuala Lumpur Airport who cast a perfunctory glance at my expired visa and invalid passport. He yawned expansively and after applying the proper stamp handed the document back to me. I was astounded!

At the taxi stand I shared a ride with a newly arrived Canadian volunteer on his way to Sarawak. We sat in the back of the air-conditioned Mercedes Benz taxi and entered the reinforced concrete citadel. My companion had a free room at the Hotel Grand Central and generously offered to share his room to save me the ordeal of searching for a room at this late hour. A porter carried his suitcase and my jungle pack to the room. I took a cold shower, and when I stepped from the bathroom, wrapped in a towel, I noticed a teddy bear on the pillow of the only bed. The volunteer knew from our conversation in the taxi that I had spent some time in Sarawak and was attentively perched at the foot of the bed with a notepad and pen. "Advice?" he asked. I glanced from the volunteer to the stuffed-animal toy and back to the volunteer.

"Go back!" was all that came to my mind, but I was incapable of uttering a word. I could only laugh. Unmercifully, I bent over double and laughed. I couldn't help myself. Advice?! What could I say to a grown man with a teddy bear about a culture still centered on basic life-and-death activities. I pulled myself together enough to describe the attractions of Kuching. Partially satisfied, the volunteer stepped into the bathroom for his shower. Without waiting for him to reappear, I dressed and went for a walk through the open-air night market, wondering about that teddy bear. That night I rolled out my rattan bed mat for the last time and slept on the carpeted floor.

In the morning my passport was renewed at the U.S. embassy, and I sent my pack and parang to San Francisco by surface mail.

I stuffed my journals, camera, film, and a change of clothing into a flight bag and caught the night train to Singapore to sell the last of my trade goods: two kilos of super grade A *gaharu* and fifty grams of fine gold. Once I had completed the sale of those items the barter trade cycle would be ended. So would my journey.

In Singapore I took a room in a small Chinese hotel around the corner from the famous hotel, Raffles. I easily sold the gold at the market rate to an Indian jeweller, and a day later I located a dealer in *gaharu*. At first the man didn't want to buy such an insignificant quantity from a stranger, but after we had drunk tea mixed with sweetened condensed milk, and I had told him the story of how I had come by the *gaharu*, he paid me slightly less than the going rate of 650 Singapore dollars per *kati*. With my profits I went to the Bank of Shanghai to convert to U.S. currency then to the UTA airline office, where I bought a ticket to San Francisco via Sydney, Australia.

I handed eight hundred U.S. dollars over the counter and watched as the airline ticket agent counted the eight one-hundred-dollar bills. "A stopover in Sydney with an open on-ward flight," I reminded the woman.

The computer printed my ticket while I recalled where the money for its purchase had come from. Six weeks earlier, at the headwaters of the Mahakam River, a chicken had been sacrificed to the spirit of a *gaharu* tree. Then, with an egg, Bungan, the white goddess, had been called up for clearance to fell the tree. *Gaharu* was extracted with jungle knives and traded for shotgun shells. The gold had been obtained from the Christian gold miners from Mahak Baru, who had carefully sifted through the remains of Noah's rejects with shallow, wooden, cone-shaped bowls. The smell of smoke was in my clothes, leech bites were still visible on my ankles. I looked up to find the smiling, uniformed ticket agent handing me my ticket.

"I hope you enjoyed your holiday. Come back to Singapore soon," she said in a soft, efficient voice.

"Yes," I mumbled.

My Australian visa was delayed, and for two days I slogged my way through Singapore's crush of people and traffic. The noise level was unbearable, and I exhausted myself shuttling between banks, embassies, money changers, taxi stands, bus stops, open-air restaurants, and the relative peace of my hotel room. Within the multistoried shopping complexes I drifted up and down silent, rubber-cushioned escalators. Floating through perfumed and air-conditioned time and space, I was dumbfounded by the endless variety of consumer items, especially a battery-operated musical toothbrush that played "Oh, What a Beautiful Morning." I imagined myself back at the Penan camp at Pa Tik leading a church choir with this marvel of dental hygiene. But it would be false of me to deny my attraction to the toothbrush. I bought one with my *gaharu* money. It seemed like a fitting tribute from the tree spirit to the spirit of injection-molded plastics.

It was dark when the big plane took off. I sat by the window, and a three-quarter moon was up. The Kenyah recognize fifteen phases of the moon, and this was *bulan manuk*, the moon phase by which to plant tapioca, rice, and peanuts. It is also an auspicious time for marriage. The increasing bulge of the moon represents the swelling belly of the newlywed wife. Dinner was brought to me on a neat, compartmentalized, plastic tray. The cutlery was sealed in a plastic bag inscribed with the airline's logo. I set the geometrically perfect food aside. I was drifting in time again. I remembered the airliner that had passed over my jungle camp months earlier, sending a glimmer of golden light into the forest. Sitting in the plane, I knew there was only water beneath us, but I looked into the darkness and searched for a pinpoint of firelight from a lonely jungle camp. I slept intermittently and was still looking for the campfire as the unmistakable predawn orange-red light of central Australia appeared on the eastern horizon. The land became visible, and I could make out a waterless plain that swept to the horizon without interruption. Instead of the lush jungle canopy of giant hardwood trees festooned with orchids and ferns, I looked down at a landscape stripped bare of green vegetation and trees — an arid, red plain of undulating sand hills, dry riverbeds, spinifex, and salt pans. I imagined the jungle had been peeled back from the earth with a knife, leaving the soil naked and unprotected. Moving through Sydney's Kingsford Smith Airport, I felt much the same until I walked through the last customs barrier and into the arms of a waiting friend.

EPILOGUE

FOUR YEARS elapsed between my departure from Sarawak and the completion of this book. In that time development projects have moved ahead unchecked in the upriver areas. One event in particular has a bearing on my journey.

In September 1985 representatives of twelve Penan groups living between the Tutoh River and Limbang River met in Long Seridan. The Kelabit people in Long Seridan helped the Penan write a declaration to the government and the timber concession licensees stating their desire to keep their traditional forestland untouched. This is the area where I spent my first month with Tingang Na and John Bong and the Ba'Talun Penan.

A month later an iron logging bridge was constructed at Long Bekawa on the upper Tutoh River by Samling Timber Company (contractor to Wan Abdul Rahman Timber Company). This bridge provided bulldozer access to the virgin jungle that lies between the Limbang and Tutoh rivers. Timber operations commenced immediately.

The Penan have no legal rights in this situation and were not consulted. Prior to 1959 all land that had previously been burned off for farms was considered to be native customary-rights land. The Penan were not included in this scheme because they don't practice shifting cultivation like the longhouse people. The Penan management of wild sago palms and their utilization of forest products are not enough to establish land tenure and qualify them for native customary-rights land. The Sarawak government has ignored the fact that the Penan have successfully managed natural resources for hundreds of years on a sustainable-yield basis and have a well-defined sense of tribal boundaries in the forest. The Penan are competing for forest resources that provide the government with millions of dollars of royalties each year. Despite the slump in world hardwood prices, the logging continues because this revenue is the major source of political funds in Sarawak.

Early in 1986 several Penan families responded to the invasion of their traditional land. Dressed in loincloths and hornbill-feathered caps, the men stopped the bulldozers at the logging bridge with their blowguns. Numerous arrests have been made by the police, and the logging companies are presently (1987) offering bribes to the Penan headmen in an effort to control the people. Meanwhile, the network of logging roads expands towards the highland community of Bario. The Penan response to the bribes has been an emphatic, "Keep your money. You can print money, but you can't print land. We want our land."

ACKNOWLEDGMENTS

I would like to thank the following people, who generously assisted in the preparation of the manuscript by making available their published and unpublished research material: Cynthia Mackie, for help in developing the section on successional vegetation in secondary forests of East Kalimantan; Timothy Jessup and Nancy Peluso, for information regarding the use of minor jungle products; Peter Kedit, Sarawak Museum ethnologist, for his comments on Penan nomadism and the Iban tradition of *bejelai*; and Dr. Paul Chai, from the National Parks and Wildlife Office in Kuching, for his work on ethnobotany in Sarawak.

This book could not have been written without the encouragement and support of many people. Special thanks are expressed to Ted Simon, Margaret Shuk, and Jim Williams.

E. H.

BIBLIOGRAPHY

Aichner, P. "Adat Bungan." *Sarawak Museum Journal,* 1956.

Arnold, Guy. *Longhouse and Jungle.* London: Chatto & Windus, 1959.

Baring-Gould and Bampfylde. *A History of Sarawak Under Its Two White Rajahs.* London, 1909.

Beccari, Odoardo. *Wanderings in the Great Forests of Borneo.* London, 1904.

Caldecott, Julian. "Hunting and Wildlife Management in Sarawak." Kuala Lumpur: World Wildlife Fund, 1986.

Caldecott, Julian and Serena. "A Horde of Pork." *New Scientist,* August 1985.

Caufield, Catherine. *In the Rainforest.* New York: Alfred A. Knopf, 1985.

Chin, Lucas. *Cultural Heritage of Sarawak.* Kuching, 1980.

Conley, William. *The Kalimantan Kenyah: A Study of Tribal Conversion.* New Jersey: Presbyterian and Reformed Publishing Co., 1975.

Conrad, Joseph. *Alamayer's Folly: A Story of an Eastern River and Tales of Unrest.* London: T. Fisher Unwin, 1895.

————. *Heart of Darkness.* New York: Heritage, 1969.

Douglas, R. S. "An Expedition to the Bah Country of Central Borneo." *Sarawak Museum Journal,* 1911.

Dunn, F. L. "Rain-forest Collectors and Traders: A Study of Resource Utilization in Modern and Ancient Malaya." Monographs of the Malaysian Branch of the Royal Asiatic Society, no. 5. Kuala Lumpur, 1975.

Eberhardt, Isabelle. *The Oblivion Seekers.* San Francisco: City Lights Books, 1975.

Geddes, W. R. *Nine Dayak Nights.* London: Oxford University Press, 1957.

Gimlette, J. D. *Malay Poisons and Charm Cures.* London: J. and A. Churchill, 1923.

Hanbury-Tenison, Robin. *Mulu, the Rain Forest.* London: Weidenfeld and Nicolson, 1980.

Hansen, Eric, and Robin Williams. "The Politics of Resource Development. Hill Logging in Sarawak." ABC Radio, The Science Show, no. 521. Sydney, Australia.

Harrisson, Tom, *World Within: A Borneo Story*. Singapore: Oxford University Press, 1986.

Hong, Evelyne. Natives of Sarawak, Survival in Borneo's Vanishing Forest. Penang, Malaysia: Institut Masyarakat, 1987.

Hose, Charles. *The Field-book of a Jungle-Wallah*. London: H. F. & G. Witherby, 1929.

———. *Fifty Years of Romance and Research*. London: Hutchinson & Company, 1927.

Hose, Charles, and W. McDougall. *The Pagan Tribes of Borneo*. London: Macmillan, 1912.

Jessup, Timothy. "Why Do Apo Kayan Shifting Cultivators Move?" *Borneo Research Bulletin*, 1981.

Kedit, Peter. "Gunong Mulu Report: A Human-Ecological Survey of Nomadic/Settled Penan Within the Gunong Mulu National Park Area Fourth/Fifth Division, Sarawak." *Sarawak Museum Journal*, 1978.

Kipling, Rudyard. *The Jungle Book*. New York: Doubleday, 1946.

Mohun, Janet, and Omar Sattaur. "The Drowning of a Culture." *New Scientist*, January 1987.

Morrison, Hedda; Leigh Wright; and K. F. Wong. *Vanishing World*. New York: Weatherhill, n.d.

Myers, Norman. *The Primary Source: Tropical Forests and Our Future*. New York: Norton, 1984.

Nieuwenhuis, A. W. *Quer durch Borneo*. 2 vols. Leiden, 1904.

Posewitz, Dr. Theodor. *Borneo: Its Geology and Mineral Resources*. Translated by Frederick H. Hatch. 1892.

Prattis, Ian. "The Kayan-Kenyah 'Bungan Cult.'" *Sarawak Museum Journal*, 1963.

Roth, Henry Ling. *The Natives of Sarawak and British North Borneo*. 2 vols. London: Truslove & Hanson, 1896.

Rousseau, J. "The Peoples of Central Borneo." *Sarawak Museum Special Issue*, 1974.

Rubenstein, Carol. "Poems of Indigenous Peoples of Sarawak: Some of the Songs and Chants." *Sarawak Museum Journal*, Special Monograph, no. 2, vol. XXI, parts I and II, July 1973.

St. John, Spenser. *Life in the Forest of the Far East; or Travels in Northern Borneo*. 2 vols. London: Smith Eider, 1863.

Smythies, B. E. "Dr. A. W. Nieuwenhuis — A Borneo Livingston." *Sarawak Museum Journal*, n.d.

Wallace, Alfred Russel. *The Malay Archipelago: The Land of the Orang-Utan and the Bird of Paradise. A Narrative of Travel, with Studies of Man and Nature*. New York: Dover, 1962.

Whittier, Herbert and Patricia. "The Apo Kayan Area of East Kalimantan." *Sarawak Museum Journal*, 1973.